The Campus History Series

UNIVERSITY OF TOLEDO

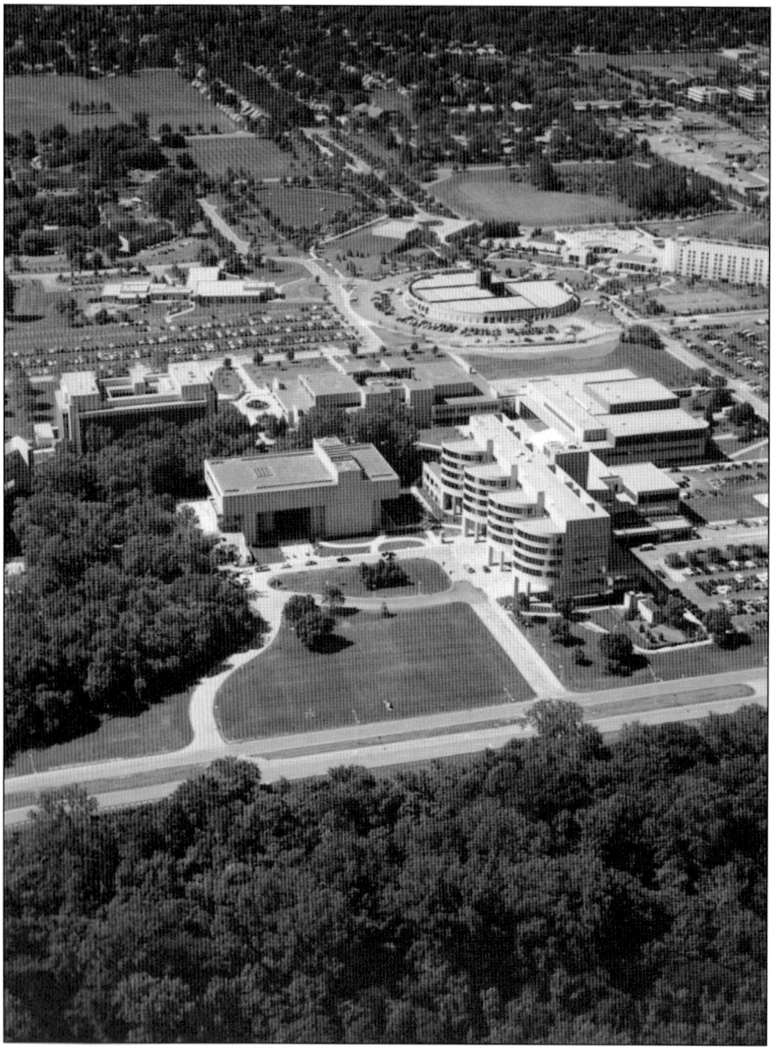

The campus of the former Medical College of Ohio, founded in 1964, is pictured in this aerial view. The college merged with the University of Toledo in 2006. (Courtesy of the University of Toledo Archives.)

On the Front Cover: This photograph of a student on her way to commencement was taken by an unknown photographer in the 1950s. (Courtesy of the University of Toledo Archives, Ward M. Canaday Center for Special Collections, the University of Toledo.)

Cover Background: This 1938 aerial view of the University of Toledo shows the first buildings of the Bancroft Street campus. (Photograph by Maurice Wallace, courtesy of the University of Toledo Archives, Ward M. Canaday Center for Special Collections, the University of Toledo.)

The Campus History Series

UNIVERSITY OF TOLEDO

BARBARA L. FLOYD

ARCADIA
PUBLISHING

ISBN 978-1-4671-2724-0

Published by Arcadia Publishing
Charleston, South Carolina

Printed in the United States of America

Library of Congress Control Number: 2017940419

For all general information, please contact Arcadia Publishing:
Telephone 843-853-2070
Fax 843-853-0044
E-mail sales@arcadiapublishing.com
For customer service and orders:
Toll-Free 1-888-313-2665

Visit us on the Internet at www.arcadiapublishing.com

This book is dedicated to the thousands of people—most of whom are not named within these pages—who have labored every day since 1872 to make the University of Toledo a success.

CONTENTS

ACKNOWLEDGMENTS

I would like to thank Brenda Lee and the University of Toledo (UT) Foundation, and Dan Saevig and the UT Alumni Association, for their generous support for this publication.

This book would not have been possible without the incredible images preserved in university archives created by photographers both known and unknown. The archives house well over 15,000 images, and sifting through them to decide which 240 should be included has been a labor of love. While most of the early images are from anonymous sources, those from the 1960s to 2000s were taken by the late longtime university photographer Bill Hartough. Many of the images in chapter five were taken by Medical College of Ohio photographer Jack Meade. Most of those in chapter six were captured by Dan Miller, current university photographer. My thanks for your keen eye and for capturing events both big and small. I apologize for not being able to label each photograph with the name of its creator, but I hope this acknowledgment will suffice.

I would also like to thank the staff of the Ward M. Canaday Center for Special Collections for their support during the process of writing this book.

It is impossible to include many people who have played important roles in the history of the University of Toledo in the limited space available in this book. My apologies to all who I was not able to include. You should know that your contributions are documented in university archives, and your work is a part of our institutional memory. Because the focus of this book is on the major events that have shaped the university, there was little space for athletics, student organizations, and individual faculty and staff. That is a lot to exclude. This is also not a volume that dwells on the controversial, but rather speaks to the celebration of our growth as an institution. Sources used to research the book include Frank Hickerson's *The Tower Builders: The Centennial Story of the University of Toledo,* published in 1972, and *A Community of Scholars: Recollections of the Early Years of the Medical College of Ohio*, published in 2011. I also drew upon my own previous work, *The Tower's Lengthening Shadow: 125 Years of the University of Toledo.*

Unless otherwise noted, all images are from the University of Toledo Archives, or the online photograph archive of the UT Department of Marketing and Communication.

INTRODUCTION

The University of Toledo began as one man's dream. But it required the labor of thousands of others to see it become a reality. More than once in its 145-year history, it seemed like a dream that was destined to fail. If there is one theme in the history of this institution, it is survival against incredible odds. More than once, the university nearly closed, and without perseverance by those who believed in it—and some incredible luck—its continuing history would not be written today.

From the beginning, what became the University of Toledo seemed like a long shot, largely because Toledo itself seemed like a long shot. The city had been founded in 1837, just 35 years before the university was founded. While the rest of the state had developed and prospered after Ohio's statehood in 1803, northwest Ohio sat largely dormant. Toledo was surrounded by the Great Black Swamp, which made it difficult for anyone to get to the area. Those who did settle here lived in the Graveyard of the Midwest, a nickname given the city because of the epidemics of malaria, cholera, and other deadly diseases that regularly swept through and decimated the population. It was not until the Miami and Erie Canal was proposed in 1835 that anyone had much interest in Toledo. Ironically, after years of being ignored, once there was a shot at economic development, residents had to fight a war with their neighbors to the north over who would get to claim Toledo.

The Toledo that Jesup Scott came to in the early 1830s was hardly one that anyone besides Scott would have believed could be the "Future Great City of the World." But as a real estate investor, Scott saw the location of Toledo on railroad lines, on the Great Lakes, and near rich farmland as elements that could create an industrial powerhouse. And that Future Great City would need a university.

Unfortunately for Scott, his dream failed. The Toledo University of Arts and Trades that was endowed by Scott in 1872 closed by 1878—the first time financial constraints would affect the institution. It was born again in 1884 by Scott's sons, who donated what was left of the university's assets to the City of Toledo if it agreed to operate an institution that fulfilled the terms of their father's bequest.

The Toledo University Manual Training School established with Scott's trust was successful in its early years. But the decision of Scott's sons to give the institution to the city nearly killed it. Constant infighting between the board of directors and the Toledo Board of Education over who controlled the school was almost fatal on more than one occasion. In 1905, the board of education refused to levy taxes to support the school, and it closed for a month. In 1908, the directors had to embarrass the city into providing financial support by pointing out that if the city could afford to spend $2,400 on an elephant for the zoo, it could surely afford to fund a university. Pres. Jerome Raymond, who worked to convert what was basically an advanced high school into a real university, could not stand the stress, and resigned after one year.

In 1911, the issue of who controlled the school was settled by the Ohio Supreme Court, making it clear the directors, not the board of education, did. But that did little to quell the criticism by its detractors, one of whom described the university as a "blunder and a crime." Also in 1911, another near fatal blow was delivered when a classroom building burned nearly to the ground. The directors were ready to walk away when a last-minute deal provided classroom space in a downtown office building. Administrators also added to the precarious state of the university. One president refused to leave his office when he was fired, and his successor had to change the locks to keep him out.

The various locations of the school in makeshift spaces around Toledo also limited its growth and threatened its future. In its early years, classes were held in locations like an old elementary school building in a blighted, crime-ridden part of town, and in unused buildings constructed by the city for World War I troop training. In 1928, newly appointed president Henry Doermann was convinced that the only way to ensure the future of the university was to build a new campus, one with beautiful architecture that would inspire the students. This effort, too, almost failed. The city taxpayers did approve $2.8 million for a new campus on Bancroft Street, but did so less than a year before the start of the worst economic depression of modern times. If Dr. Doermann had waited until 1929 to put the bond levy before voters, the chances of the university surviving might have been much bleaker. And it is certain that the campus today would not reflect Dr. Doermann's stunning architectural vision.

Financial constraints seem always to be looming over the institution. From 1884 to 1967, the University of Toledo was a municipal institution supported by the taxpayers of Toledo. By the time Dr. William Carlson took over as president in 1958, over 12 percent of the city's entire budget was going to support the university, a situation that Toledo City Council made clear could not continue. A desperately needed tax levy to support the university was approved by Toledo voters in 1959—by 144 votes. Dr. Carlson realized that UT's potential was limited as long as it remained a municipal university. After much political maneuvering, UT became part of Ohio's system of higher education in 1967.

Medical education in Toledo had an equally difficult journey. The Toledo Medical College, the first medical school in the city, was founded in 1882. But at a time when medical education was unregulated and competition for students drove down quality, the school's diplomas were not worth the paper they were printed on, and finances were always stretched. In an effort to stabilize the Toledo Medical College, in 1904, it merged with the struggling Toledo University—the same university that could hardly pay its own bills. Needless to say, this was not a good solution. As medical education became regulated and the move to license physicians took hold, the school was doomed. Its graduates were unable to pass professional licensure requirements, and the Flexner report of 1910 was the final nail in the school's coffin. By 1918, the Toledo Medical College was closed by the Toledo University Board of Directors.

But some in Toledo continued to dream of a medical school, particularly the publisher of the city's major newspaper, Paul Block Jr. By the early 1960s, after numerous studies, years of lobbying, and many events that might have spelled its end, in 1964, the state chartered what was then called the Medical College of Ohio at Toledo. The school was housed in a former tuberculosis hospital in its early years and used the outdated and inadequate Maumee Valley Hospital for its clinical training. The young college struggled to attract top-level faculty to what must have seemed to many like a pipe dream. But the school did just that and thrived as an independent school for 40 years.

In 2006, the two institutions that seemed like long shots for much of their separate histories joined together.

Today, Toledo may not have become the Future Great City of the World as Jesup Scott believed it would, but there is no doubt that the university he founded has shaped the world through generations of students who have been provided a chance for a better life through the institution he created.

One

Founding and Early Struggles to Survive

> Cities are organisms that grow up as naturally as men. They develop where human faculties are most effective, and because these faculties can be more effective there than elsewhere.
>
> —Jesup Wakeman Scott
> *A Presentation of Causes Tending to Fix the Position of the Future Great City of the World,* 1868

It is not uncommon that universities begin as the dream of one man or woman who wishes to create an educational institutional they believe can change the world. Jesup W. Scott believed that if he endowed an institution of higher learning in Toledo, Ohio, it would help propel the city to be not just a great city, but the greatest city in the world—bigger than London, Paris, Rome, or New York.

Scott had always been interested in how geography influenced the development of cities. Through articles he published in some of the major magazines of the time, he theorized about what attributes would be necessary to create the next great city. For Scott, the location of Toledo in a temperate climate zone, near one of the Great Lakes, at the mouth of a river, on major rail lines running between east and west, and with farmlands surrounding it all signaled that Toledo was singularly suited for the development as this future great city. And if it was to be that great city, it would need a university where its young people could be trained to assume their roles in its great future.

It did not hurt that Scott was a real estate investor who owned many large parcels of land in the city, including much of what is today downtown. If Toledo did become "the future great city of the world," Scott stood to profit handsomely.

Scott donated land near what was to be a railroad terminal as an endowment for "an institution for the promoting of knowledge, in the arts and trades and related sciences . . . to furnish artists and artizans with the best faculties for high culture, in their respective occupations, in addition to what are furnished by the public schools." With his donation, Scott established the Toledo University of Arts and Trades on October 12, 1872.

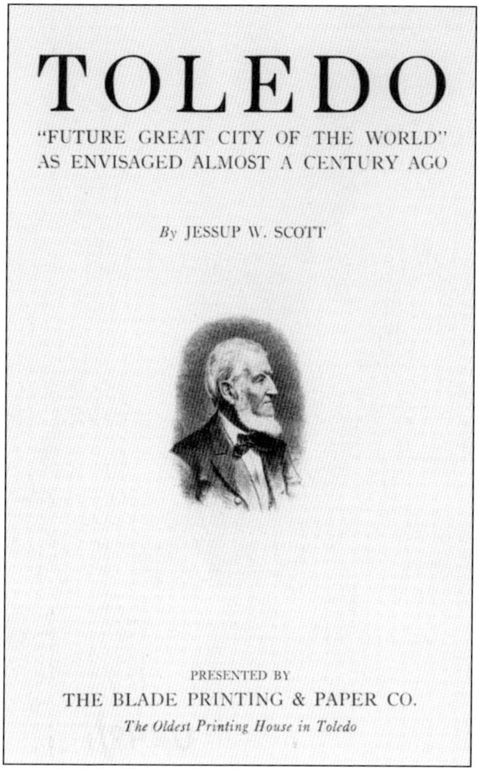

The land Scott donated as an endowment for the university was located near Nebraska Avenue. The land was valued at $80,000 in 1872, but the value was sure to rise once the Lake Shore & Michigan Southern Railroad built a terminal near what was then farmland. The growing value of the land would underwrite operation of the university, and once established, Scott believed other Toledo businessmen would step forward with additional financial support.

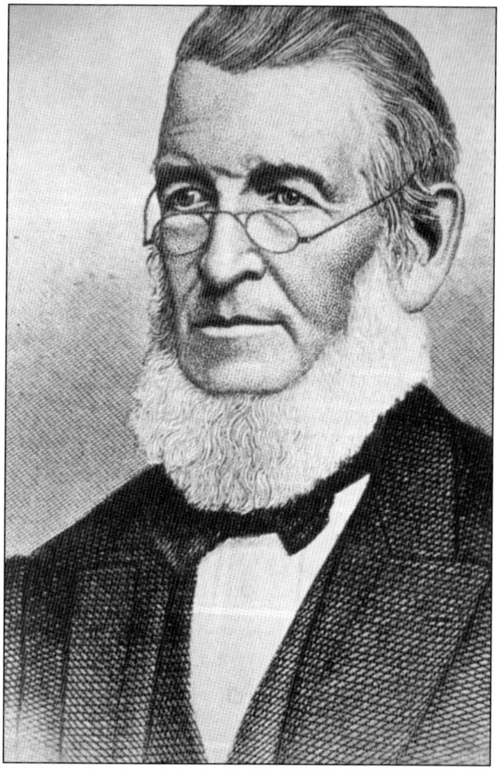

The university as established by Scott had a board of directors that included two of his sons, William and Frank. Others included businessmen William H. Raymond, Albert E. Macomber, and Charles Hill, along with Sarah R.L. Williams, a suffragette and author. The articles of incorporation stated that classes were to be offered "free of cost to all pupils who have not the means to pay for the same, and all others are to pay such tuition and other fees as the trustees may require." Scott did not live to see his dream become a reality, as he died in January 1874.

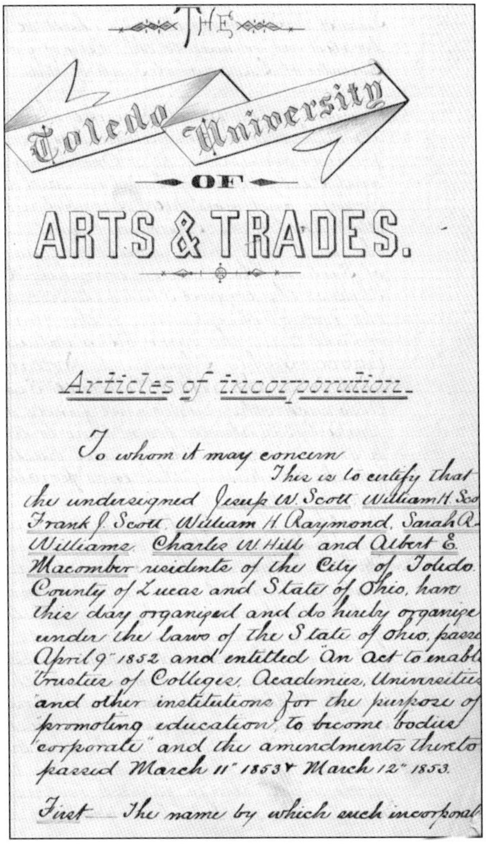

The Toledo University of Arts & Trades.

Articles of Incorporation.

To whom it may concern

This is to certify that the undersigned Jesup W. Scott William H. Scott Frank J. Scott William H. Raymond, Sarah R. Williams Charles W. Hill and Albert E. Macomber residents of the City of Toledo County of Lucas and State of Ohio, have this day organized and do hereby organize under the laws of the State of Ohio, passed April 9th 1852 and entitled An act to enable Trustees of Colleges, Academies, Universities and other institutions for the purpose of promoting education, to become bodies corporate" and the amendments thereto passed March 11th 1853 & March 12th 1853.

First The name by which such incorporat

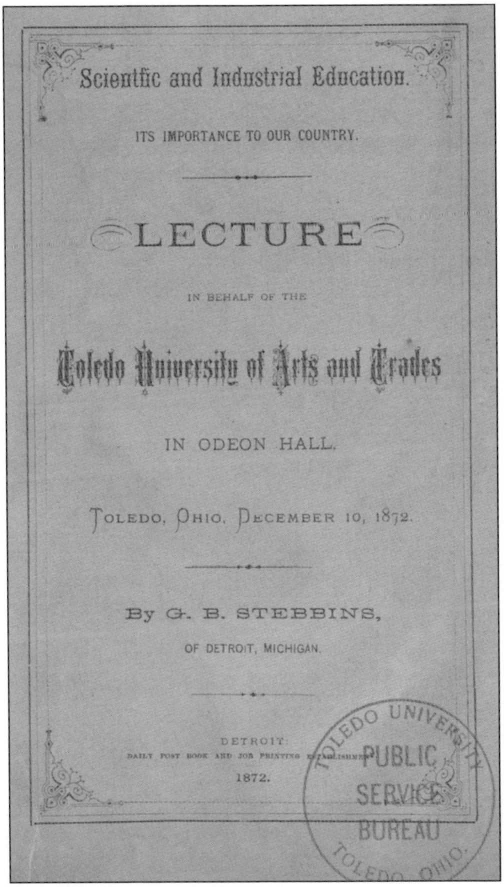

The Toledo University of Arts and Trades opened a year later in a converted church building at 10th and Adams Streets downtown. The building was named Raymond Hall for the trustee who donated the money for its purchase. Almost immediately, there were financial problems. The railroad terminal that was to make the Scott land valuable enough to endow the university was never built. The Scott family donated additional parcels of land, and the trustees tried to raise funds by selling subscriptions to the school. Due to the cost of renovating the building, there was no money to hire instructors the first year. The only subjects offered were architecture and painting.

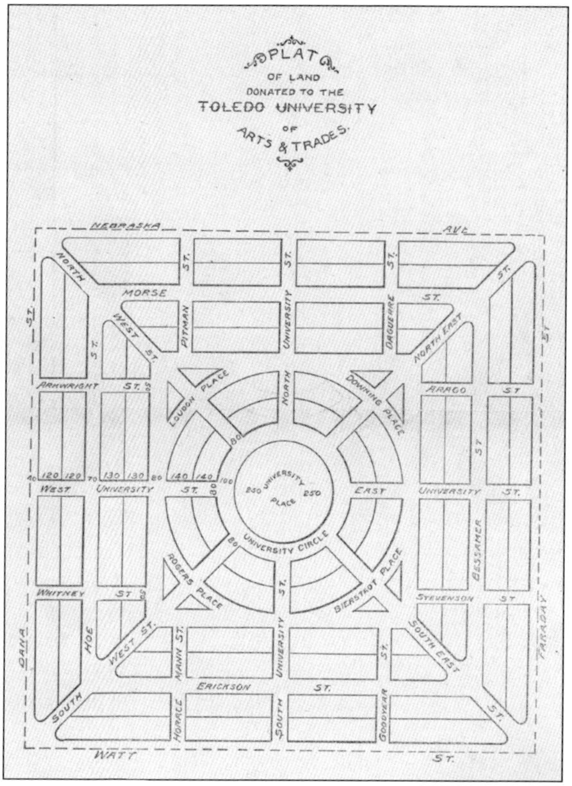

The value of the Scott land continued to depreciate, and by 1878, the school had no money to operate. The Scott endowment was completely spent, and the school closed. Jesup Scott's dream of a future great city and a university located in that city seemed unlikely to happen.

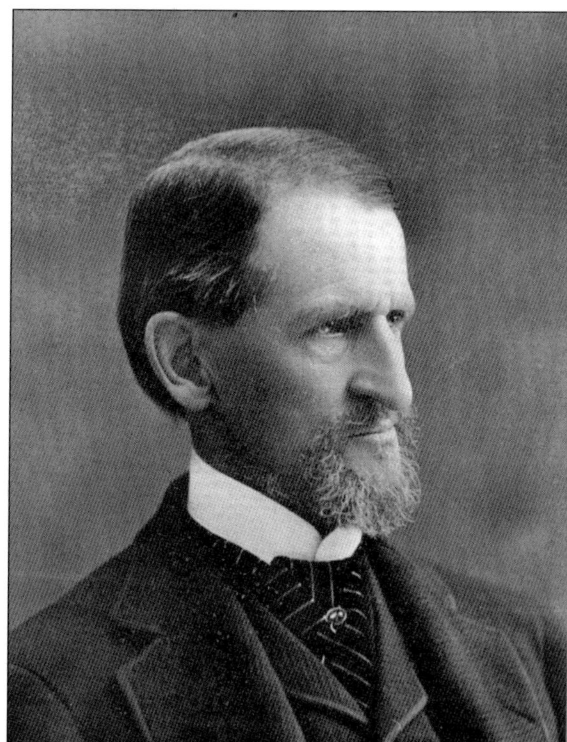

Scott's three sons—Frank, William, and Maurice—were not willing to give up on their father's dream. Frank Scott (shown here) became interested in a new educational concept called manual training, and felt that it met the requirements of his father's original trust for the university.

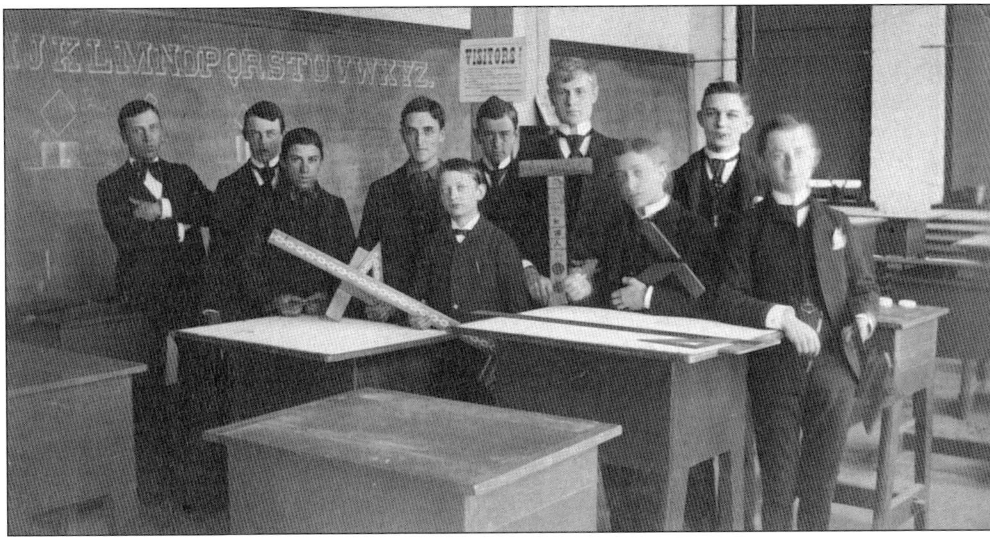

Manual training was an idea developed and promoted by Calvin M. Woodward at Washington University in St. Louis. Students would spend half of their day learning traditional academic subjects and half of their day learning vocational skills like woodworking, metalsmithing, or mechanical drawing. Students did not specialize in a specific trade, but rather were exposed to many. Through this type of educational experience, it was believed that students would learn the dignity of labor while at the same time develop their academic skills to be prepared for any career path they might choose.

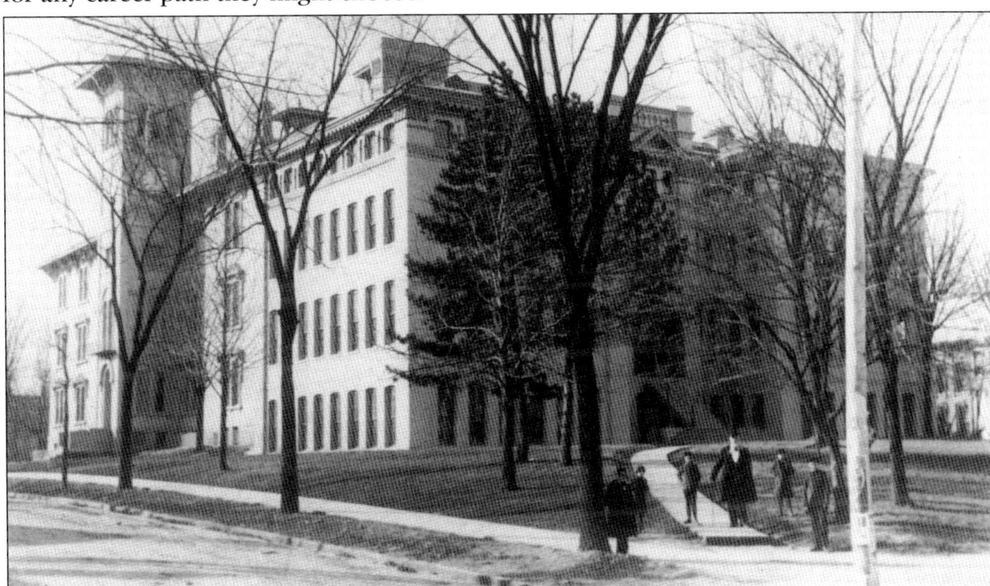

On January 8, 1884, the trustees agreed to donate the remaining assets of the Toledo University of Arts and Trades to the City of Toledo on the condition that the city carry out the terms of the original Scott trust. The city accepted in March. The new institution was known as Toledo University, and its first department was the Manual Training School. In May 1884, city council approved a levy to support the school. A new building was constructed adjacent to the Central High School that included a blacksmith and machine shop, carpenter shop and finishing room, and drawing and design rooms.

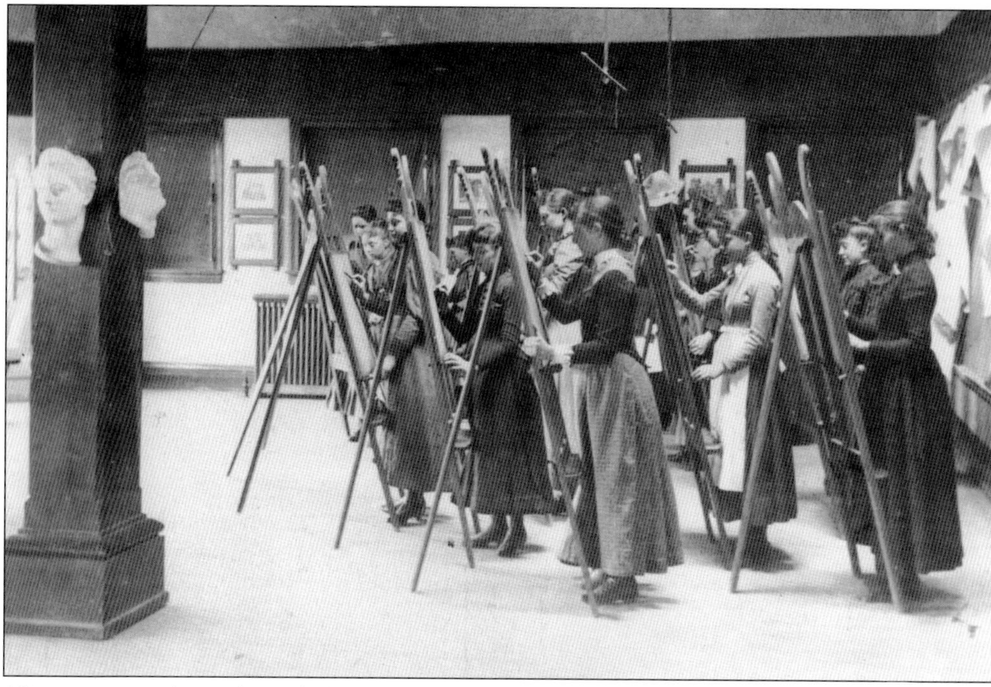

After agitation from the Toledo Woman's Suffrage Association and Sarah Williams, one of the original trustees of the Toledo University of Arts and Trades, the Manual Training School admitted both boys and girls beginning in 1886. That year, 40 girls and 22 boys enrolled in courses in the domestic economy department. Girls also took classes in carpentry and metalworking. As a reporter for *The Blade* remarked, "It is worth going a long way to see the girls dressed in gingham aprons, with little turbans on their heads, shoving the plane, swinging the hammer and yielding the saw." In 1905, Wood Design and Construction was taught by Mary H. Barkdull.

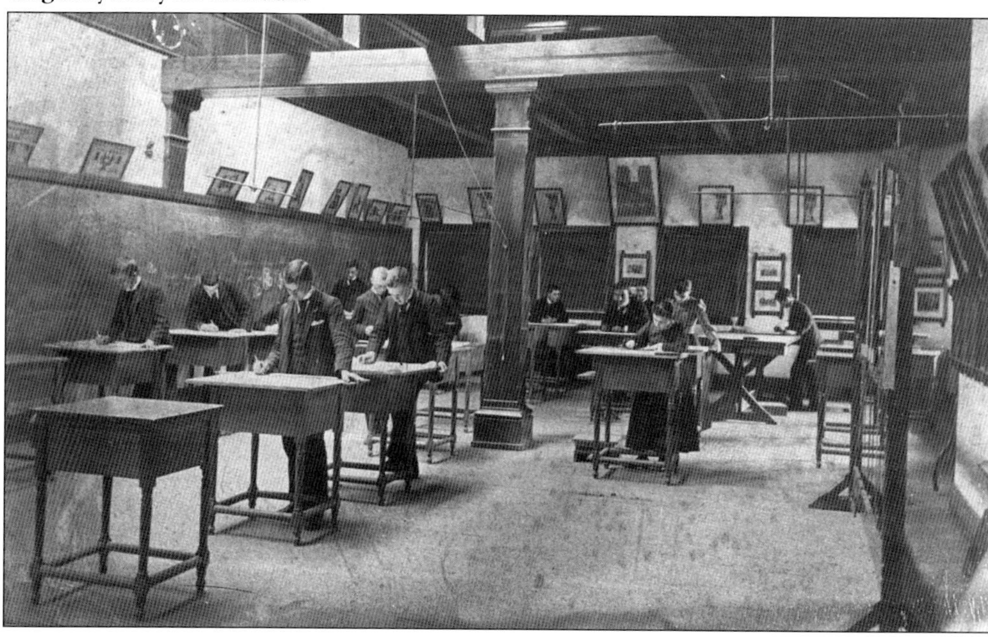

In 1900, Toledo University passed up one of the greatest opportunities ever presented to it by a donor. On February 27, William Tucker (shown here), then postmaster, met with the board and indicated a wealthy donor wanted to create an institution of higher learning in Toledo. Because of the secrecy of the proposal and restrictions on the gift, it was turned down. Only after rejecting the gift did the directors discover that the would-be benefactor was Andrew Carnegie. The directors attempted to reopen negotiations with Carnegie, but he did not respond. He went on to found the Carnegie Technical Schools in Pittsburgh, forerunner of Carnegie Mellon University.

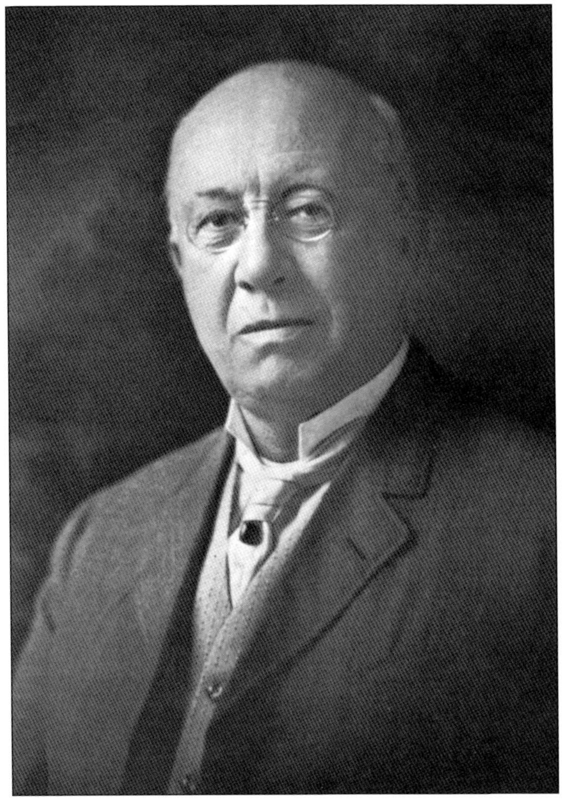

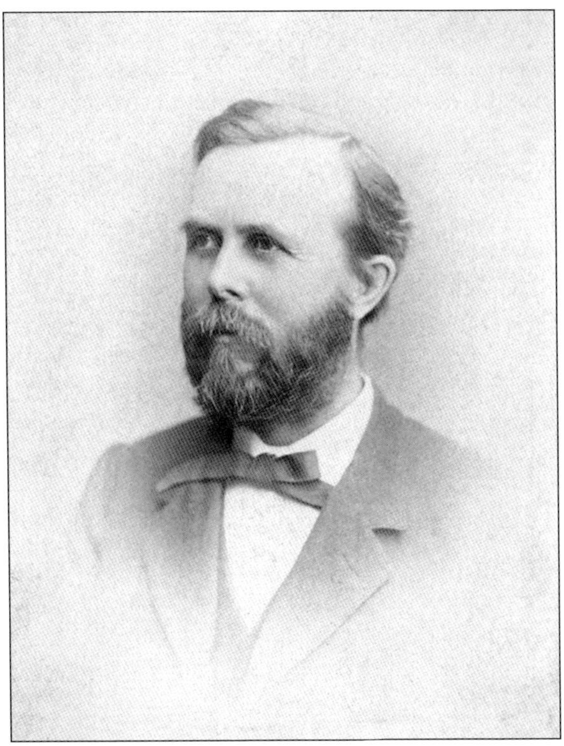

In 1900, the school changed its name to the Toledo University Polytechnic School. Albert E. Macomber, one of the original trustees of the university in 1872, suddenly turned on it because he believed the polytechnic school did not abide by the terms of the original Scott trust. Maurice Scott agreed. Fueling the dispute was a proposal of the board to sell the original Scott property to pay for a new building. A battle ensued between the Toledo Board of Education and the board of directors over control of the school. In 1905, the board of education refused to levy taxes to support the school, and it could not open for one month. Several members of the board of education barricaded themselves in the building and refused to leave. The board of directors asked the city to file a lawsuit to settle the question of control.

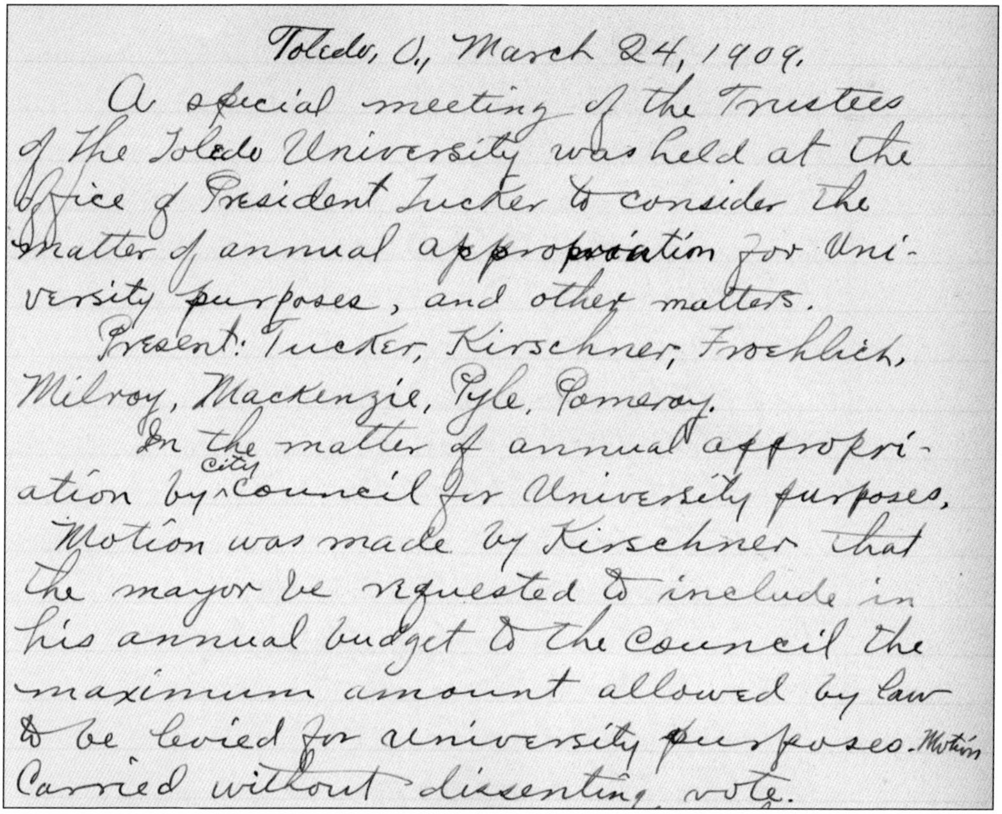

Toledo, O., March 24, 1909.

A special meeting of the Trustees of the Toledo University was held at the office of President Tucker to consider the matter of annual appropriation for University purposes, and other matters.

Present: Tucker, Kirschner, Froehlich, Milroy, Mackenzie, Pyle, Pomeroy.

In the matter of annual appropriation by city council for University purposes, Motion was made by Kirschner that the mayor be requested to include in his annual budget to the council the maximum amount allowed by law to be levied for university purposes. Motion Carried without dissenting vote.

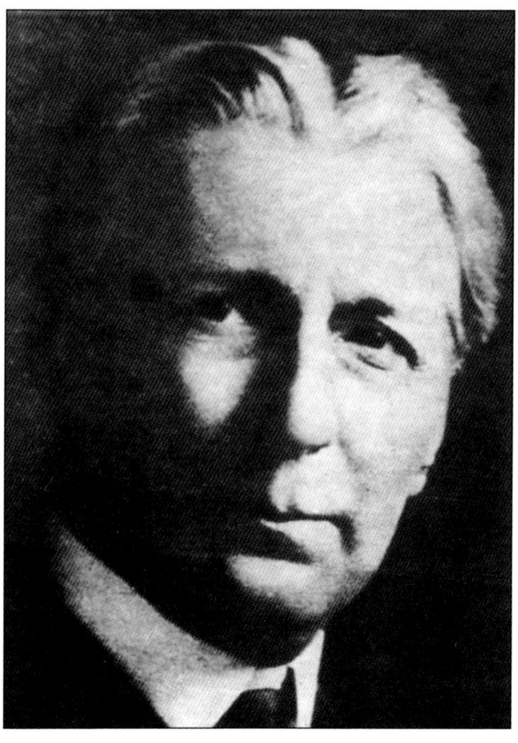

In 1908, the city tried again to levy taxes to support the university. Albert Macomber published a scathing pamphlet criticizing the university and viciously attacked the effort to collect the taxes. The city refused to turn over any money to operate the university until board of directors member Dr. John Pyle (pictured at left) embarrassed them by noting the city's willingness to spend $2,400 to purchase an elephant for the zoo, but allocate no money for the university. The tactic worked, and on June 15, 1909, the city granted exactly $2,400 to the institution.

Toledo University began to move away from its manual training school roots in 1904. That year, it affiliated with the Toledo Medical College, a struggling institution located at the corner of Cherry and Page Streets downtown. At this time, there were no licensure requirements for doctors, and the quality of students was poor. Trustees of the medical college felt that affiliation with Toledo University, which had its own financial problems, would bring stability.

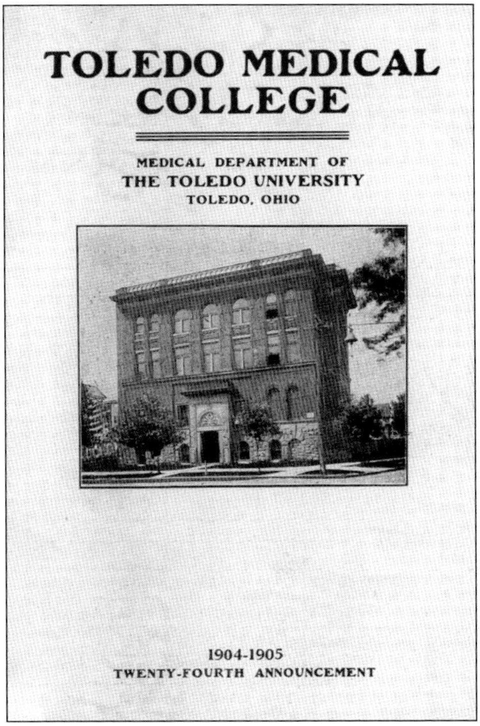
TOLEDO MEDICAL COLLEGE

MEDICAL DEPARTMENT OF
THE TOLEDO UNIVERSITY
TOLEDO, OHIO

1904-1905
TWENTY-FOURTH ANNOUNCEMENT

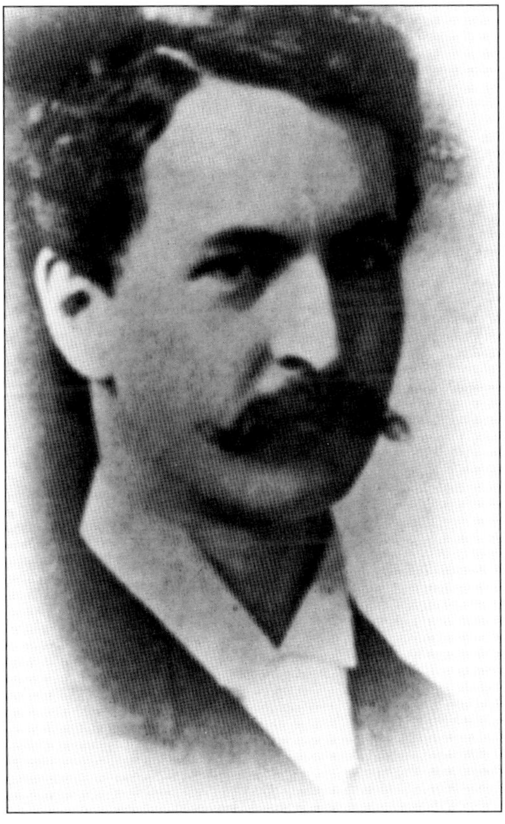

In 1909, Dr. Jerome Raymond was appointed the first president of Toledo University. Dr. Raymond continued the move towards becoming a post-baccalaureate university despite ongoing financial problems and questions over legality of the institution's existence and control. He affiliated with the Toledo Conservatory of Music and created the College of Arts and Sciences. He resigned after one year due to the stress of inadequate finances and the unresolved political issues. Dr. Charles A. Cockayne, a faculty member, was appointed acting president and held the position for four years.

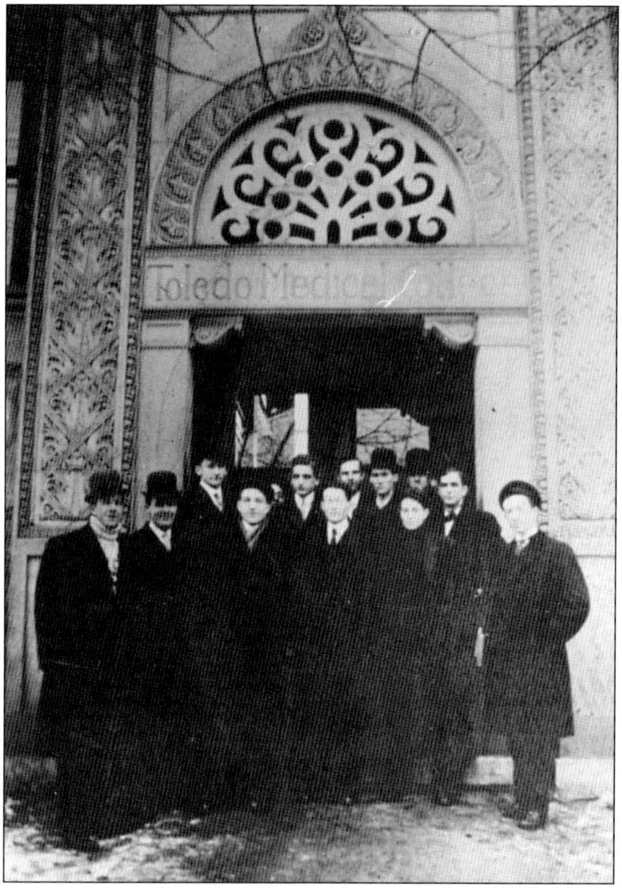

Classes for Toledo University were held at two locations—the Manual Training School building adjacent to Central High School, and at the Toledo Medical College building (pictured). On January 9, 1911, a fire nearly destroyed the medical college building. It was a devastating blow for the university, which lost its laboratories and many classrooms.

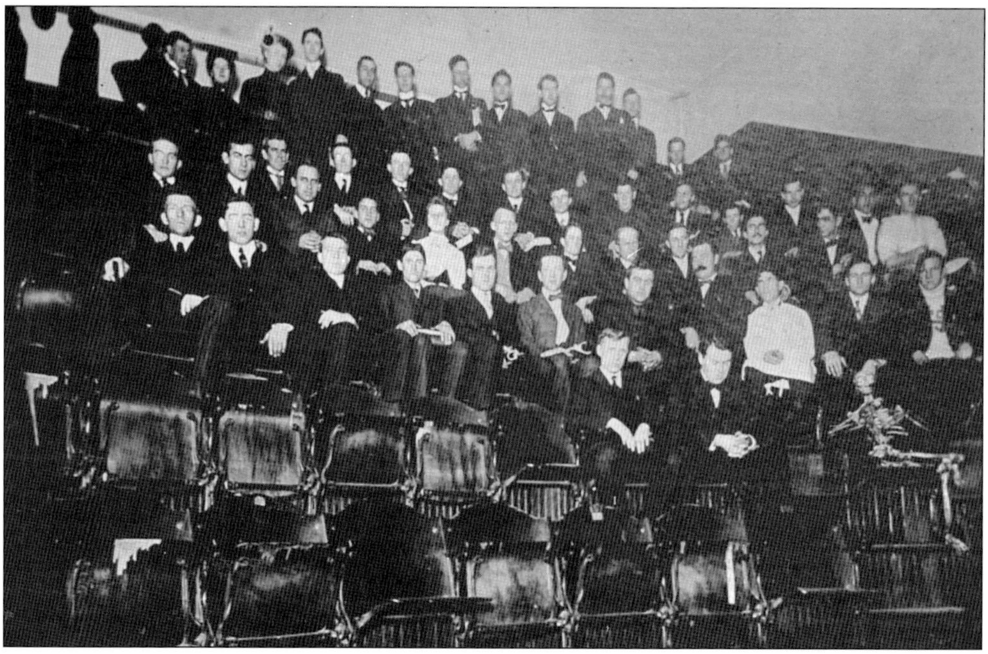

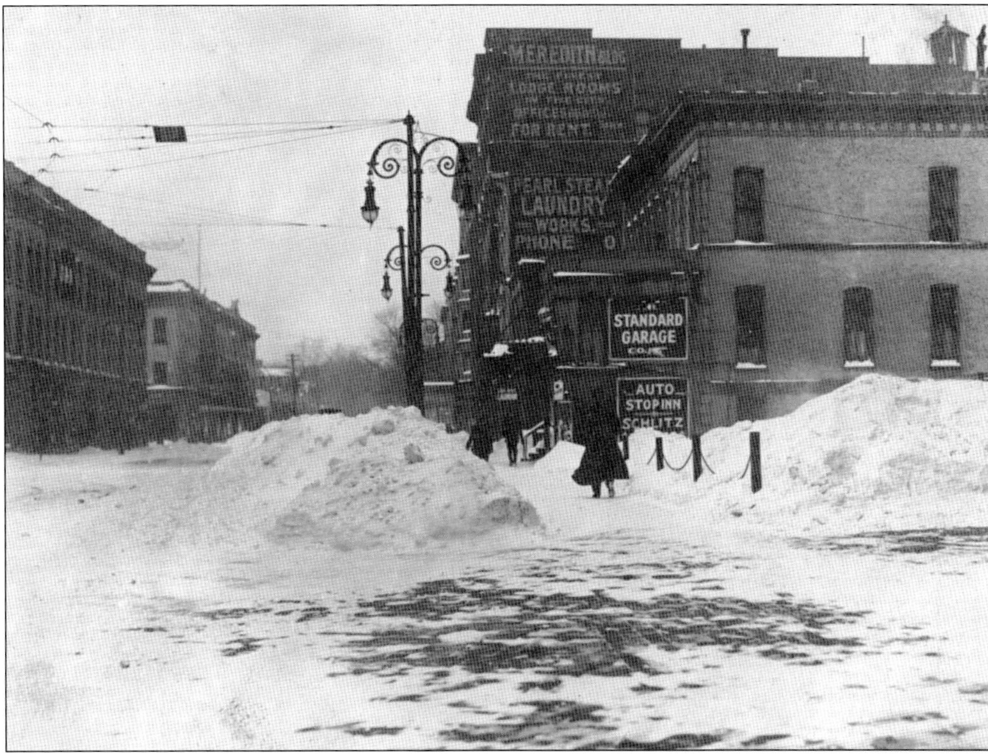

The directors were ready to give up and close the university. Fortunately, last-minute arrangements were made to hold classes in the Meredith Building, an office building located at Michigan Street and Jefferson Avenue. (Courtesy of the Toledo Lucas County Public Library.)

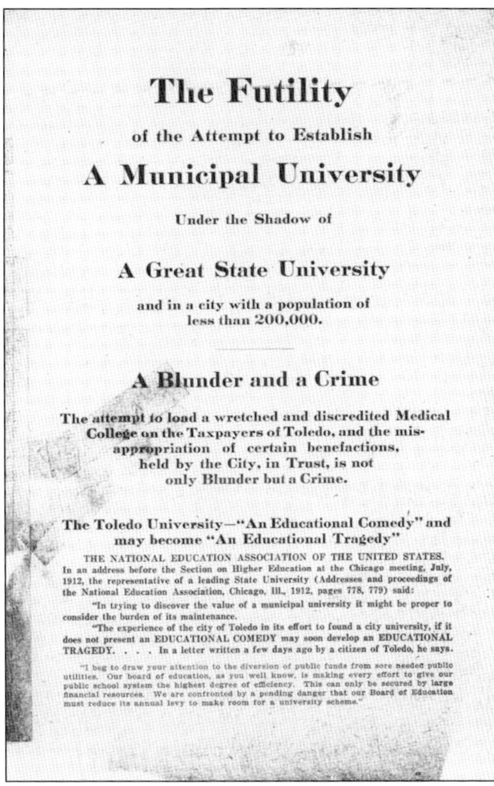

The Futility

of the Attempt to Establish

A Municipal University

Under the Shadow of

A Great State University

and in a city with a population of less than 200,000.

A Blunder and a Crime

The attempt to load a wretched and discredited Medical College on the Taxpayers of Toledo, and the misappropriation of certain benefactions, held by the City, in Trust, is not only Blunder but a Crime.

The Toledo University—"An Educational Comedy" and may become "An Educational Tragedy"

THE NATIONAL EDUCATION ASSOCIATION OF THE UNITED STATES. In an address before the Section on Higher Education at the Chicago meeting, July, 1912, the representative of a leading State University (Addresses and proceedings of the National Education Association, Chicago, Ill., 1912, pages 778, 779) said:

"In trying to discover the value of a municipal university it might be proper to consider the burden of its maintenance.

"The experience of the city of Toledo in its effort to found a city university, if it does not present an EDUCATIONAL COMEDY may soon develop an EDUCATIONAL TRAGEDY. . . . In a letter written a few days ago by a citizen of Toledo, he says.

"I beg to draw your attention to the diversion of public funds from sore needed public utilities. Our board of education, as you well know, is making every effort to give our public school system the highest degree of efficiency. This can only be secured by large financial resources. We are confronted by a pending danger that our Board of Education must reduce its annual levy to make room for a university scheme."

The issue of the legality of Toledo University as a body separate from the board of education was finally resolved on January 24, 1911, in the case of *Toledo v. Seiders et al.*, which established the university's legal right to exist and the board of directors as its governing body. The city raised the institution's operating budget to $5,000, and it seemed like the university might survive. In 1913, Albert Macomber published this pamphlet—one of many such treatises he circulated—calling the university a "blunder and a crime." Macomber said the directors of Toledo University were extorting money from taxpayers, and the institution was little more than a diploma mill.

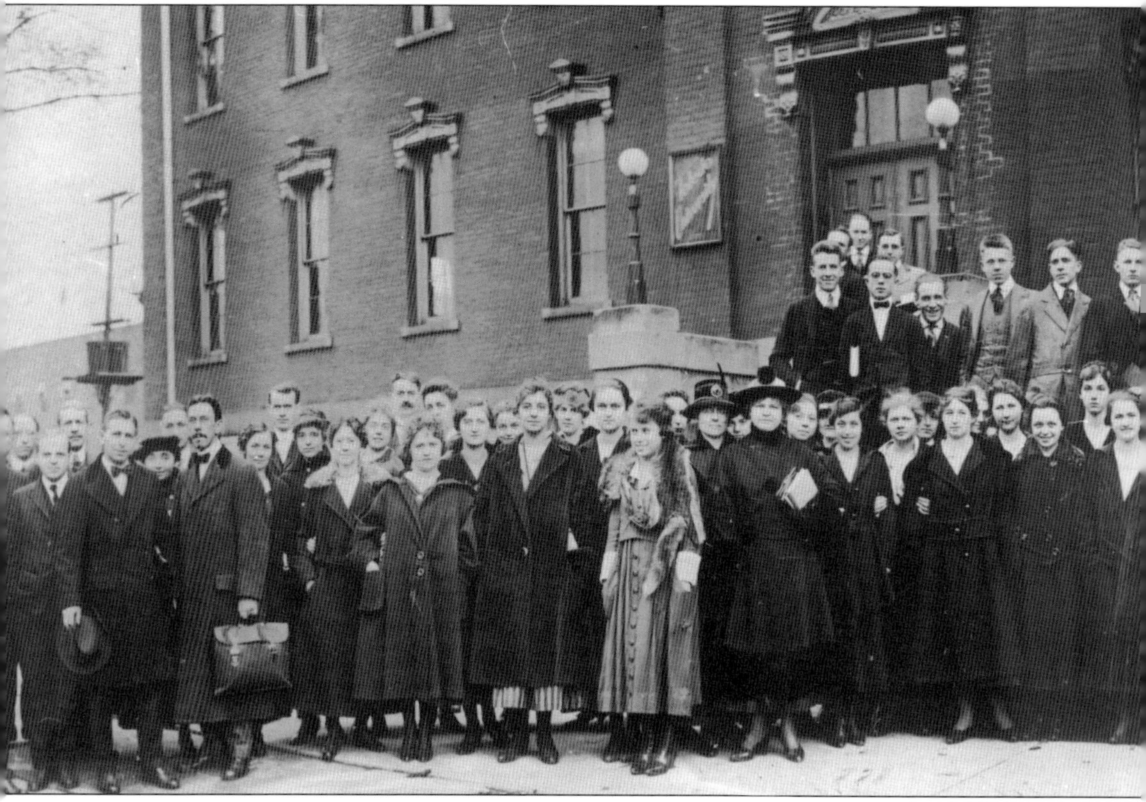

The directors made a deal with the board of education to swap the Manual Training School building for an old elementary school at the corner of 11th and Illinois Streets downtown. But this building was in a crime-ridden part of town, and required extensive renovation after

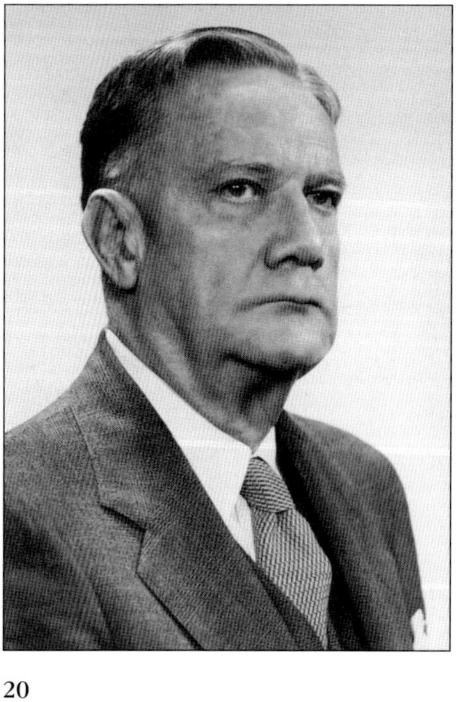

Dr. Cockayne was removed as acting president in 1914, although he refused to leave, and his successor, Dr. Allen Cullimore, had to change the locks on the president's office door to keep him out. Dr. Cullimore served as acting president for five months until a permanent president, Dr. A. Monroe Stowe, took office in July 1914.

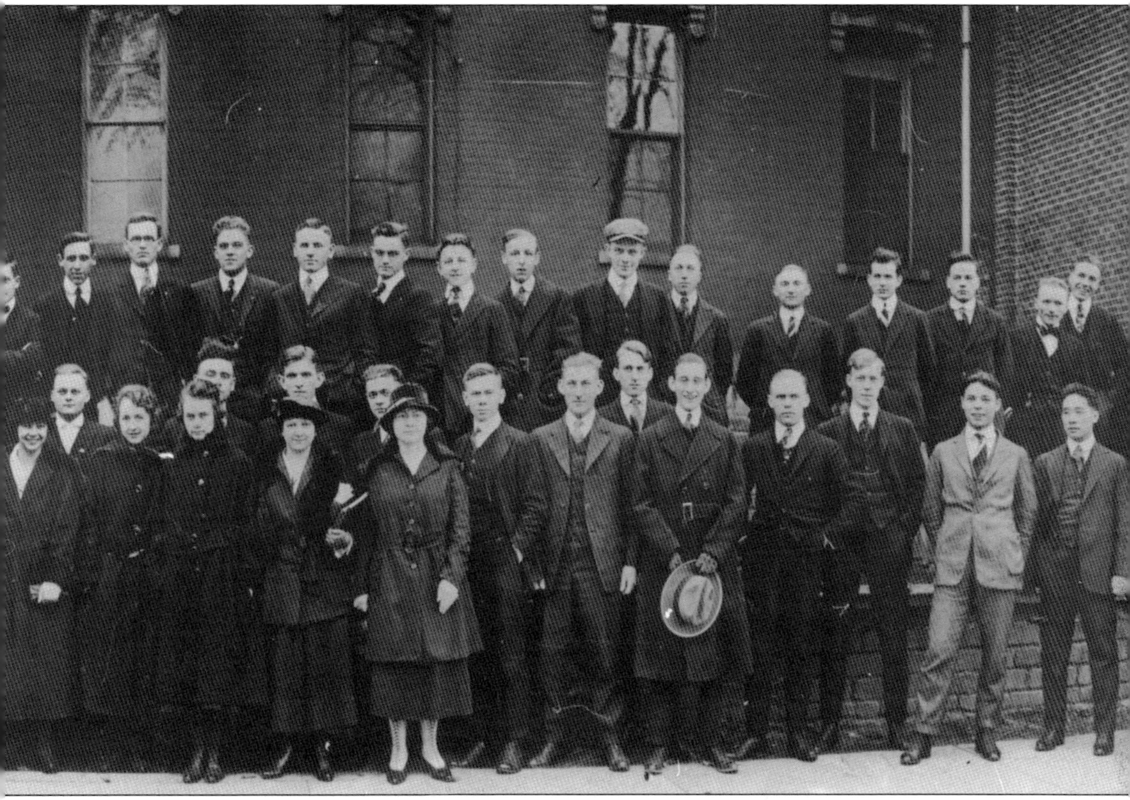

being empty for years. It was also more than a mile from the Toledo Medical College which, after repairs, was again the site for classes. This photograph shows many students gathered on the steps of the building.

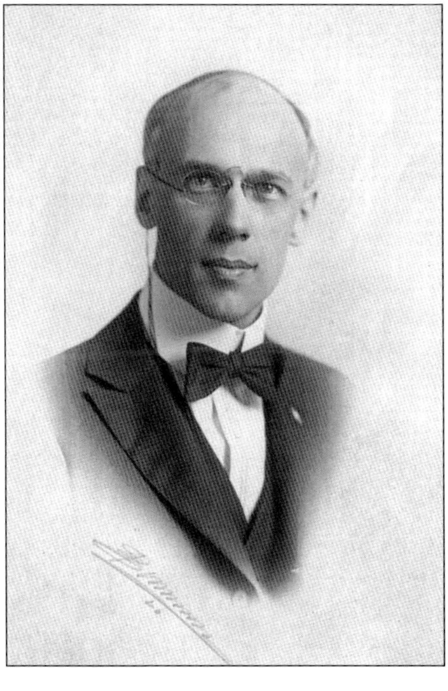

Dr. Stowe was successful in moving Toledo University forward in several respects. He established educational standards, admission requirements, and a formal curriculum. He founded the College of Commerce and Industry in 1914, and the College of Education in 1916. Enrollment grew from 200 students to 1,400, and the budget increased to $200,000. He also took the first steps toward becoming accredited by the North Central Association of Colleges and Secondary Schools, which was granted in 1920.

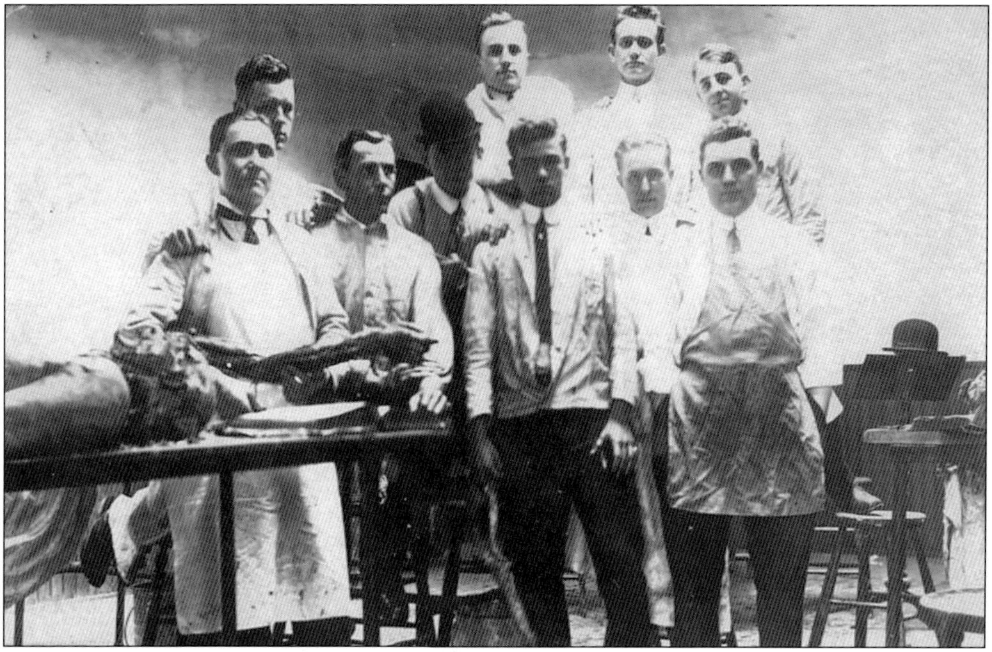

Dr. Stowe faced many of the same challenges as previous presidents, and some new ones. A review of the Toledo Medical College produced for the Carnegie Foundation in 1910 described the school as "the medical department of Toledo University, a municipal institution of uncertain status without substantial resources." In 1913, the American Medical Association produced its own negative report, noting a lack of clinical arrangements with local hospitals and a meager budget. In 1914, the Ohio State Medical Board stopped accepting credit for courses taken at the school. Efforts to save the school failed, and in January 1918, the board of directors of Toledo University closed the school.

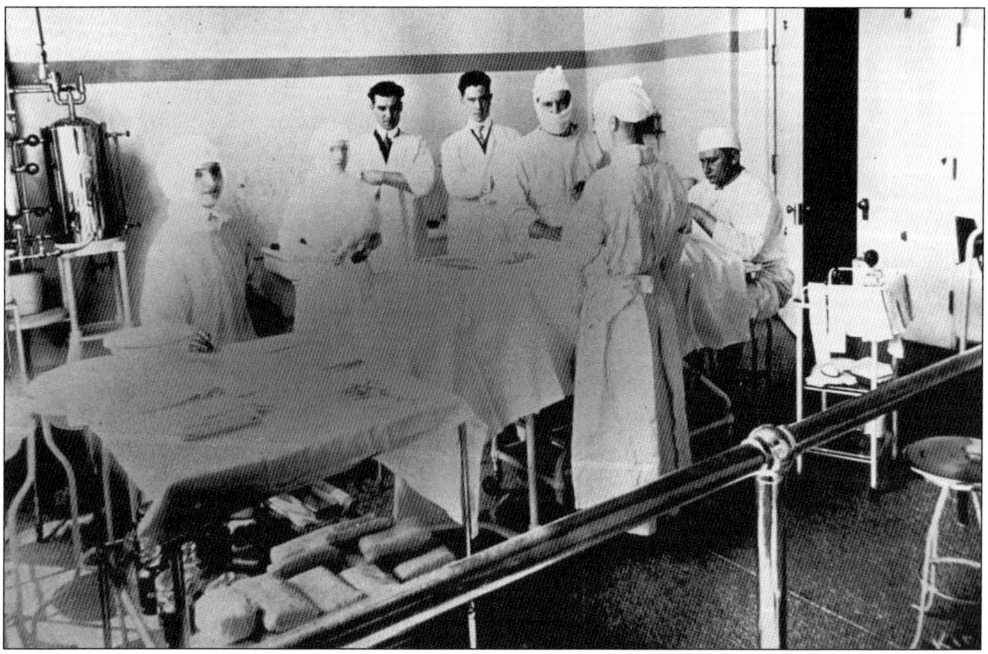

In 1915, the university found itself embroiled in political controversy involving Dr. Scott Nearing, who was appointed professor of economics and dean of the College of Arts and Sciences that year. Dr. Nearing had been dismissed from his previous position at the University of Pennsylvania for his radical views. In Toledo, he continued to be outspoken as an advocate for the working class, and some accused him of promoting Socialism. In 1917, the board of directors dismissed Nearing for what they perceived as his radical teaching.

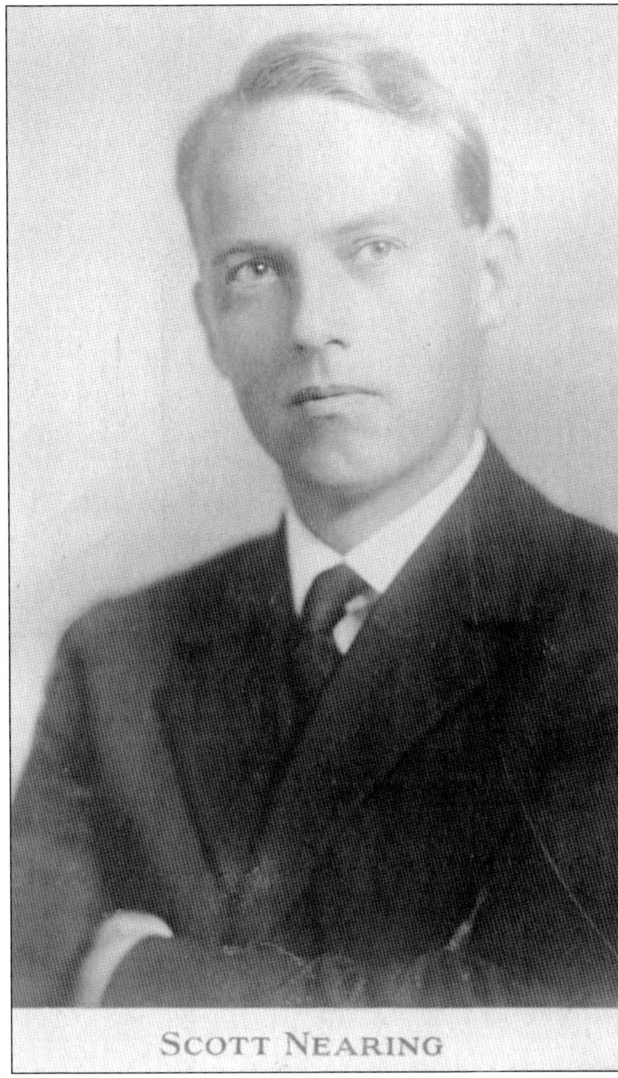

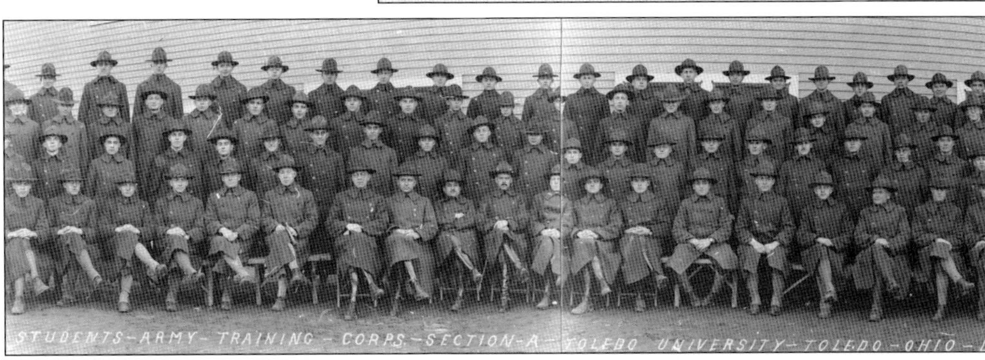

World War I had an impact on the university. Enrollment dropped in 1917 as many left to serve their country. A Toledo University section of the Students Army Training Corps, a forerunner of ROTC, was established by the US War Department. A building to house the students during their training was constructed on the original Scott property on Nebraska Avenue.

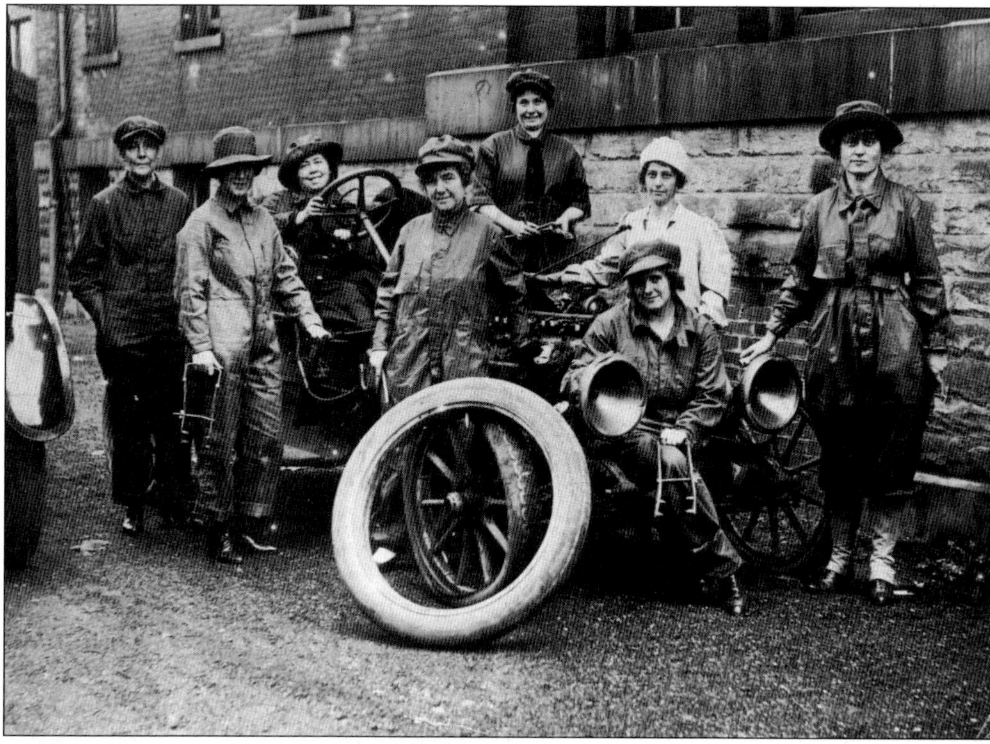

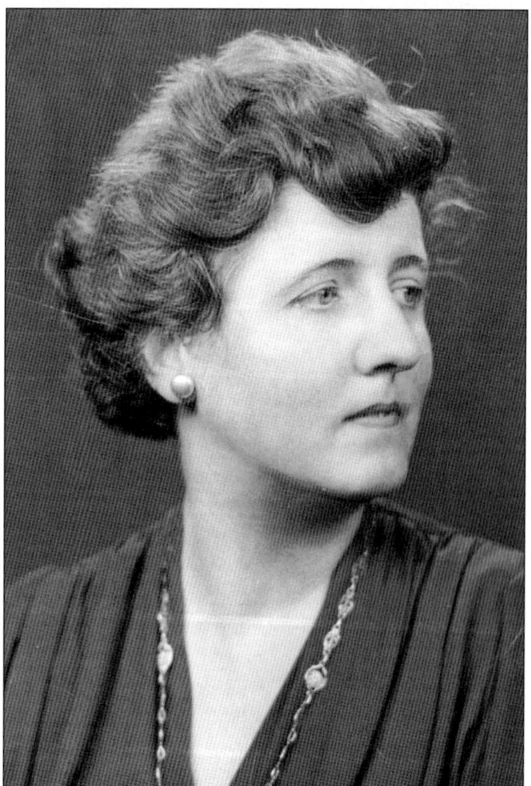

The War Department also proposed a program to train automobile mechanics for the war effort. World War I was the first war to use automobiles, particularly as ambulances on the front lines. A building to house the program was constructed on the Scott land adjacent to the dormitory in 1918. As part of the effort, women also enrolled in an automobile mechanics class. It was held at the university's building at 11th and Illinois Streets.

President Stowe created a new library for the university in 1917. Prior to that time, students used the city's library. In 1921, Mary Mewborn Gillham was appointed librarian, and she held that position for 48 years.

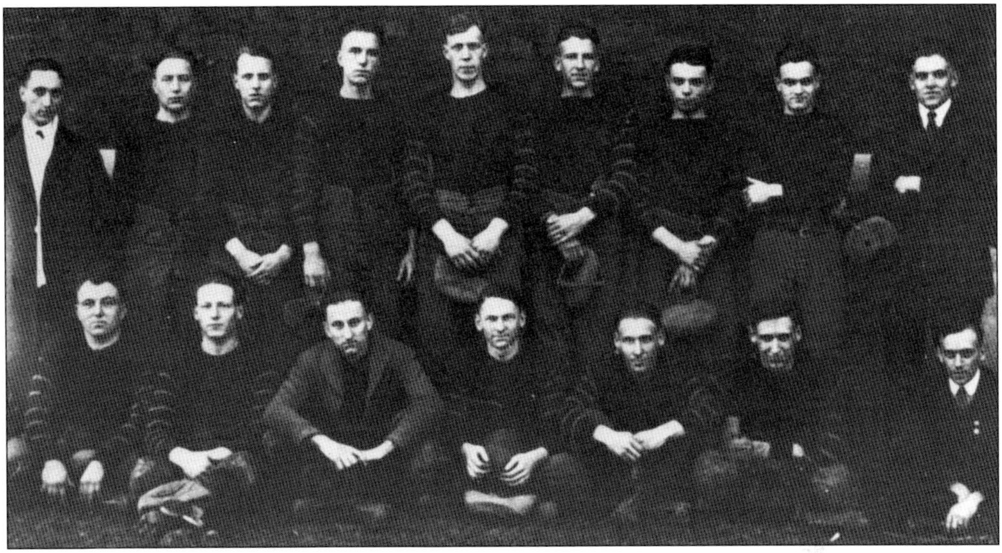

Also in 1917, the university's football team was organized. The team's first game was against the University of Detroit, and they lost by a score of 145 to 0. The football team quickly improved, and in a game against the Carnegie Institute of Technology in 1923, the team was given its nickname "Rockets" by a sportswriter for the *Toledo Times* after some fast moves by one of the players. The name stuck.

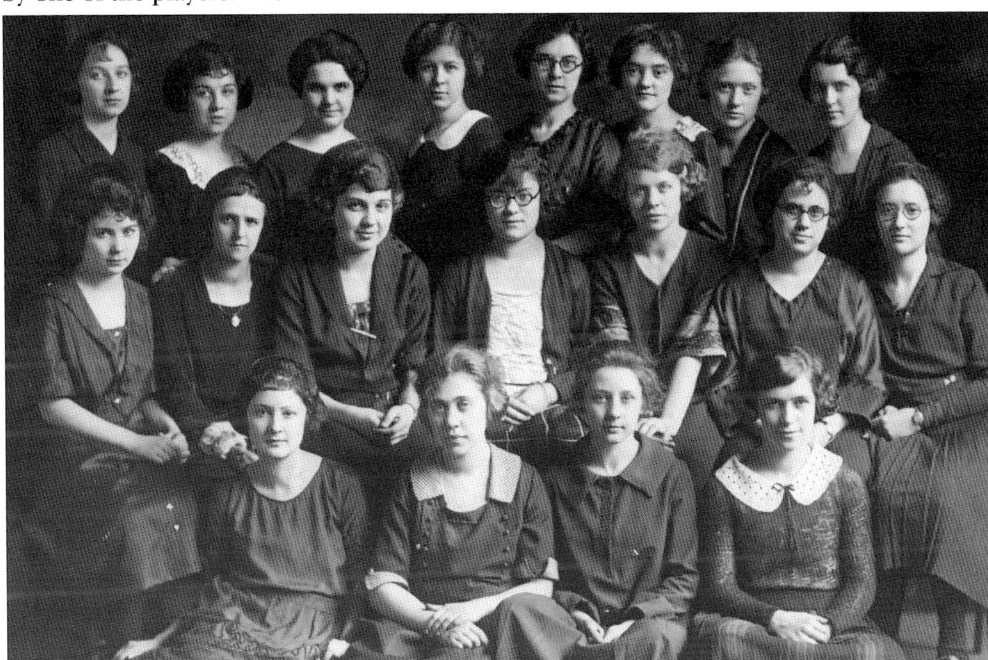

As the university matured, the student body began to seek extracurricular activities. Student Council was created in 1919. Also that year, Samuel Steinbeck and Leo Steinem started a student newspaper called the *Universi-Teaser*. A yearbook, called *The Blockhouse* (for the symbol of the city of Toledo) was published in 1922. In 1920, the Panhellenic Council was formed to oversee the numerous Greek organizations. One of the sororities on campus was Kappa Pi Epsilon, whose members are shown here.

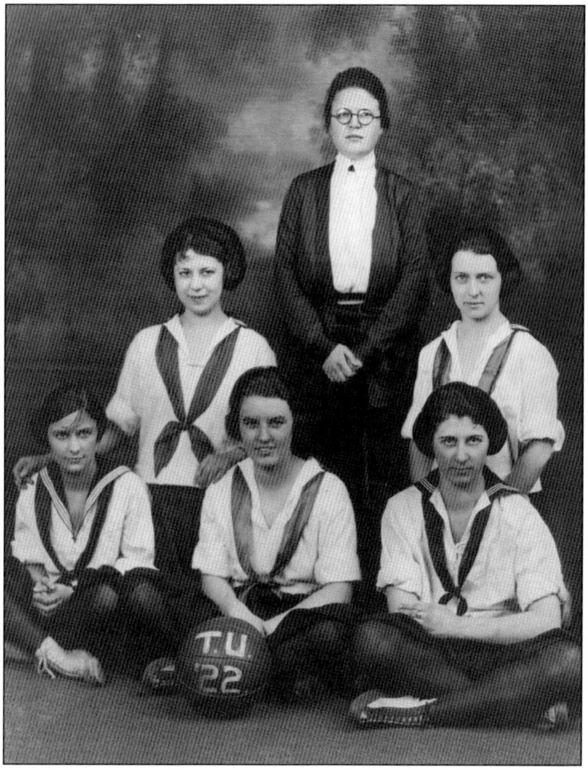

The first women's basketball team was organized in 1922. Also that year, C.J. Dyer wrote the institution's first fight song, "Fight for Dear Old 'T.' 'U.'"

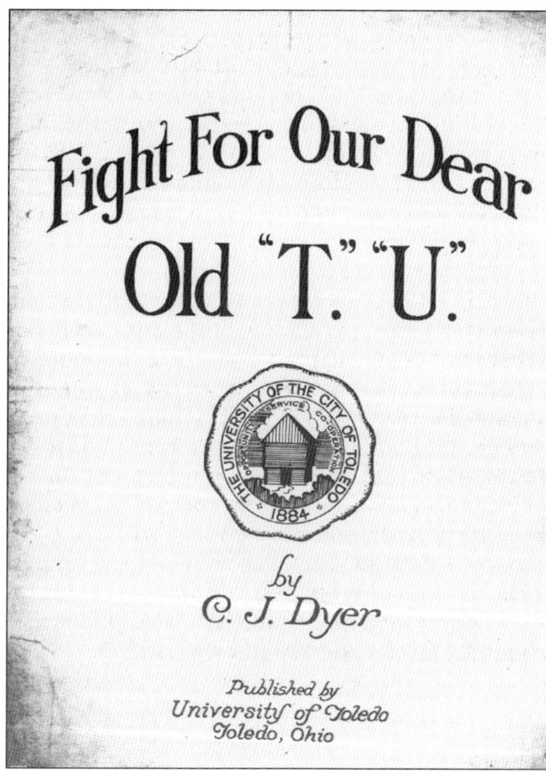

Two

Finding a Permanent Home

By the 1920s, classes for Toledo University were held in three inadequate buildings—the converted elementary school at 11th and Illinois Streets, the Toledo Medical College building a mile away, and in the Meredith Building downtown. Enrollment had grown to 1,500, and there was not enough room for everyone. Clearly, the university needed new facilities if it was to continue to grow. In 1921, city council agreed to spend $50,000 to renovate the unfinished automobile mechanics training facility and Students Army Training Corps dormitory that had been built on the original Scott farm land for World War I to house the university.

While the proposed buildings were twice the size of the building at 11th and Illinois Streets, the location was less than ideal. It was in the middle of an industrial area at the end of the street car line. The main building, renamed the Science Building, looked like a factory. The second floor of the dormitory building that had housed soldiers training for World War I was removed, and it became the gymnasium. Some classes were still held at the 11th and Illinois Streets building, although in 1926 there was a push to close it after a student returning from evening classes was beaten to death.

Clearly, if the University of Toledo was to have any kind of stability and a chance to prosper, it required a new, permanent home, preferably one built exclusively to house the institution rather than being adapted from some other use.

Recognizing the limitations of the university's facilities, in 1926, Toledo City Council appointed a subcommittee to determine a new, permanent location for the university's campus. Sites considered included Ottawa Park and Detweiler Park among 34 other sites. The firm Bartholomew Inc. of St. Louis was hired by the city in 1928 to identify the best location for a new university campus. The company was charged with finding land that was central to the student body, and large enough to allow the university to grow to accommodate 3,000 students within 10 years. The site had to be located away from noisy railroads and industrial areas, odor, smoke, billboards, and undesirable neighborhoods. "All things being equal, the best possible neighbor would be a large public park, an impressive public building group, or a quiet high-class residential neighborhood," Bartholomew's report concluded.

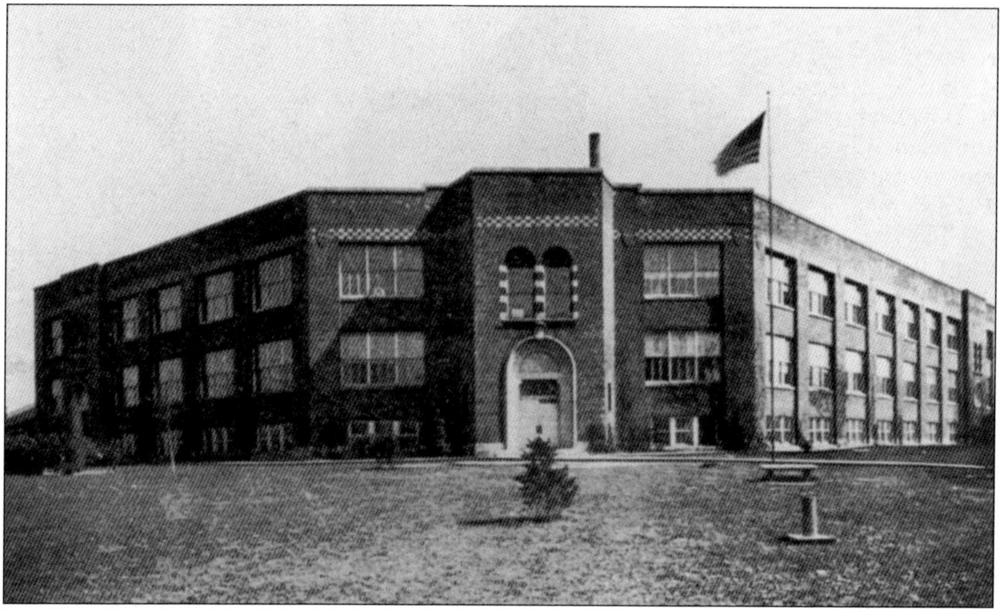

These buildings, converted World War I training facilities, became the new home of the university in 1922. The larger building was called the Science Building, and the smaller one was the gymnasium. The buildings were located on the original land donated by Jesup Scott on Nebraska Avenue.

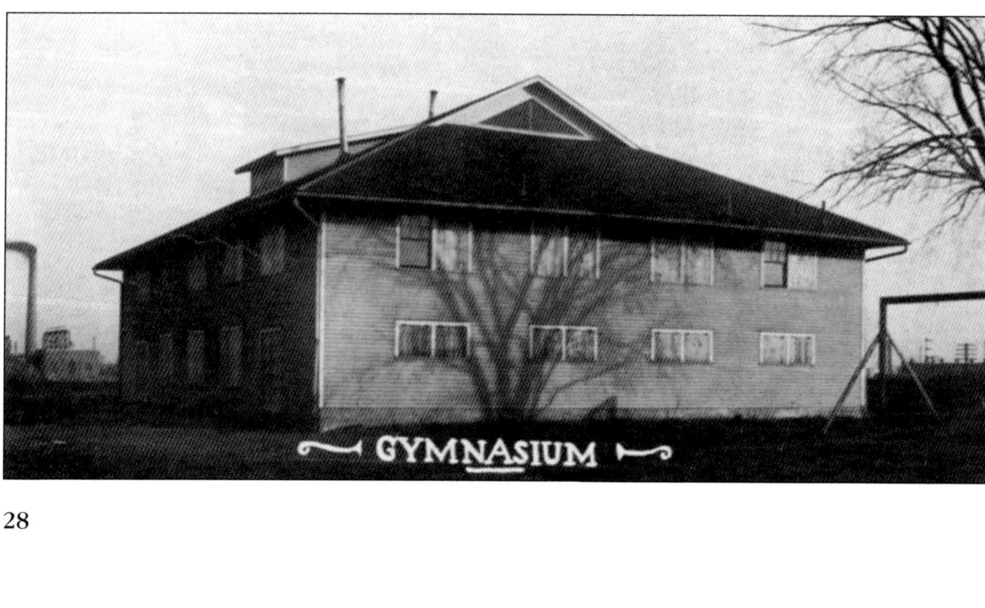

In 1925, A. Monroe Stowe resigned after relations with the faculty deteriorated. John W. Dowd, who taught history and math, was appointed his replacement on March 28, 1925. He was 78 years old when appointed to the position, and he died on May 13, 1926, after becoming ill.

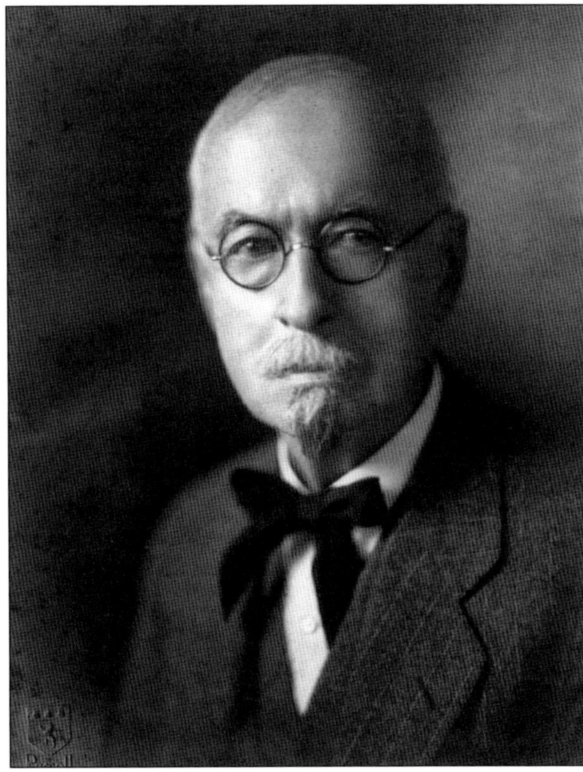

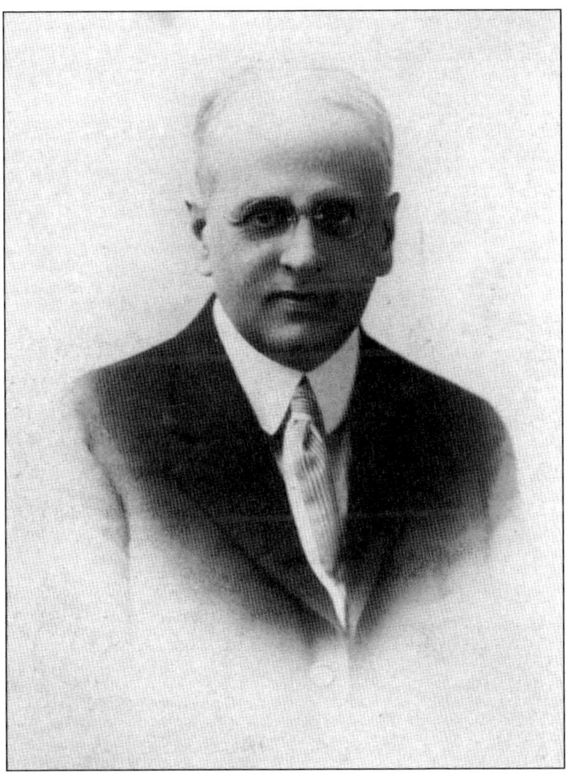

Dr. Lee MacKinnon was appointed chief administrative officer as Dowd's replacement. He did not want to be president, but would serve in this role three times during his tenure at the university. The quick succession of leaders continued. In 1926, Ernest Ashton Smith was appointed president but died of a heart attack after only one year in office. Dr. MacKinnon again stepped in to lead the university.

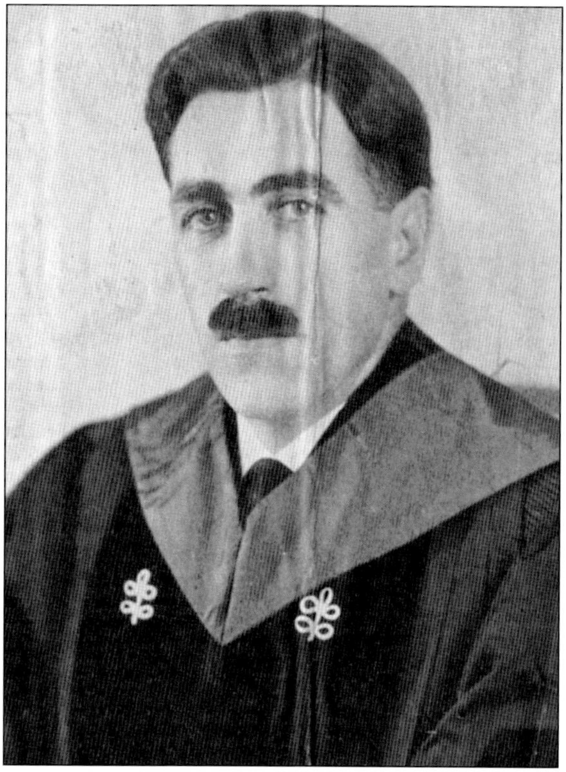

In 1927, the board of directors announced the appointment of a new president, Dr. Henry J. Doermann, who was just 37 years old and acting president of the University of Puerto Rico. He was inaugurated on March 19, 1928, and immediately began planning for a new campus. Dr. Doermann and the board hoped to pay for it by selling the university properties at Cherry and Page Streets, 11th and Illinois Streets, and the Scott Park farm. But because of legal issues with the Scott trust, instead they asked city taxpayers to approve a $2.8 million bond levy.

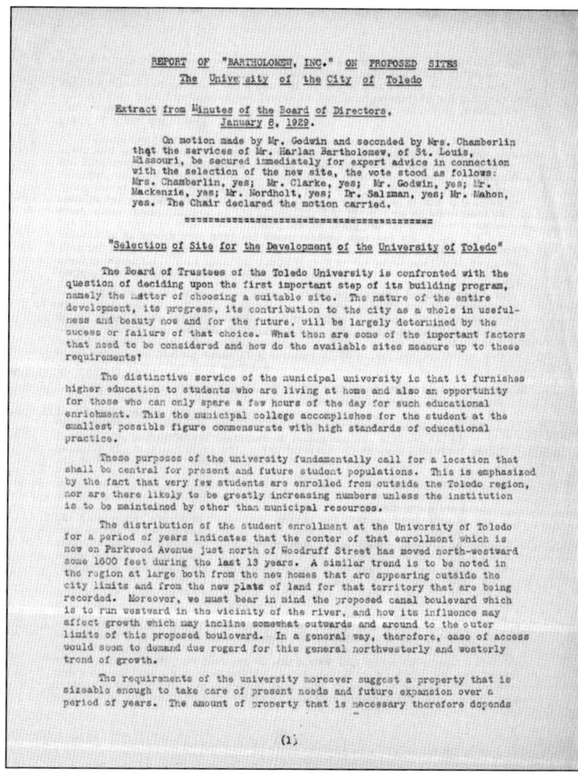

REPORT OF "BARTHOLOMEW, INC." ON PROPOSED SITES
The University of the City of Toledo

Extract from Minutes of the Board of Directors,
January 8, 1929.

On motion made by Mr. Godwin and seconded by Mrs. Chamberlin that the services of Mr. Harlan Bartholomew, of St. Louis, Missouri, be secured immediately for expert advice in connection with the selection of the new site, the vote stood as follows: Mrs. Chamberlin, yes; Mr. Clarke, yes; Mr. Godwin, yes; Mr. Mackenzie, yes; Mr. Nordholt, yes; Dr. Salzman, yes; Mr. Mahon, yes. The Chair declared the motion carried.

==

"Selection of Site for the Development of the University of Toledo"

The Board of Trustees of the Toledo University is confronted with the question of deciding upon the first important step of its building program, namely the matter of choosing a suitable site. The nature of the entire development, its progress, its contribution to the city as a whole in usefulness and beauty now and for the future, will be largely determined by the sucess or failure of that choice. What then are some of the important factors that need to be considered and how do the available sites measure up to these requirements?

The distinctive service of the municipal university is that it furnishes higher education to students who are living at home and also an opportunity for those who can only spare a few hours of the day for such educational enrichment. This the municipal college accomplishes for the student at the smallest possible figure commensurate with high standards of educational practice.

These purposes of the university fundamentally call for a location that shall be central for present and future student populations. This is emphasized by the fact that very few students are enrolled from outside the Toledo region, nor are there likely to be greatly increasing numbers unless the institution is to be maintained by other than municipal resources.

The distribution of the student enrollment at the University of Toledo for a period of years indicates that the center of that enrollment which is now on Parkwood Avenue just north of Woodruff Street has moved north-westward some 1600 feet during the last 13 years. A similar trend is to be noted in the region at large both from the new homes that are appearing outside the city limits and from the new plats of land for that territory that are being recorded. Moreover, we must bear in mind the proposed canal boulevard which is to run westward in the vicinity of the river, and how its influence may affect growth which may incline somewhat outwards and around to the outer limits of this proposed boulevard. In a general way, therefore, ease of access would seem to demand due regard for this general northwesterly and westerly trend of growth.

The requirements of the university moreover suggest a property that is sizeable enough to take care of present needs and future expansion over a period of years. The amount of property that is necessary therefore depends

(1)

The new campus required a location. One attractive site recommended by Bartholomew Inc. was the Rufus Wright farm on Bancroft Street. The firm's report noted that "the area along the street should give opportunity for an imposing building group with the Administration building as the center, perhaps, and commanding interest and attention along the approach to Bancroft street." At a public hearing to consider the matter, Albert Macomber, then age 92, surprised all by supporting the move and suggesting the Wright farm as the best site.

The campaign for passage of the bond levy was led by political science professor O. Garfield Jones. Students and faculty joined the effort, knocking on doors all over the city to elicit support for the levy on the November 1928 ballot. By a vote of 48,905 to 38,477, the levy passed. The taxpayers' approval came less than a year before the start of the worst economic depression in modern times. If the 1928 vote had been unsuccessful, it is doubtful that it would have succeeded in subsequent years and the university's fortune would have been much bleaker. The Wright farm, located near a pleasant residential neighborhood and centrally accessible to most in the city, was purchased for $275,000. The local architectural firm of Mills, Rhines, Bellman, and Nordhoff was selected to design a classroom building and a multipurpose building, and Henry J. Speiker was chosen as general contractor.

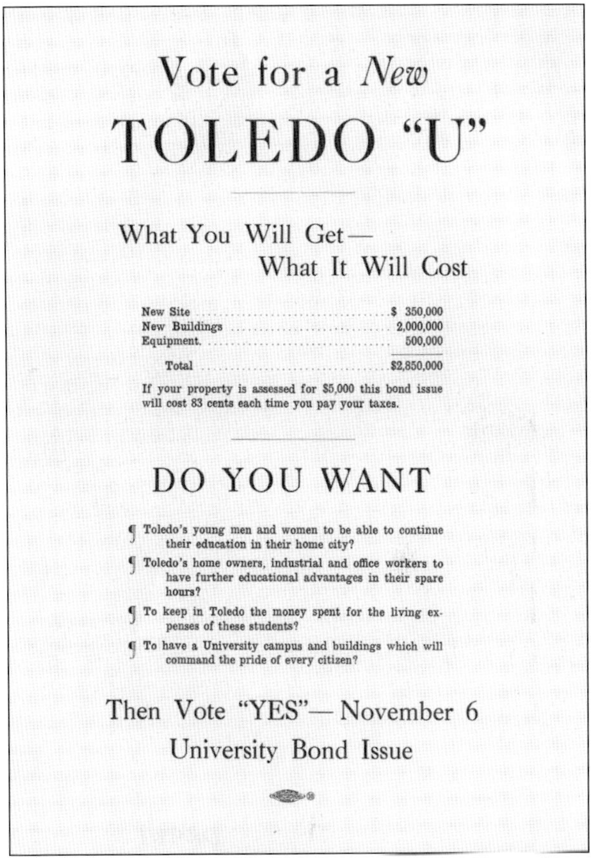

Vote for a *New*

TOLEDO "U"

What You Will Get—
What It Will Cost

New Site	$ 350,000
New Buildings	2,000,000
Equipment	500,000
Total	$2,850,000

If your property is assessed for $5,000 this bond issue will cost 83 cents each time you pay your taxes.

DO YOU WANT

¶ Toledo's young men and women to be able to continue their education in their home city?

¶ Toledo's home owners, industrial and office workers to have further educational advantages in their spare hours?

¶ To keep in Toledo the money spent for the living expenses of these students?

¶ To have a University campus and buildings which will command the pride of every citizen?

Then Vote "YES"— November 6
University Bond Issue

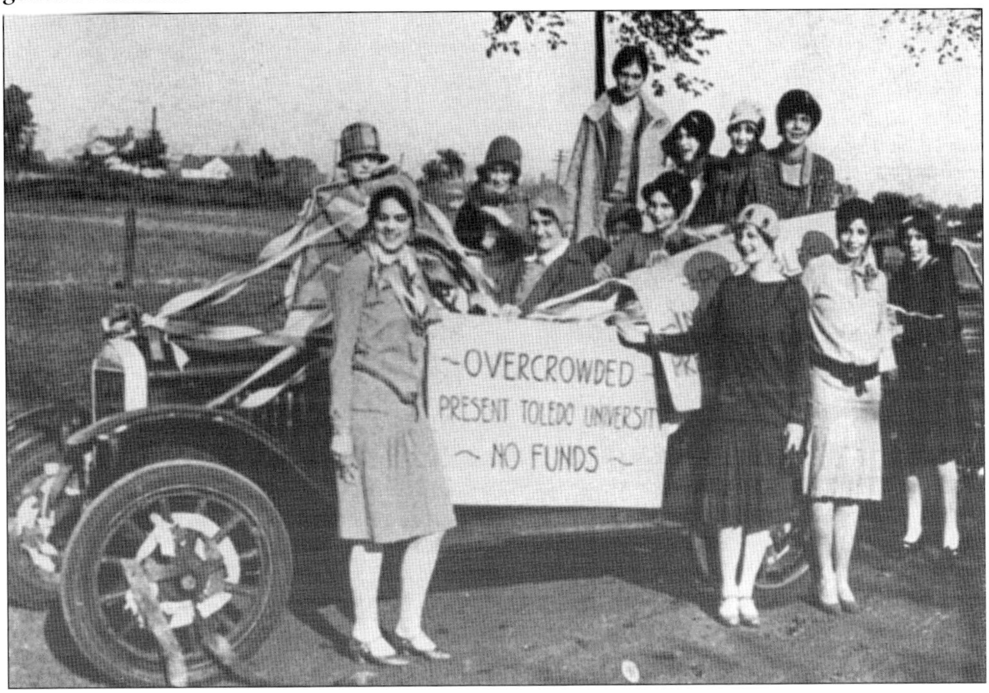

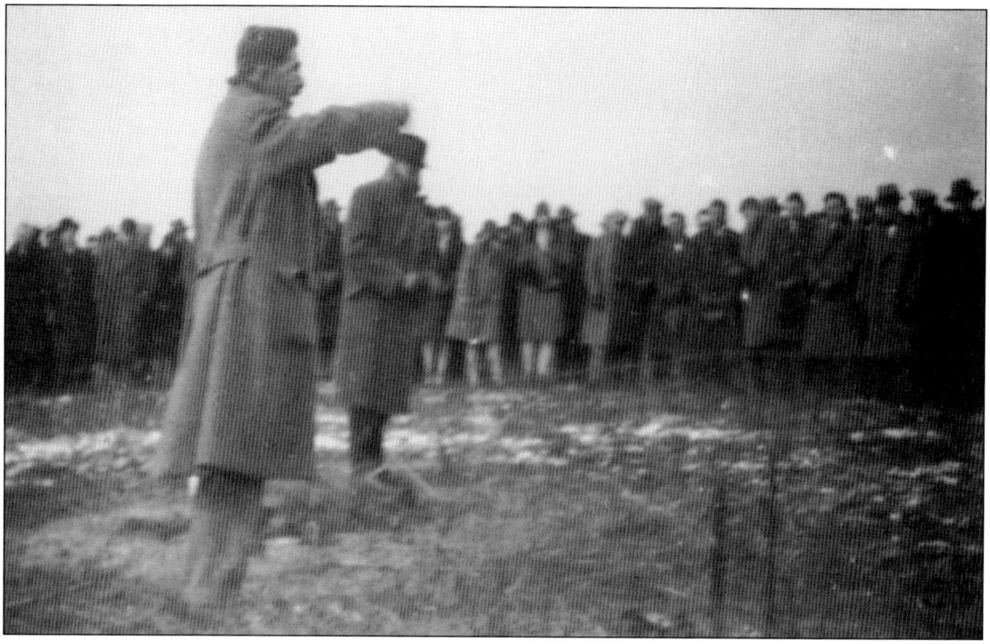

Dr. Doermann wanted the new campus to reflect the best design elements of the old universities of Europe because he felt such architecture would inspire students. A Collegiate Gothic design with a central tower and two enclosed courtyards was chosen. Many Toledoans who were suffering due to the Depression criticized the plans as extravagant, and Dr. Doermann was often forced to justify his vision. This photograph shows Dr. Doermann at the ground breaking for the new campus.

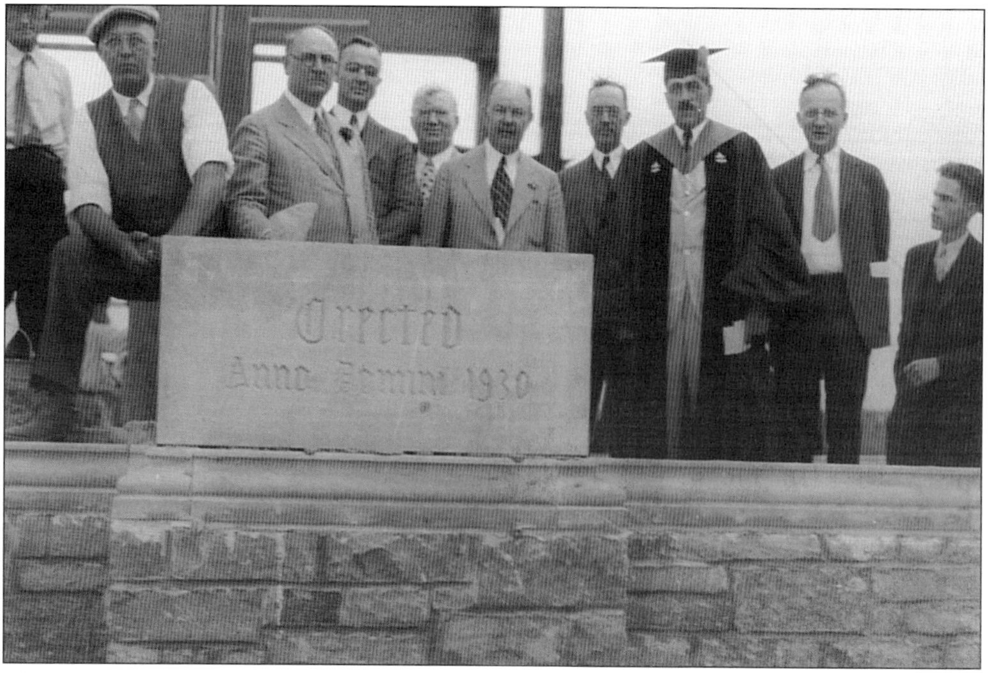

The cornerstone laying ceremony coincided with commencement on June 12, 1930. A copper box was filed with mementos of the day, and placed in the stone.

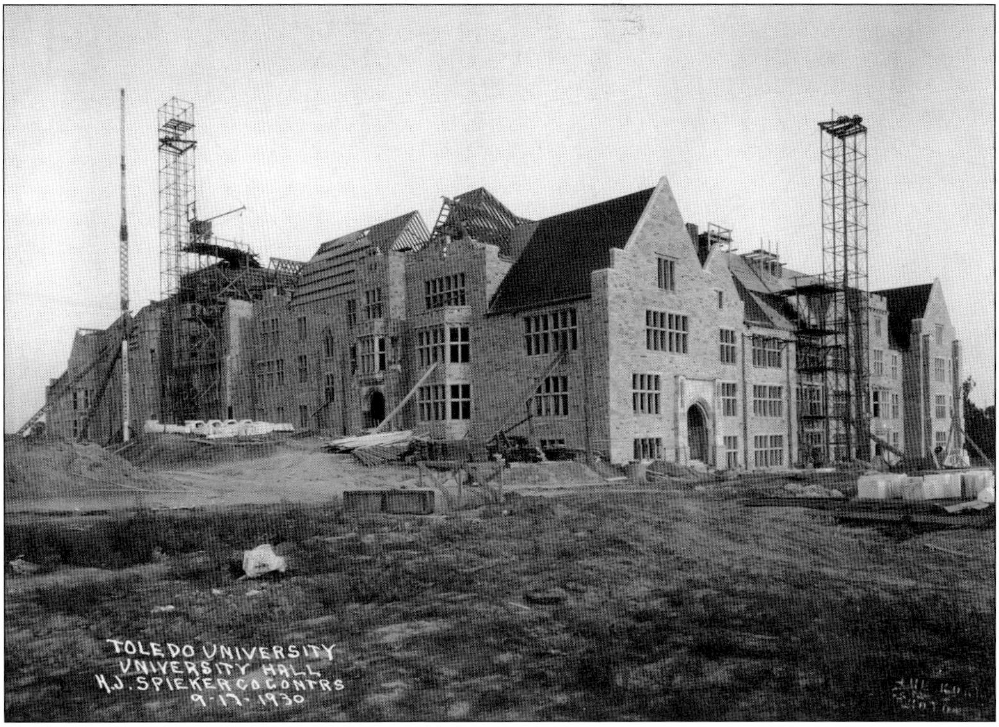

It took 400 men 11 months to complete University Hall and the Field House. When the buildings were completed, Dr. Doermann hosted a five-day open house for the citizens of Toledo to tour the campus buildings. Over 60,000 people—one-fifth of the population of the city—took him up on his offer. The new campus was about the only thing the city had to celebrate.

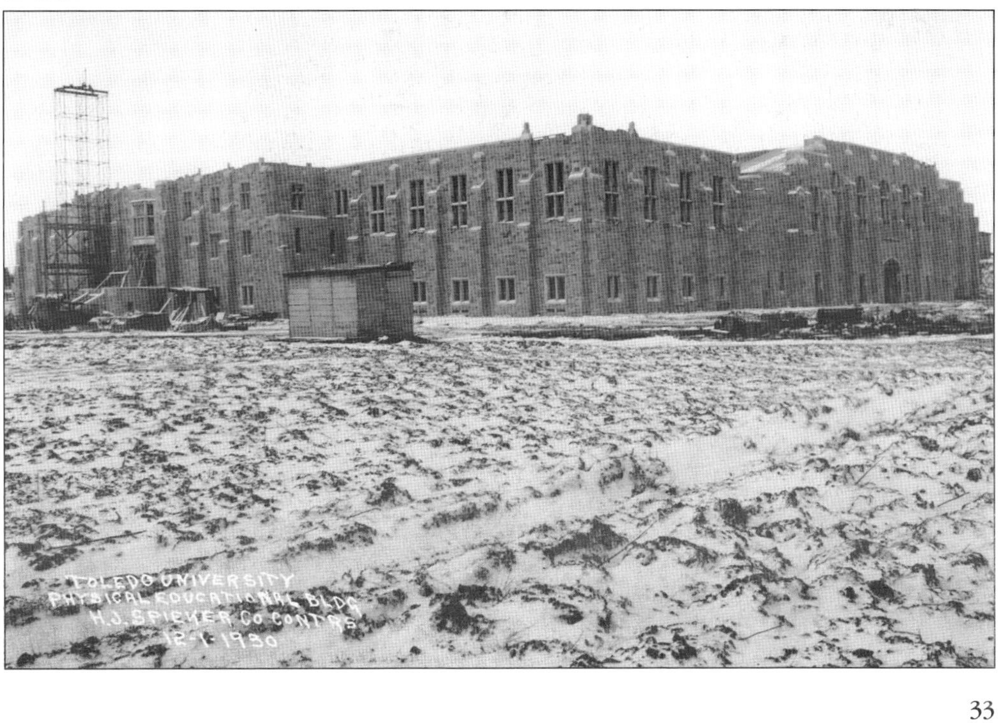

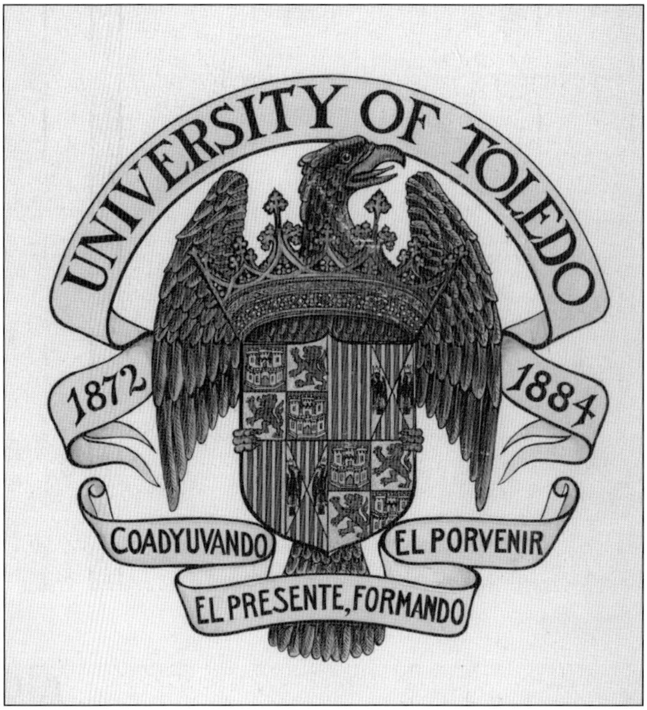

Dr. Doermann visited Spain in 1931 and worked to form a sister-city relationship with Toledo. It is believed to be the first sister-city designation ever established. Doermann also sought a new design for the university's official seal and received permission from the Spanish government to use the coat of arms of King Ferdinand and Queen Isabella. The university's motto, usually in Latin at most universities, was written in Old Spanish to reflect the relationship between the two Toledos. The motto read, "Coadyuvando El Presente, Formando El Porvenir," which was translated as "Guide to the Present, Moulder of the Future."

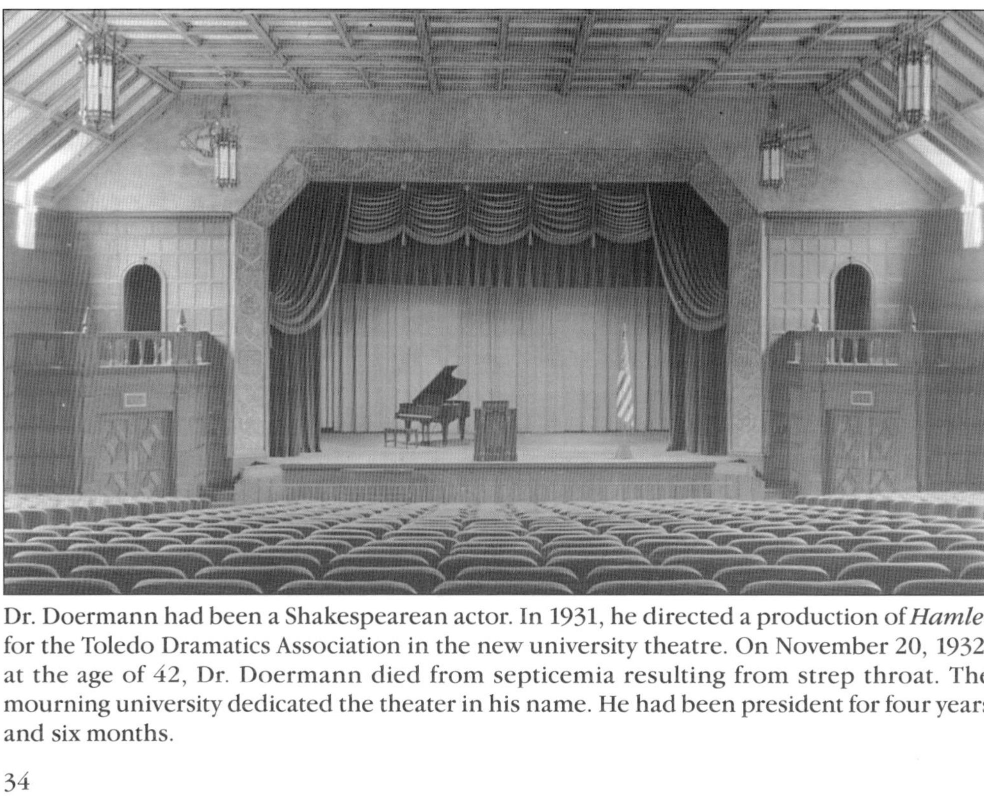

Dr. Doermann had been a Shakespearean actor. In 1931, he directed a production of *Hamlet* for the Toledo Dramatics Association in the new university theatre. On November 20, 1932, at the age of 42, Dr. Doermann died from septicemia resulting from strep throat. The mourning university dedicated the theater in his name. He had been president for four years and six months.

Dr. Lee MacKinnon again took over as administrative officer for the third time. In November 1933, the board of directors appointed Philip C. Nash, dean of Antioch College, as the new president. Prior to his career in higher education, Dr. Nash had been executive director of the League of Nations Association, an organization that supported US participation in the league. World affairs remained a lifelong interest of Dr. Nash.

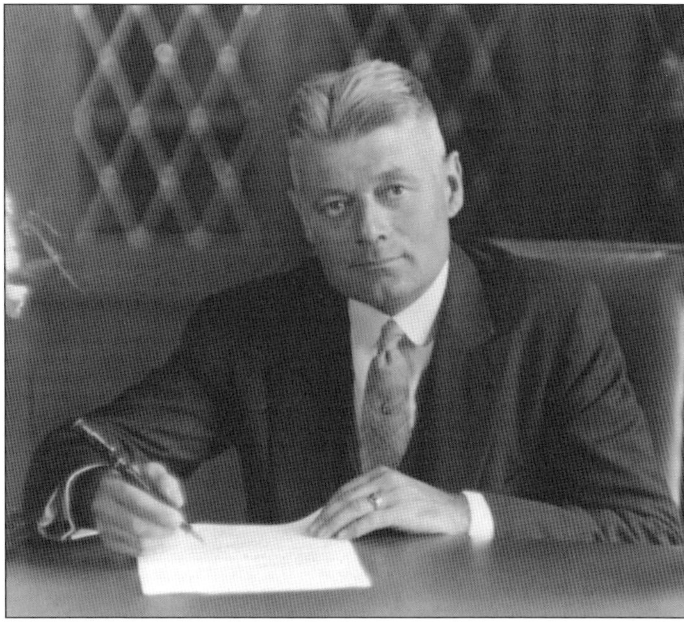

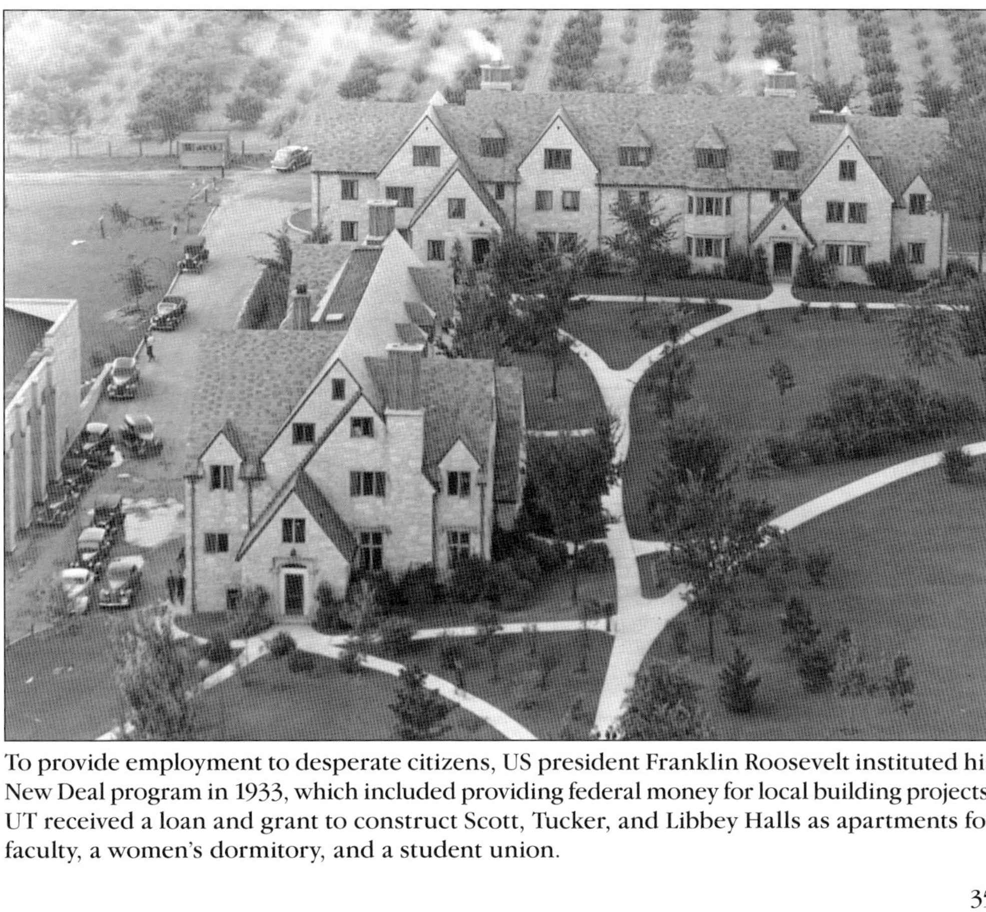

To provide employment to desperate citizens, US president Franklin Roosevelt instituted his New Deal program in 1933, which included providing federal money for local building projects. UT received a loan and grant to construct Scott, Tucker, and Libbey Halls as apartments for faculty, a women's dormitory, and a student union.

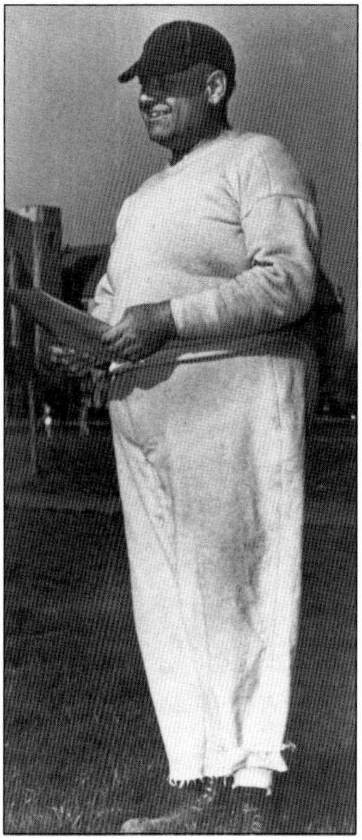

The UT football team was coached by Clarence "Doc" Spears (left). David Connelly (below, far left) coached the baseball team from 1931 to 1950 and also served during his career at UT as athletic director, track and cross-country coach, football coach, and dean of men.

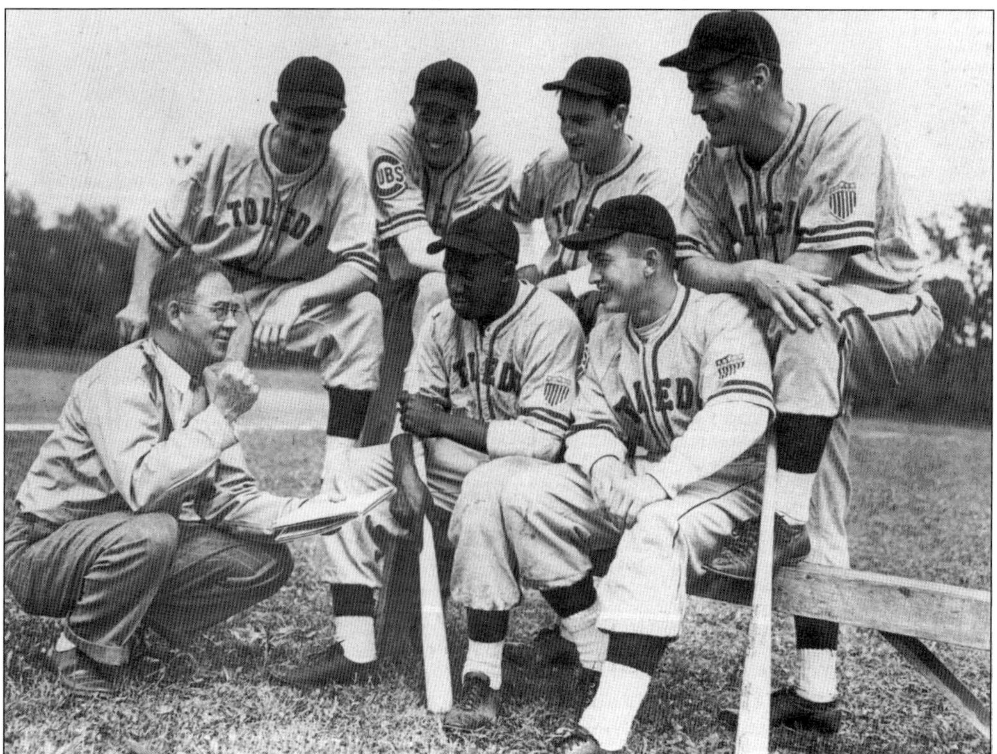

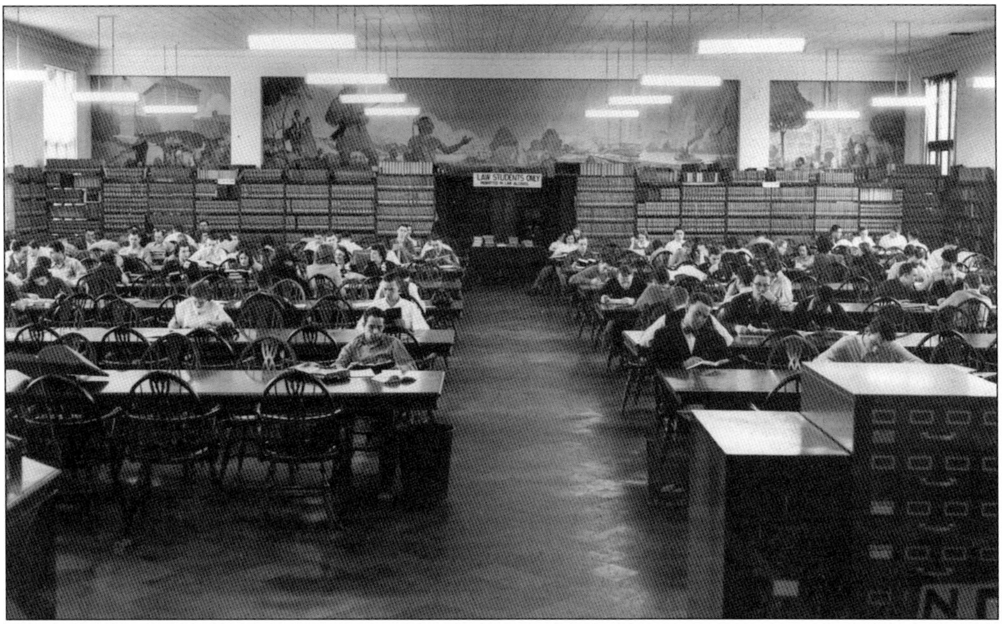

New Deal projects also included artists painting the seals of the alma maters of UT faculty on the walls of the third floor of University Hall and a mural depicting the history of Toledo on the wall of the library on the fifth floor of that building. Federal funds were also used to demolish the old Toledo Medical College building downtown.

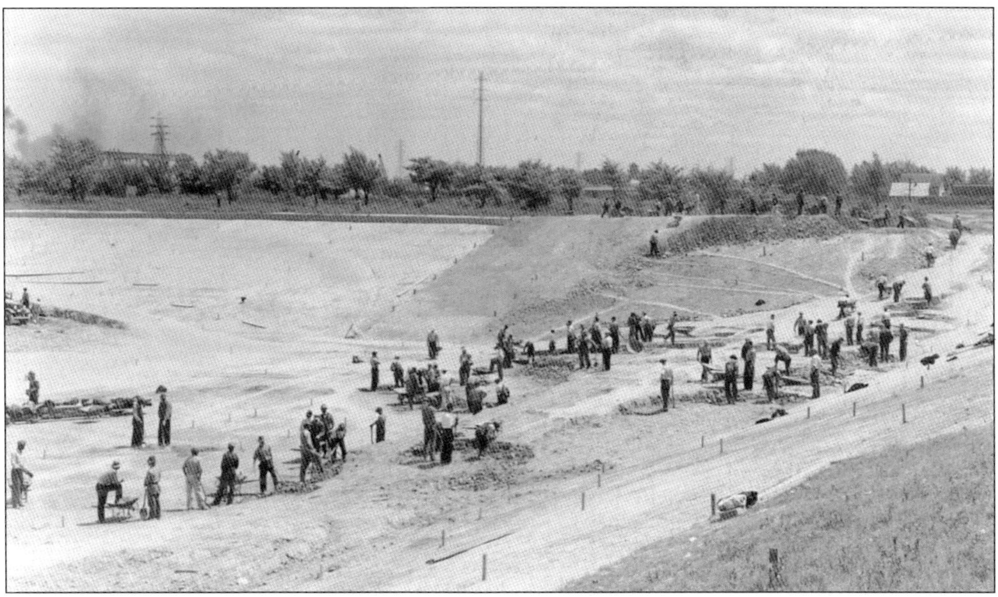

In 1936, Roosevelt's Works Progress Administration granted a contract to build an 8,000-seat stadium on the university's campus. To keep as many employed for as long a time as possible, 300 men used hand tools to excavate the stadium. This task took over one year to complete.

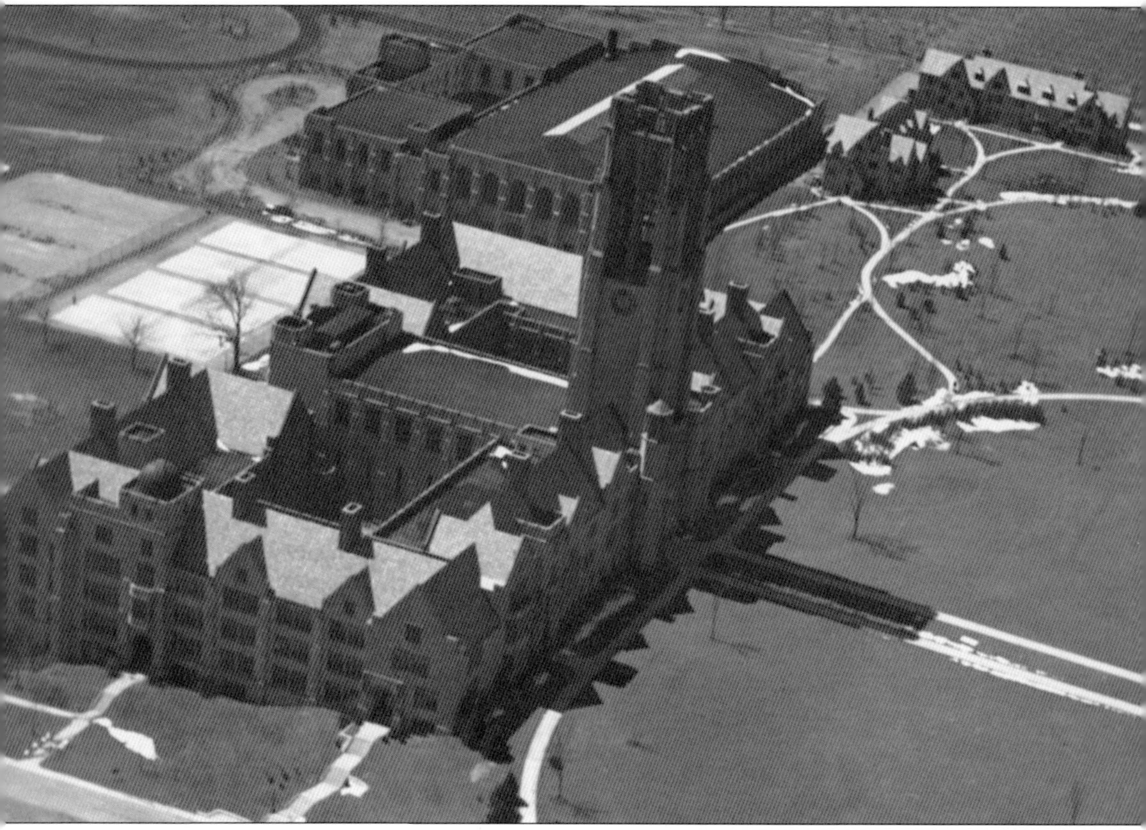

As the Depression decade came to a close, the University of Toledo had not only survived, but in many ways, had prospered. The university has a brand-new campus that was an architectural gem, New Deal funds had provided for the construction of several new buildings, and enrollments remained steady. Despite several months when payroll could not be met, the university managed to continue operations. The university's expanded campus is shown here in a 1938 photograph by Maurice Wallace.

Three

World War II and its Effects

While the Depression decade determined in many ways if the University of Toledo would survive, it was World War II that was the real watershed in the institution's history. The war transformed the university from a small, tenuous municipal institution barely able to make ends meet into the modern university it is today. Everything was changed by the war—the students, the faculty, the curriculum, and the social life. Some students who dropped out to fight for their country never returned. Thousands of others who never considered a college education possible found that military service provided them with an opportunity previously beyond their reach. Some faculty left their teaching positions for government research jobs. Those who remained often had to fill in and teach courses outside their specialty areas. New programs of study supported the war effort, including pilot training and military nursing. Campus activities changed from dances and parties to those with a civic purpose like war bond drives. Women assumed leadership roles in most campus organizations as the number of men declined.

Before the bombing of Pearl Harbor, student sentiment at UT was largely against military engagement in Europe's problems. On April 20, 1939, students rallied at University Peace Day, an annual event, where UT president Philip Nash spoke. While Hitler's invasion of Poland and France was months away, Dr. Nash felt war was inevitable. President Nash, who had long advocated for an international organization to promote peace, told students that "even after spending much of my life resisting war, I nevertheless believe that war would be better than the surrender of freedom by democracies."

Enrollment began to decline in 1940 and took a major downward tumble after Pearl Harbor. The College of Engineering's enrollment dropped by 90 percent, and the College of Arts and Sciences by 50 percent.

After war was declared, universities across the country were asked to help the government by making available facilities and programs for the war effort. UT quickly revised its curriculum to allow for accelerated degree programs. Students who completed 12 weeks of the semester were given full credit if they left to join the war. After the draft age was dropped to 18 in 1942, the university established Saturday and summer session classes for high school students to allow them to be admitted at the end of their junior year.

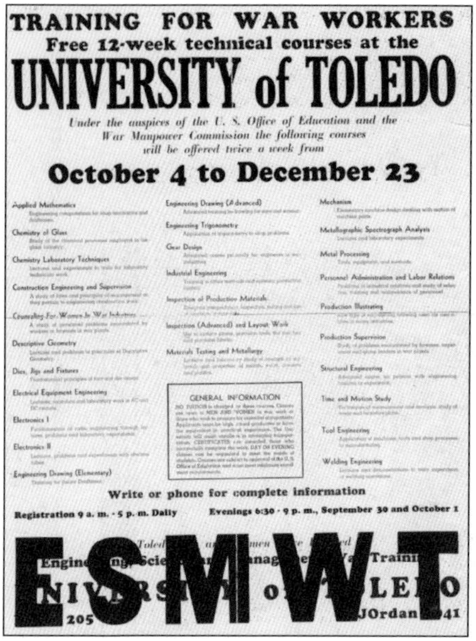

Faculty also left to join the war. Others helped organize war-related programs, including College of Engineering dean Delos Palmer, who helped establish the Engineering, Science, and Management War Training Program. UT was one of 200 colleges nationally to offer such training for war industry production workers. The program attracted over 1,000 students in its first semester, a significant number of whom were women. By the time the program ended in 1945, around 15,000 Toledoans had been trained.

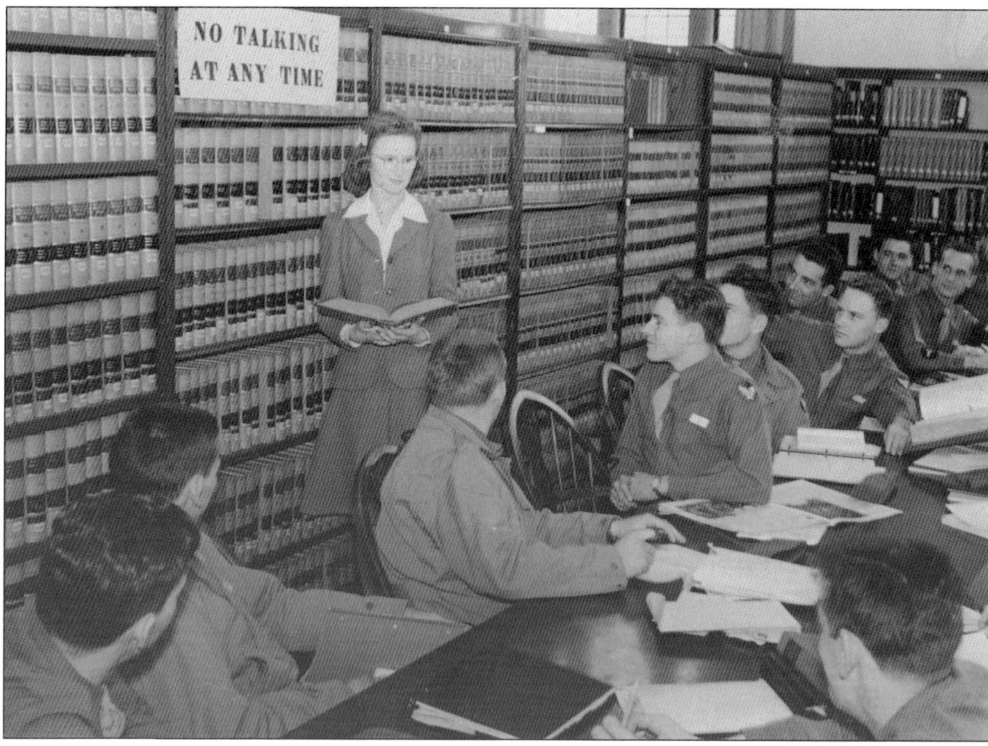

The university was a part of several air pilot training programs. In 1939, the Civilian Pilot Training Program was approved; over 100 men completed the coursework, and most entered the service after graduation. In 1943, due to a lack of space at the Miami Beach base of the 27th College Air Corps Training Unit, the government contracted with UT to house, feed, and train a detachment of the corps. The men received military, flying, physical, and academic training while living in the Field House. In the 13 months that the program ran, some 1,800 graduated.

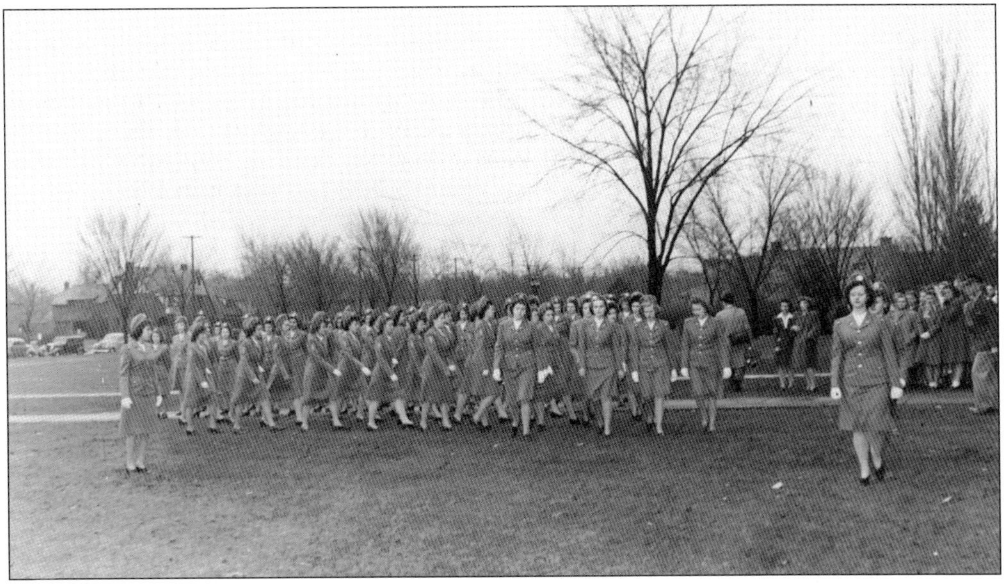

Another federal program trained women to become military nurses. The university provided academic courses, and local hospitals provided clinical training. The women also practiced military drills under the direction of several UT faculty. More than 300 graduated from the US Cadet Nurse Corps program.

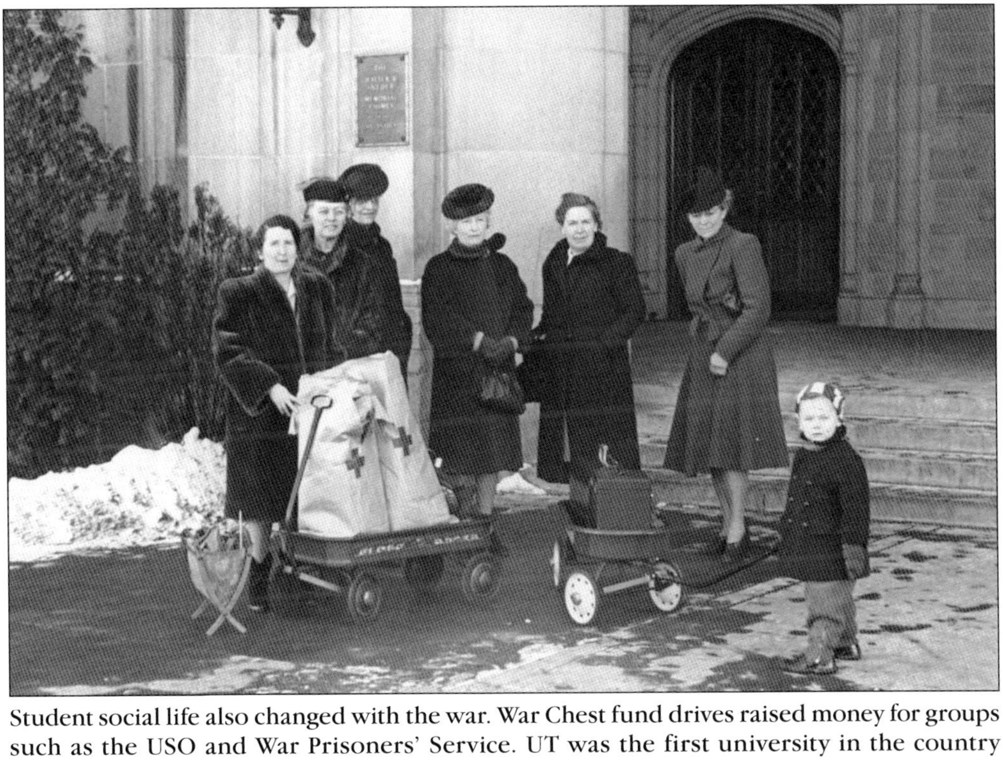

Student social life also changed with the war. War Chest fund drives raised money for groups such as the USO and War Prisoners' Service. UT was the first university in the country with a Red Cross chapter, and wives of UT faculty collected items for the Red Cross. The group sponsored knitting bees to make sweaters for soldiers. Weekly air-raid drills were also practiced.

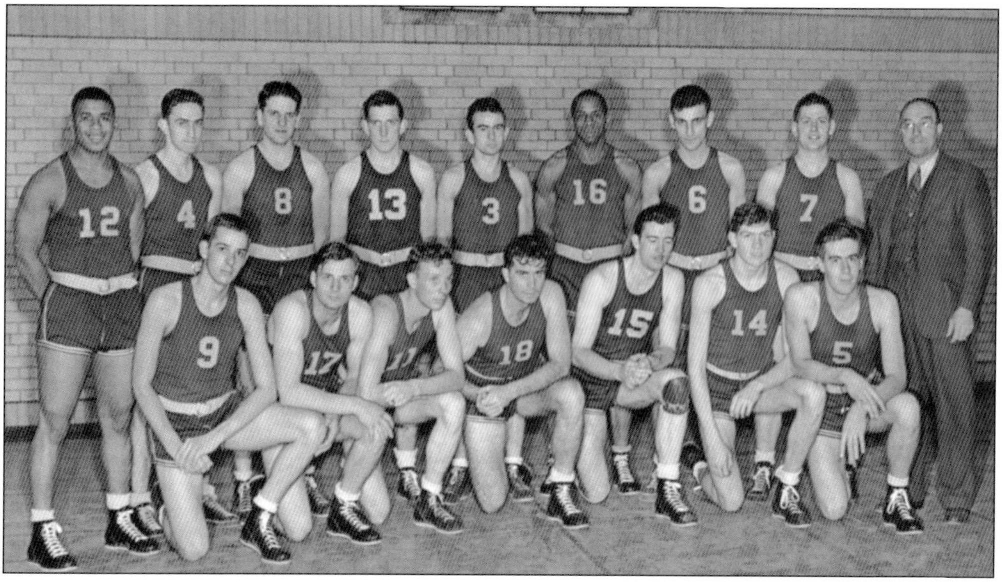

Before the war, UT's basketball team experienced several outstanding seasons under head coach W. Harold Anderson and star player Charles "Chuck" Chuckovits. The 1939, 1941, and 1943 teams played in the National Invitational Tournament in Madison Square Garden. Shown here is the 1941 team with Coach Anderson. Unlike many college teams of the day, UT's team was racially integrated. Basketball was discontinued when the Field House became the home for those in the College Air Corps program. With only 270 men on campus, football was also discontinued in 1943.

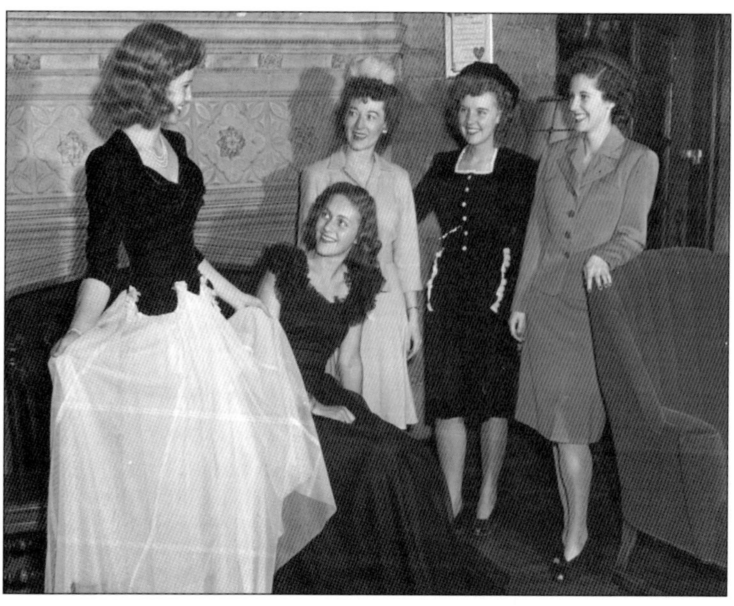

Women assumed leadership roles in most campus organizations, including president of Student Council in 1944, and editor of the *Collegian* and *Blockhouse* from 1943 to 1945. Many fraternities suspended operations, while sororities continued to be popular, including Alpha Tau Sigma, where members held a style show in 1944.

To keep track of friends serving overseas, the university posted an Armed Services Directory. Lyle Clark and Dodd Tonjes consult the directory in 1944.

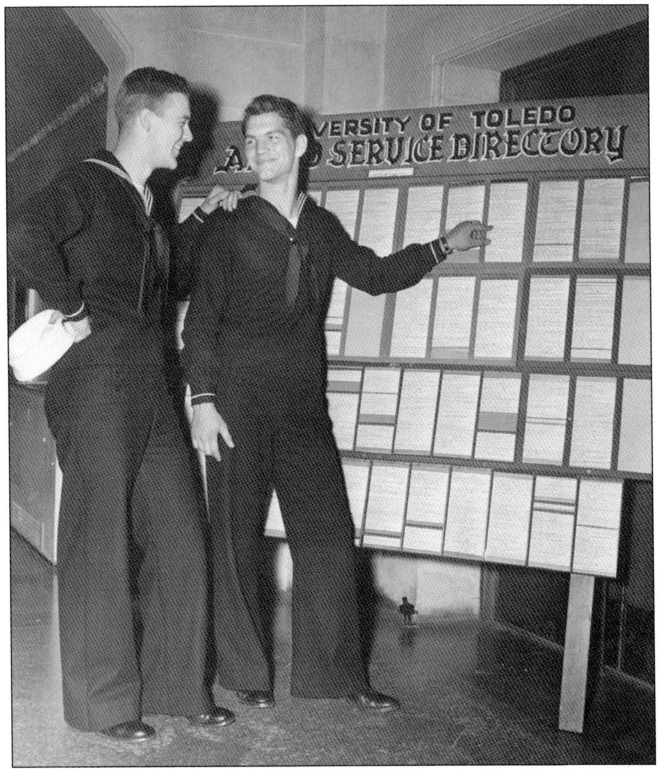

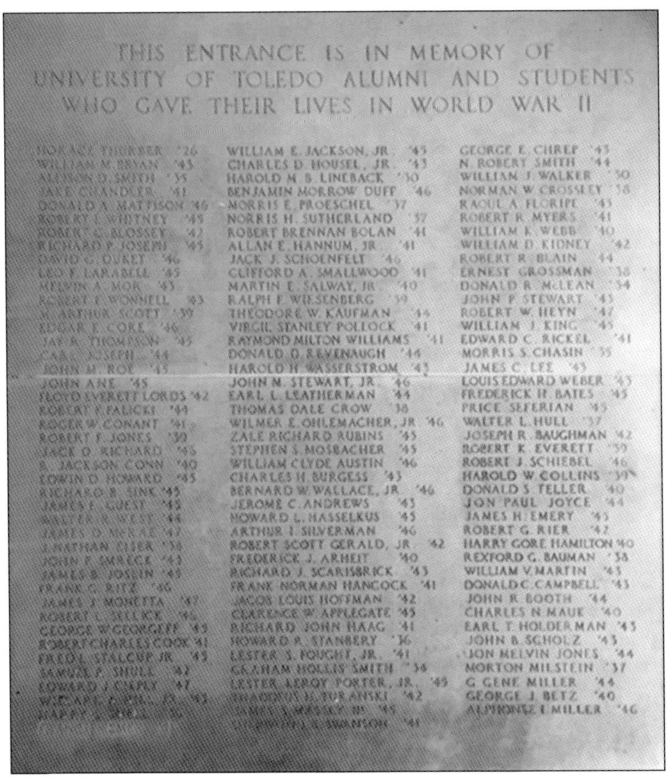

The full effect of the war on University of Toledo students was personal—disrupted lives, feelings of fear and anxiety, and more than occasionally, death. At least 108 UT students were killed in the war. A War Memorial Scholarship Fund was established in 1946 to provide money so their children could attend the university. A plaque with the names of those killed was placed at the entrance to the new library building (later named Gillham Hall) in 1953. It remains there as a lasting reminder of the impact of the war on the university.

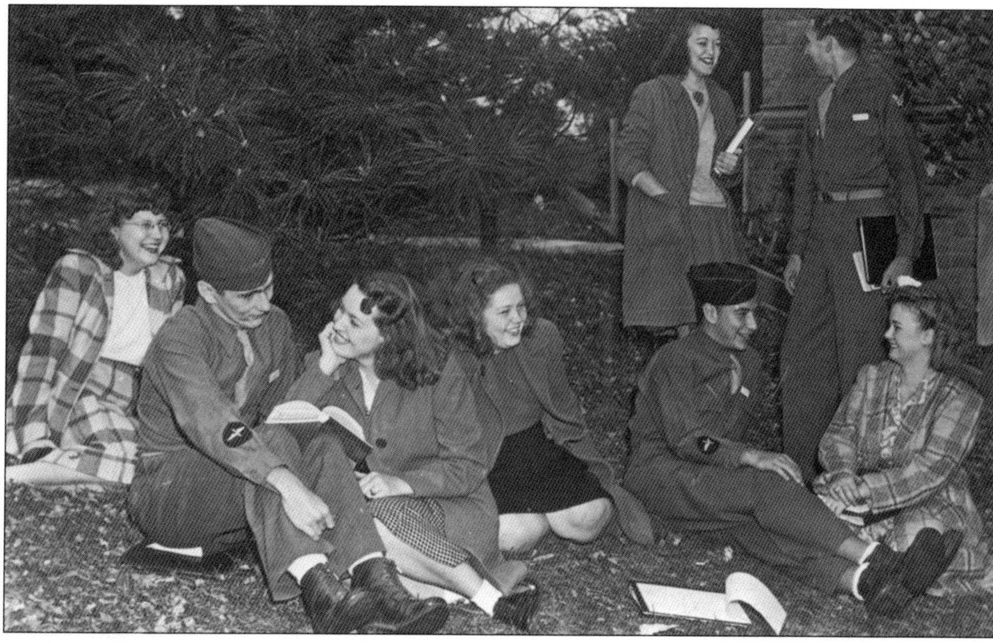

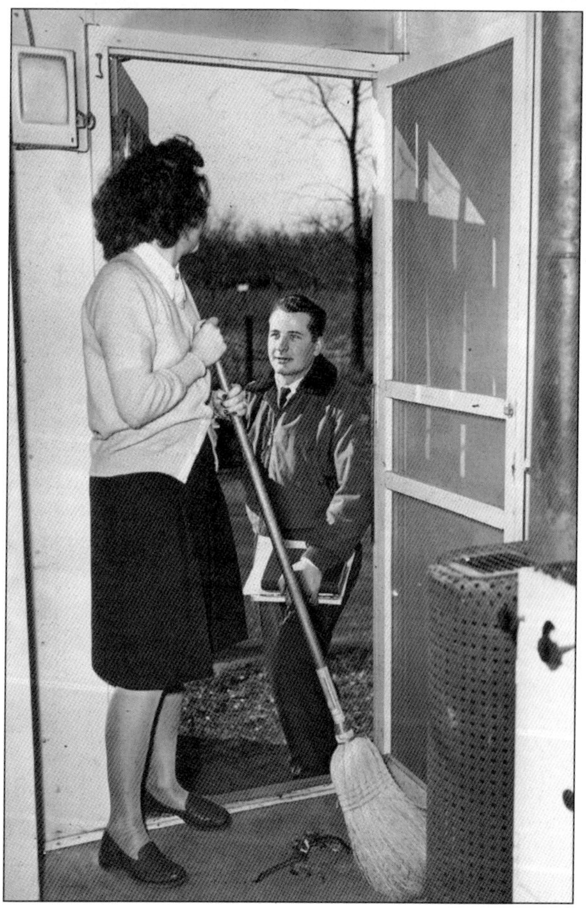

In 1944, Congress passed the Servicemen's Readjustment Act, more commonly known as the GI Bill of Rights. The intent of the bill was to reward those who had served and also cushion the economic blow as they returned looking for peacetime work. The act paid up to $500 in college tuition and provided a living allowance of between $65 and $90 per month. Over 3,000 veterans took advantage of the program at UT.

Because many of those attending on the GI Bill were married with children, they needed housing. In 1945 and 1946, UT purchased surplus units from the Federal Housing Authority and moved them to campus. The community was dubbed "Nashville" by the students in honor of President Nash, who had arranged for the housing.

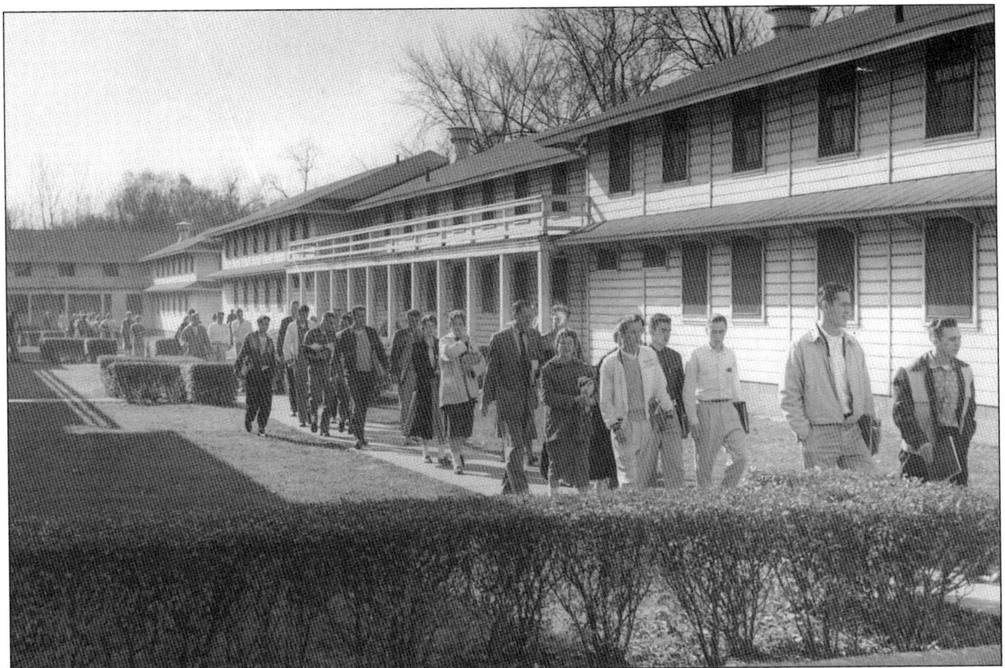

The university also purchased nine surplus Army barracks from Camp Perry in Sandusky and brought them to campus for use as classrooms and research facilities. Constructed behind University Hall, they were intended to be temporary, but a few of them stood until they were torn down in 1979.

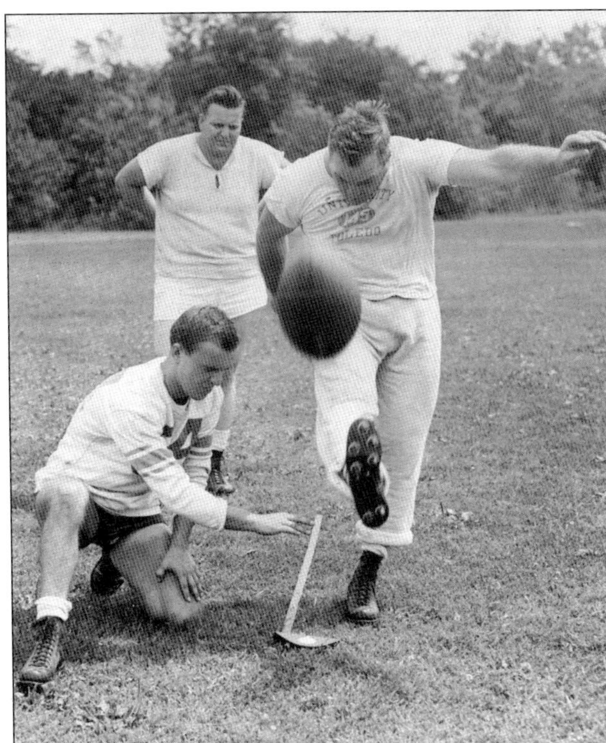

Sports returned after the war. Basketball resumed in 1945 and football in 1946. Wayne Kohn, an employee of the Toledo-based Libbey-Owens-Ford Company, suggested renovating UT's stadium to incorporate several glass additions and renaming it the Glass Bowl. Lights were also added that year.

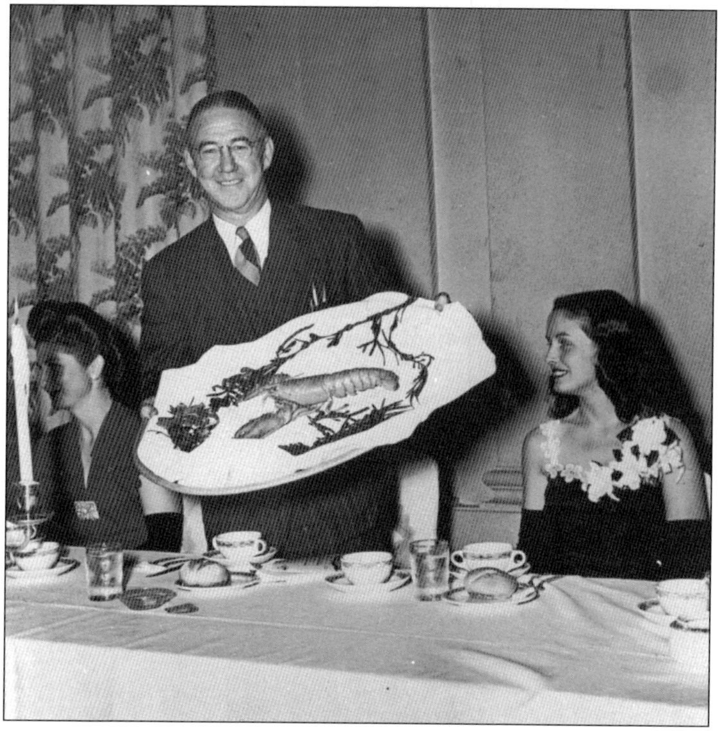

The university organized a post-season game in 1946 intended to bring in top teams from around the country to play the Rockets. That year, UT beat Bates College from Maine, which had been undefeated. At a banquet held at the Commodore Perry Hotel before the game, athletic director David Connelly showed off a lobster given to him by the governor of Maine. Two more post-season Glass Bowl tournament games were held before they were discontinued.

In honor of Pres. Philip Nash's efforts advocating for the League of Nations as an international organization that could help avoid future world wars, he was invited in 1945 to attend the United Nations Conference on International Organization, which drafted the United Nations charter. After seeing the university through the Depression and World War II, Dr. Nash's health began to fail. In August 1946, he was hospitalized for eight months with a heart ailment. He died on May 7, 1947, at the age of 56.

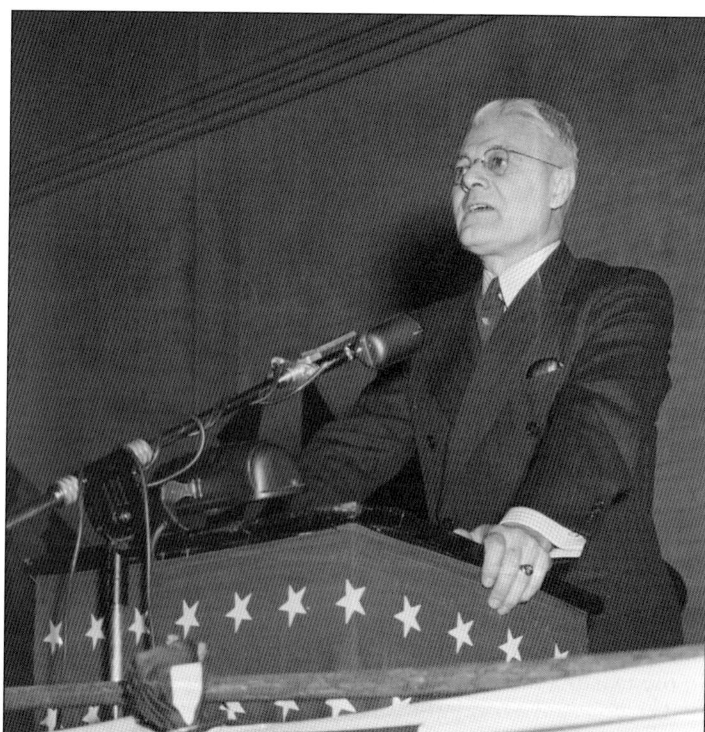

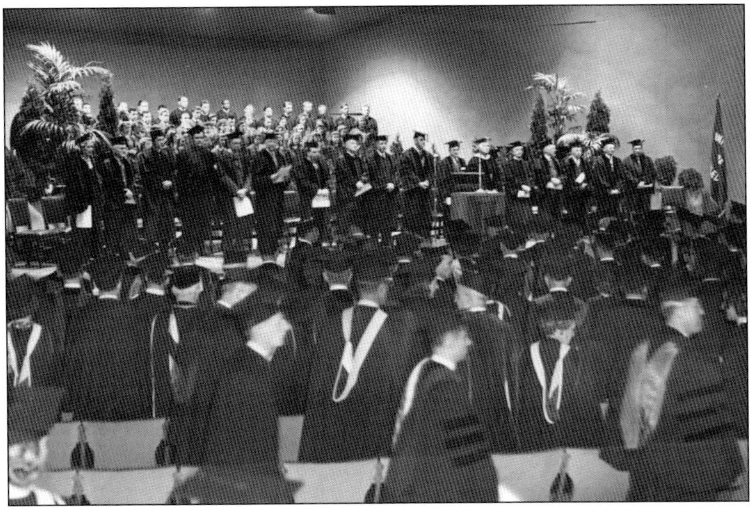

Dr. Raymond Carter took over as acting president during President Nash's extended illness. In November 1947, the board of directors appointed Wilbur W. White to the presidency. His inauguration took place in the Peristyle of the Toledo Museum of Art on May 11, 1948.

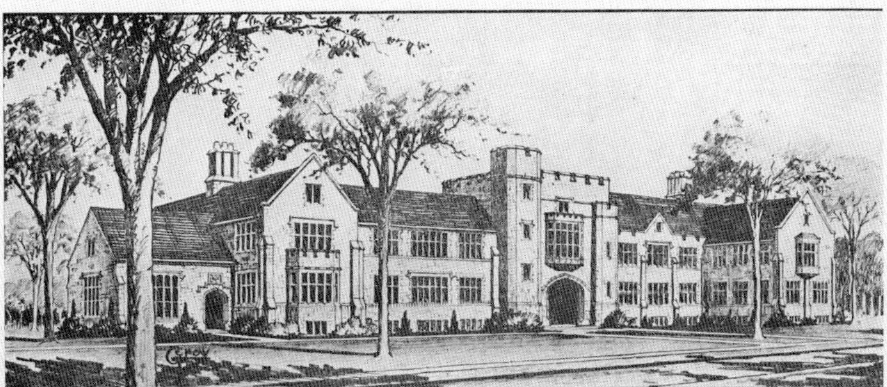

COLLEGE OF ENGINEERING - UNIVERSITY OF TOLEDO. GEROW & CONKLIN ARCHITECTS.

A separate building for the College of Engineering is one of the four which the University hopes to construct to replace the temporary structures now in use. It will provide more space for added equipment, laboratories and classrooms. All the new structures will be of Collegiate Gothic architecture in the same style as University Hall. Thus, the observance of the institution's 75th anniversary in 1947-8 finds the University of Toledo looking ahead to greater facilities for serving the city and surrounding territory.

Plans For The Future

The increase in student enrollment to the 6,000 mark has made it evident that the present facilities of the University must be expanded. The addition of temporary halls was made until plans for construction of permanent buildings could be completed.

High priority on the list of permanent structures to be erected is the Women's Building which will provide living quarters for the fast-increasing number of out-of-town students. The Home Economics Department will also be housed here.

A research building to house the University of Toledo Research Foundation is also being planned. The construction of this building will mean not only better teaching and better trained students but it will also provide for fundamental research for helping Toledo business and industry solve their more immediate problems.

In the drawing board stage is a proposed Library Building. The construction of this million dollar project will provide more room for the now overcrowded library facilities and at the same time will free almost the entire fifth floor of University Hall for classroom and office use.

President White proposed an aggressive 10-year plan for the university that focused on securing more funding from the city and from private donors, insuring that faculty had appropriate degrees, and encouraging more faculty research. White also called for a major building program, as the university's enrollment was twice what could be accommodated in the existing buildings. He sought funds from the city for a new library and law building, and established a fundraising campaign for a new engineering building.

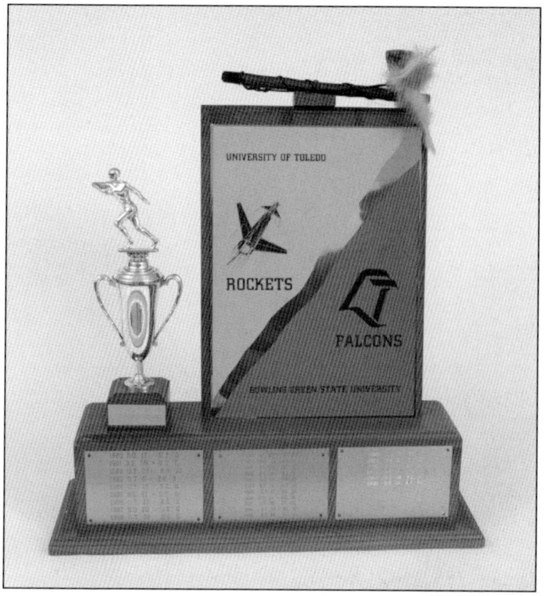

On February 22, 1947, intercollegiate athletic competition between UT and Bowling Green State University (BGSU) resumed after being suspended in 1936 due to the increasing unruliness of fans. Harold Anderson, who had been a successful coach at UT, led the BGSU basketball team to victory in that game. This trophy, known as the "peace pipe," is a symbol of the spirited yet friendly rivalry that continues today.

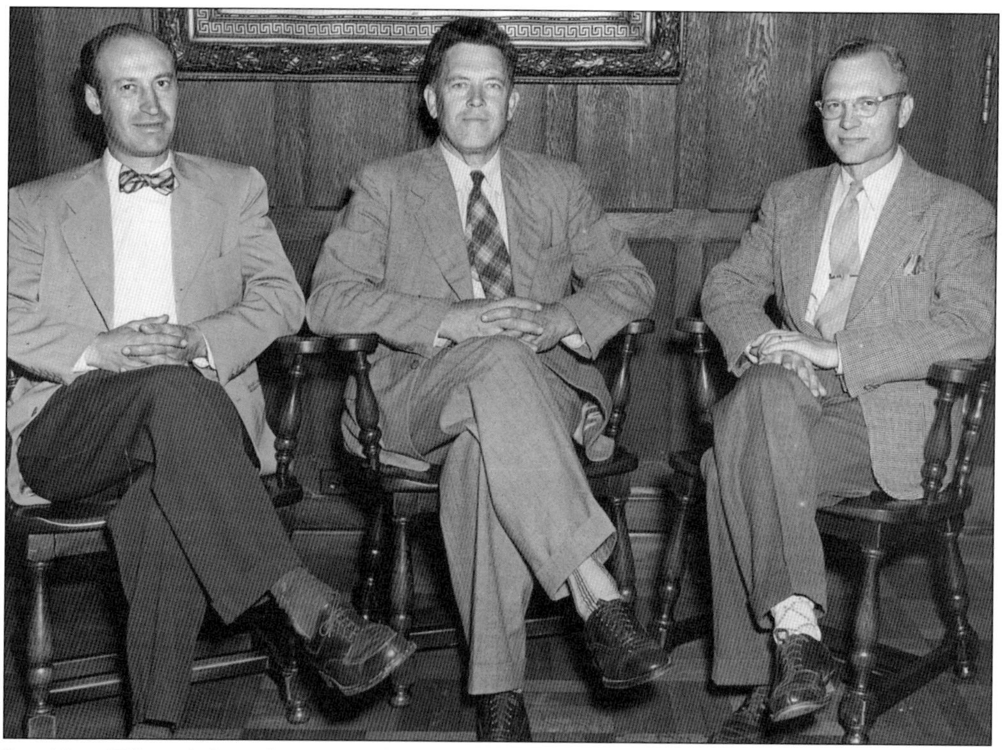

President White did not live to see his plans come to fruition. He was hospitalized in 1950 with pneumonia and a heart condition. He resigned in May 1950, and died in November. Rather than reappoint Raymond Carter as interim president, the board appointed a three-person interim operating committee to lead the institution while the search was underway for a new president. The committee consisted of, from left to right, John J. Turin, professor of physics; John B. Brandeberry, acting dean of engineering; and Jesse R. Long, director of public relations.

Dr. Asa S. Knowles, vice president at Cornell University, was appointed president of UT in 1951. The period of administrative instability that had begun with President Nash's illness in 1946 and extended through the brief tenure of President White came to an end.

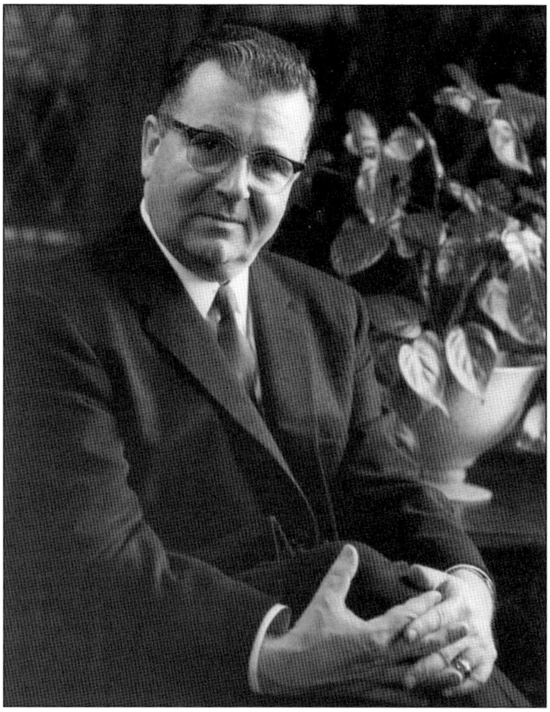

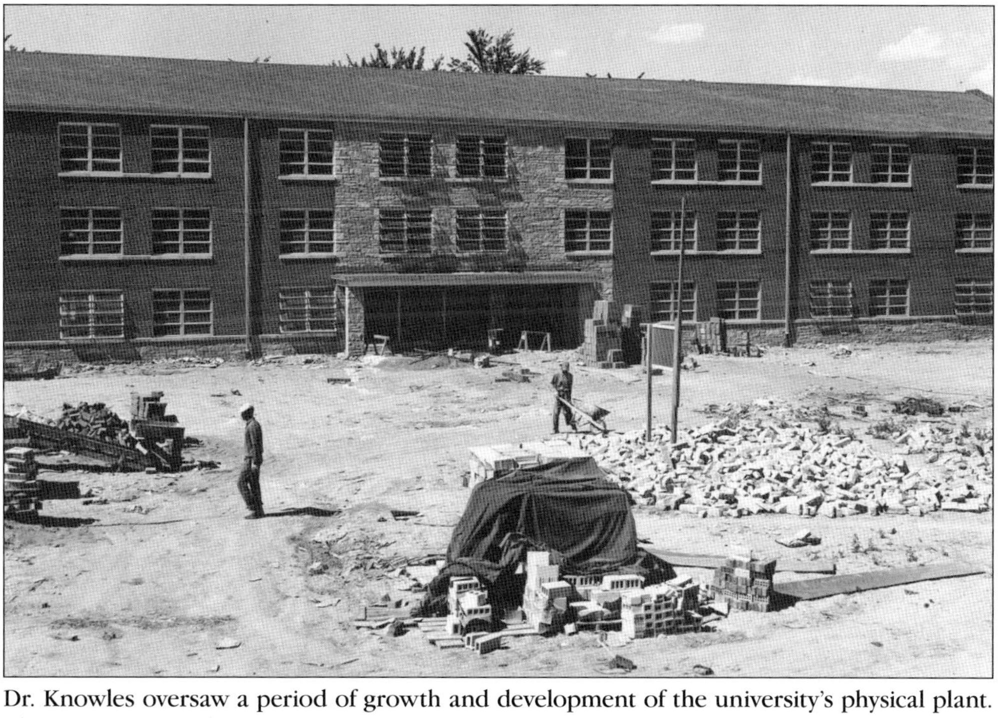

Dr. Knowles oversaw a period of growth and development of the university's physical plant. The university purchased several vacant lots on Meadowwood and Cheltenham across from the university to ensure they would not be commercially developed. In 1952, money was received from the city for construction of a new library and law building, and a new men's dormitory (pictured) named for presidents Dowd, Nash, and White, was built on the west side of campus.

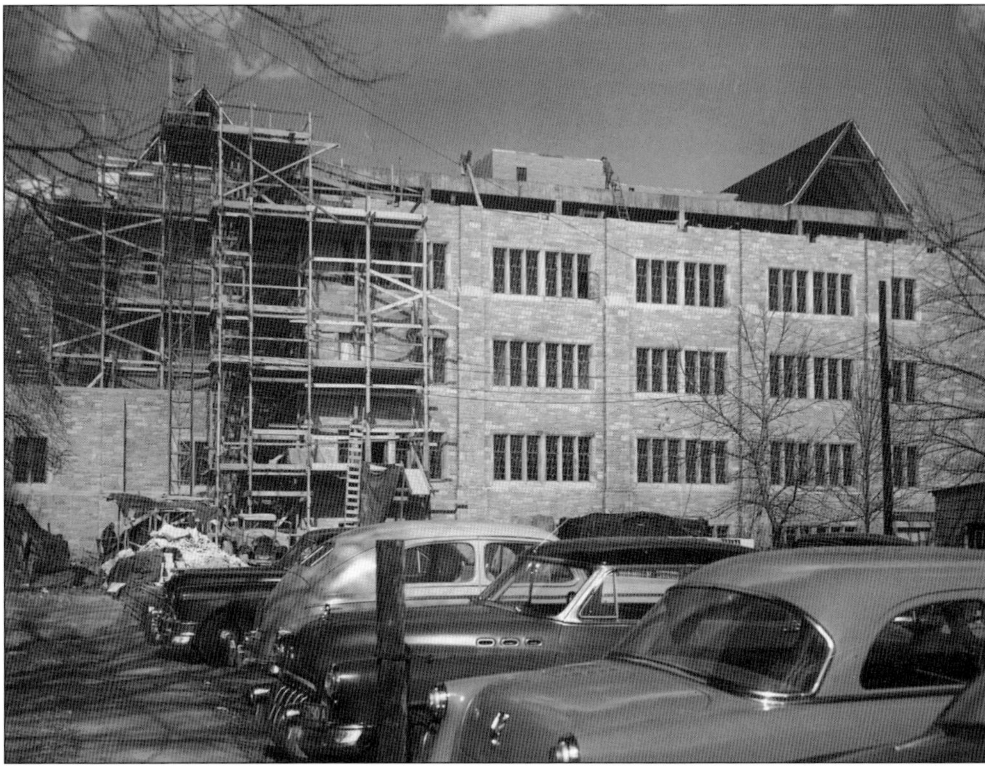

The library building replaced the library that had been on the fifth floor of University Hall. It would eventually be named for the woman who held the position of librarian for 48 years, Mary M. Gillham.

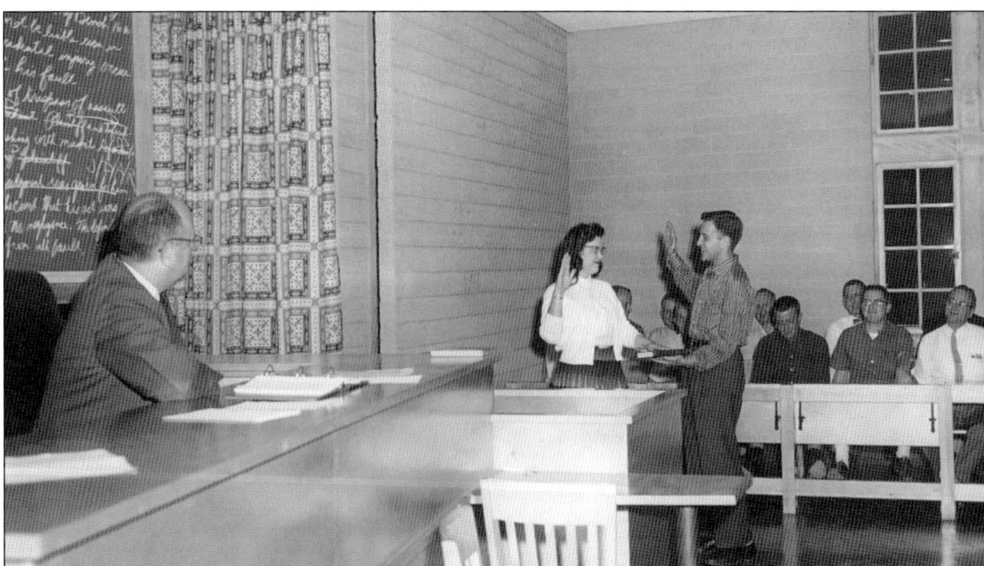

The task of moving the library's collection of books into the new building was completed in September 1953. The new library building also included the law school. The facilities included a mock courtroom so law students could practice their skills in a realistic setting.

In 1950, an athletic scandal brought the university unwanted attention. The basketball team had an exceptional winning streak of eight games, all with lopsided scores. Rumors circulated that gamblers were betting on the games. Suddenly, the team began to lose, and after a game against Niagara University, the New York district attorney charged three UT players with game fixing to benefit a New York bookmaker. The district attorney alleged that the players agreed to lose by more than seven points. The players were allowed to withdraw from the university, and Ohio law was strengthened to protect against such scandals.

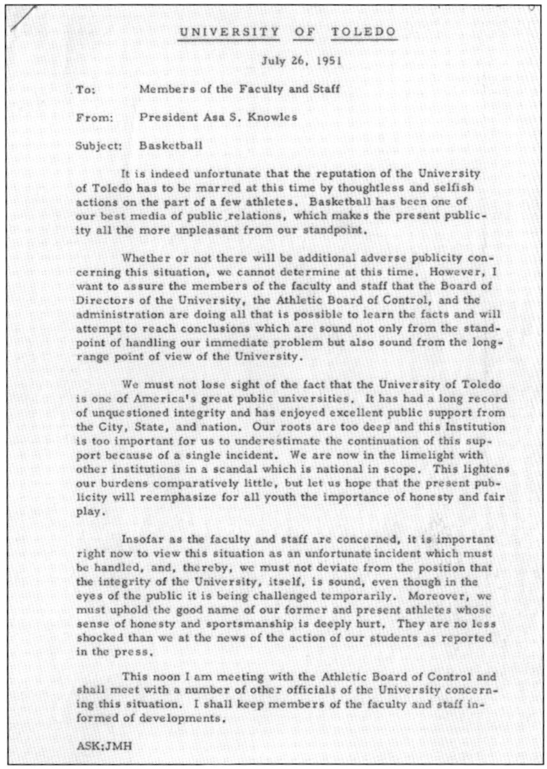

UNIVERSITY OF TOLEDO

July 26, 1951

To: Members of the Faculty and Staff

From: President Asa S. Knowles

Subject: Basketball

It is indeed unfortunate that the reputation of the University of Toledo has to be marred at this time by thoughtless and selfish actions on the part of a few athletes. Basketball has been one of our best media of public relations, which makes the present publicity all the more unpleasant from our standpoint.

Whether or not there will be additional adverse publicity concerning this situation, we cannot determine at this time. However, I want to assure the members of the faculty and staff that the Board of Directors of the University, the Athletic Board of Control, and the administration are doing all that is possible to learn the facts and will attempt to reach conclusions which are sound not only from the standpoint of handling our immediate problem but also sound from the long-range point of view of the University.

We must not lose sight of the fact that the University of Toledo is one of America's great public universities. It has had a long record of unquestioned integrity and has enjoyed excellent public support from the City, State, and nation. Our roots are too deep and this Institution is too important for us to underestimate the continuation of this support because of a single incident. We are now in the limelight with other institutions in a scandal which is national in scope. This lightens our burdens comparatively little, but let us hope that the present publicity will reemphasize for all youth the importance of honesty and fair play.

Insofar as the faculty and staff are concerned, it is important right now to view this situation as an unfortunate incident which must be handled, and, thereby, we must not deviate from the position that the integrity of the University, itself, is sound, even though in the eyes of the public it is being challenged temporarily. Moreover, we must uphold the good name of our former and present athletes whose sense of honesty and sportsmanship is deeply hurt. They are no less shocked than we at the news of the action of our students as reported in the press.

This noon I am meeting with the Athletic Board of Control and shall meet with a number of other officials of the University concerning this situation. I shall keep members of the faculty and staff informed of developments.

ASK:JMH

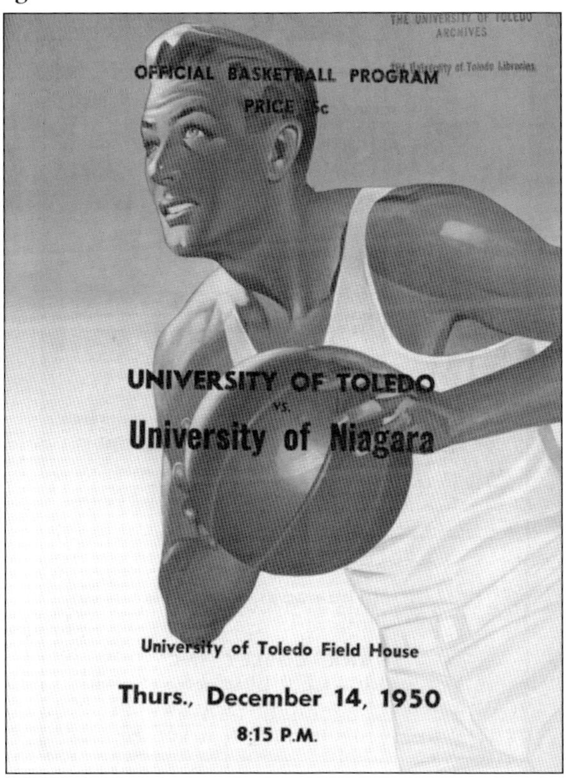

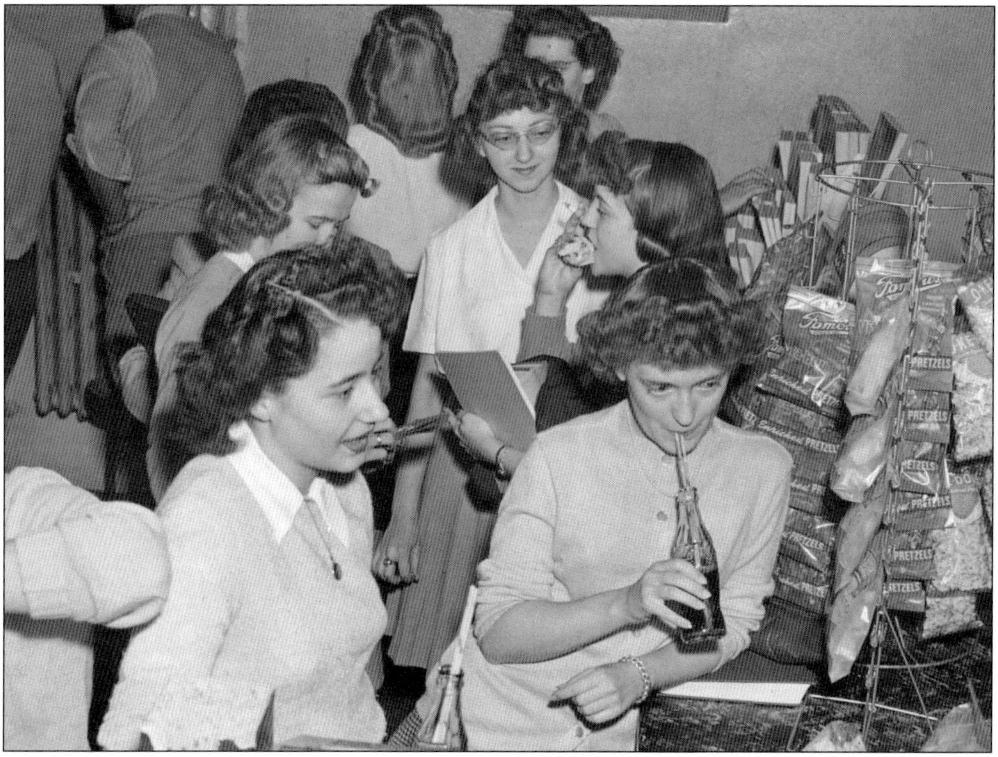

In the postwar years, college students across the country lacked interest in political affairs and were conservative in dress and attitudes. Some dubbed them the "Silent Generation." The most popular counter-culture expression of revolt was the "panty raid." At UT, this activity was given a unique twist when in 1953, a group of women raided a men's dormitory in retaliation for a raid on their dorm. A popular spot to hang out between classes was the snack bar of the Student Union, then housed in Libbey Hall.

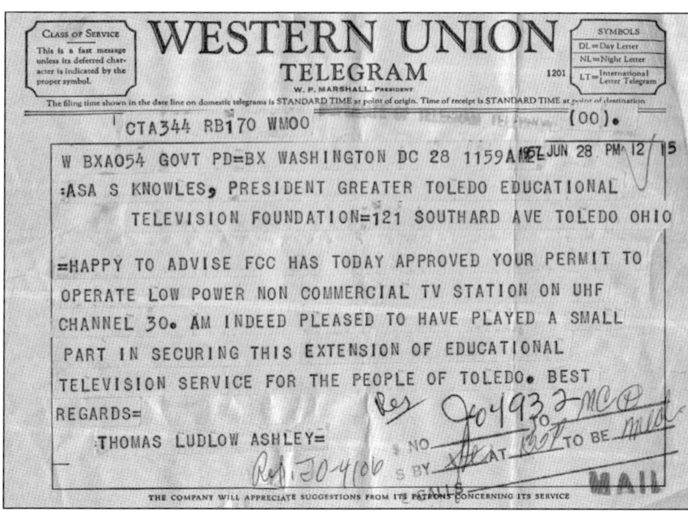

CLASS OF SERVICE
This is a fast message unless its deferred character is indicated by the proper symbol.

WESTERN UNION
TELEGRAM
W. P. MARSHALL, PRESIDENT

1201

SYMBOLS
DL=Day Letter
NL=Night Letter
LT=International Letter Telegram

The filing time shown in the date line on domestic telegrams is STANDARD TIME at point of origin. Time of receipt is STANDARD TIME at point of destination

CTA344 RB170 WMOO (00).

W BXA054 GOVT PD=BX WASHINGTON DC 28 1159AM= 1953 JUN 28 PM 12 15

:ASA S KNOWLES, PRESIDENT GREATER TOLEDO EDUCATIONAL
TELEVISION FOUNDATION=121 SOUTHARD AVE TOLEDO OHIO

=HAPPY TO ADVISE FCC HAS TODAY APPROVED YOUR PERMIT TO OPERATE LOW POWER NON COMMERCIAL TV STATION ON UHF CHANNEL 30. AM INDEED PLEASED TO HAVE PLAYED A SMALL PART IN SECURING THIS EXTENSION OF EDUCATIONAL TELEVISION SERVICE FOR THE PEOPLE OF TOLEDO. BEST REGARDS=

THOMAS LUDLOW ASHLEY=

Res 70493 2 MCP
NO. ___ AT ___ TO BE mild
BY ___
Ref. 70-4106

MAIL

THE COMPANY WILL APPRECIATE SUGGESTIONS FROM ITS PATRONS CONCERNING ITS SERVICE

In 1953, President Knowles expanded educational offerings by utilizing a new outlet—television. He invited local schools to join in the Greater Toledo Television Foundation. Studios on the fifth floor of University Hall allowed UT faculty to deliver lectures to subscribers. In 1958, the station was licensed as WTGE Channel 30, and it moved out of University Hall in 1963.

UT continued to struggle with inadequate funding from the city's budget. In 1956, a city charter amendment that included a two-mill levy for capital improvements to the university was soundly defeated. The city could provide only half of what was needed to construct the proposed engineering building, and the university raised over $1 million in private funds. The ground-breaking ceremony pictured at left included, from left to right, Mayor John Yager, President Knowles, board of directors member Walter Eversman, and Toledo businessman James Falvey.

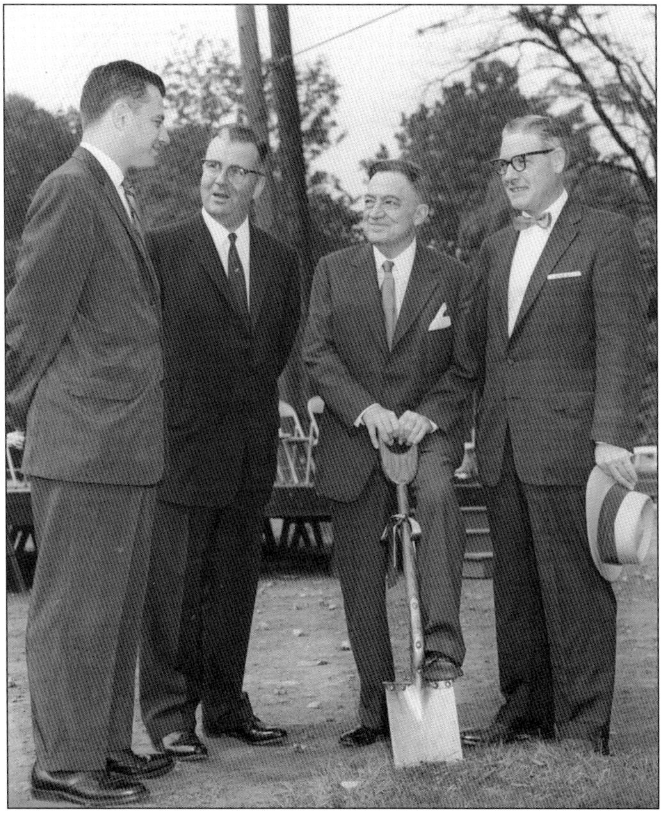

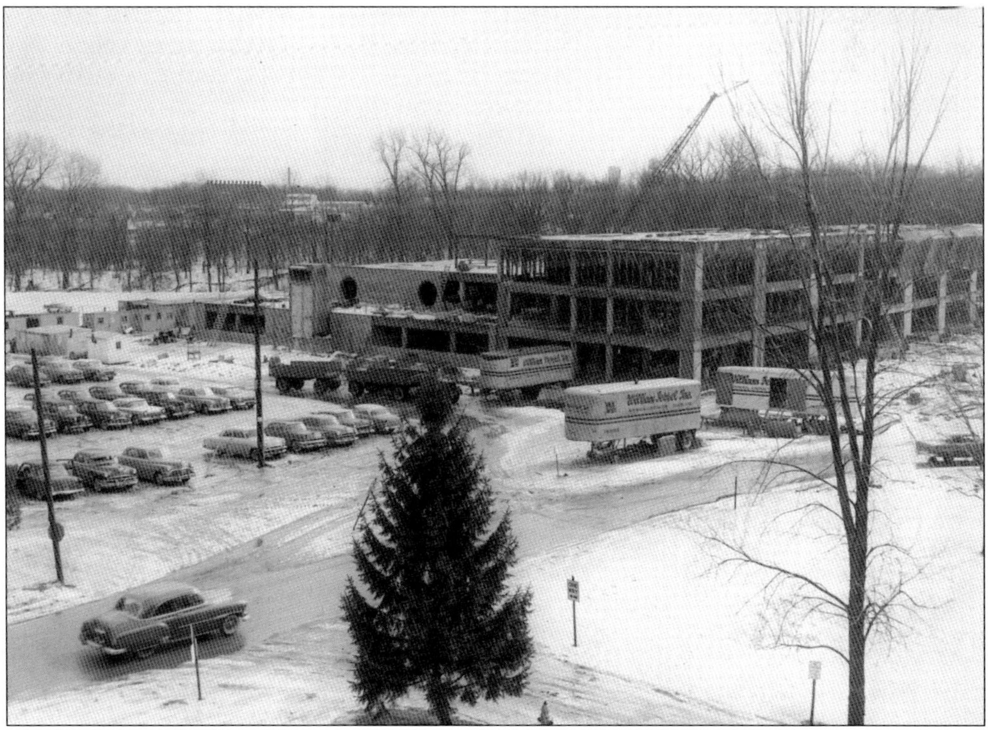

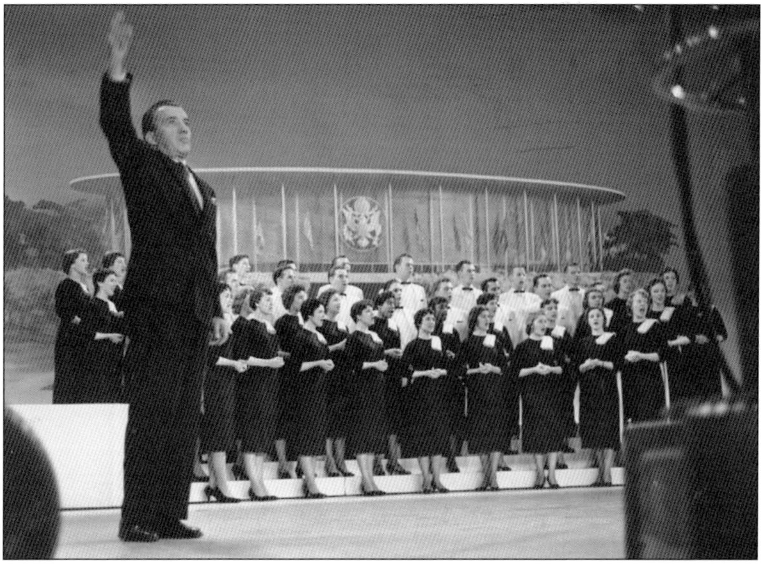

In 1958, the Rocket Choristers appeared on *The Ed Sullivan Show*. The group was directed by UT music professor Dr. Lloyd Sunderman.

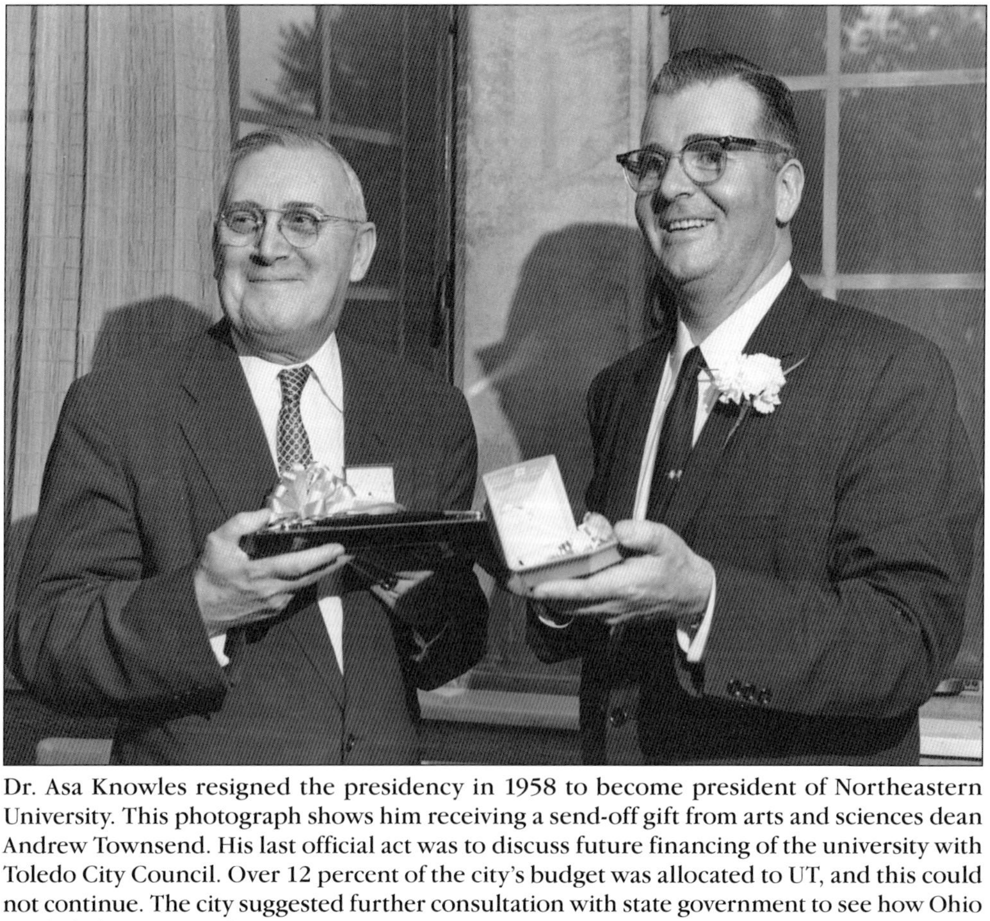

Dr. Asa Knowles resigned the presidency in 1958 to become president of Northeastern University. This photograph shows him receiving a send-off gift from arts and sciences dean Andrew Townsend. His last official act was to discuss future financing of the university with Toledo City Council. Over 12 percent of the city's budget was allocated to UT, and this could not continue. The city suggested further consultation with state government to see how Ohio might help support the institution.

Four

STATE STATUS AND EXPANSION

When Dr. Asa Knowles resigned to become president of Northeastern University in 1958, the University of Toledo was growing, but its financial situation remained dire. The North Central Association threatened to remove accreditation because of financial issues. That year, the university selected William S. Carlson as its new president. Dr. Carlson came to UT with considerable experience, having been president of the University of Delaware and chancellor of the State University of New York system.

In January 1959, a special committee of the city council met with Dr. Carlson to discuss the financial future of the institution. Toledo residents had two particular complaints—that they had to pay city taxes to support the municipal university and state taxes to support Ohio's state universities. They were also helping to underwrite the tuition of students living outside of Toledo who were attending the university.

Many in city government wanted to see the university turned over to the state. Mayor John Yager said the "ultimate, best, and inevitable solution to the financial problems of the university and the city is for the university to become state-controlled and state-operated." Three bills were introduced into the state legislature in 1959 proposing a state subsidy for Ohio's three largest municipal universities: Akron, Cincinnati, and Toledo. The bills stalled in the face of opposition from presidents of state institutions who felt any funding for municipal universities would come out of their pockets.

The financial crisis for UT worsened. Tuition was increased again, and salaries frozen. City Council placed a two-mill levy on the ballot on October 6, 1959, to raise $1.7 million a year for the university. The university launched a vigorous campaign in support of the levy, and it passed by just 144 votes. Passage of the levy stabilized the university's finances and allowed for some growth.

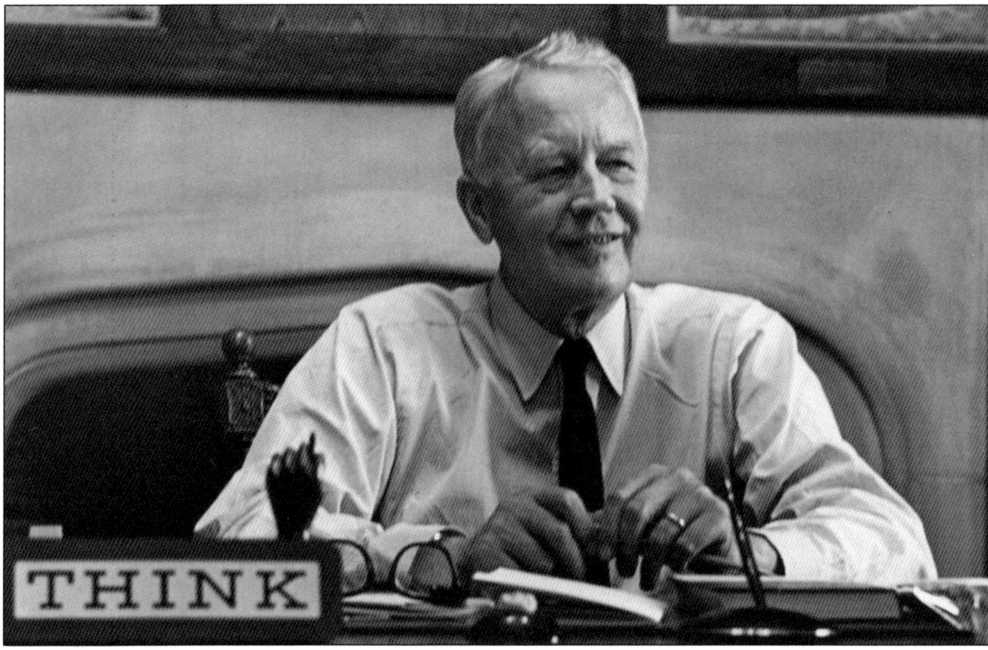

Dr. William Carlson was appointed president of UT in 1958. By the time he retired in 1972, he had overseen some of the most dramatic changes in the university's history, including its transition to a state-supported university.

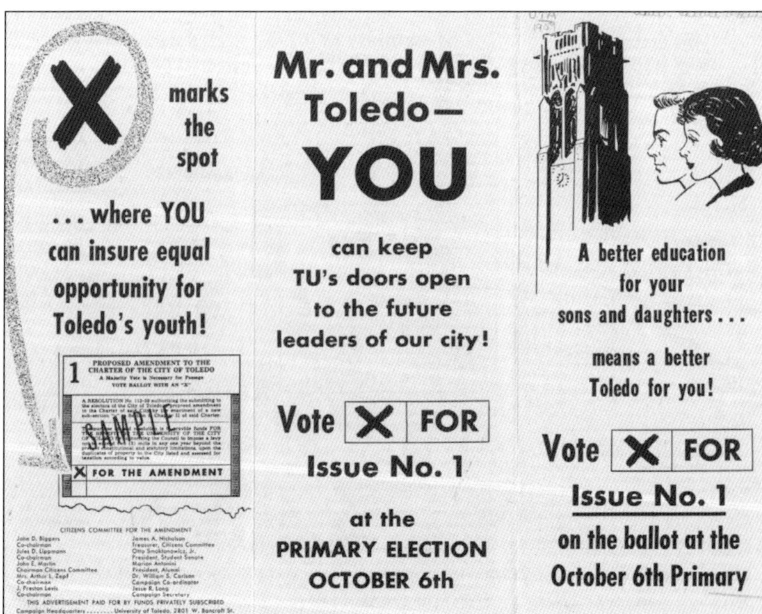

The 1959 campaign for passage of a bond levy to support the university was difficult. Flyers, bumper stickers, and campaign buttons were used to promote passage. Toledo voters approved the levy by just 144 votes.

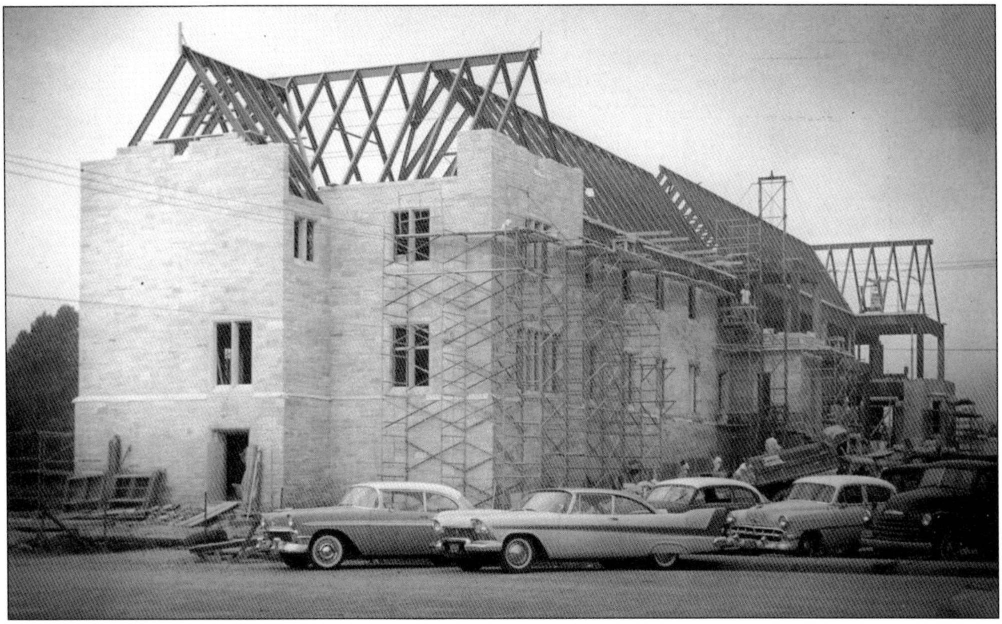

The student union located in Libbey Hall was too small for the growing student body, so the board of directors agreed to levy a $6 fee on all students to build a new one. It was completed in 1959 at a cost of $1.2 million.

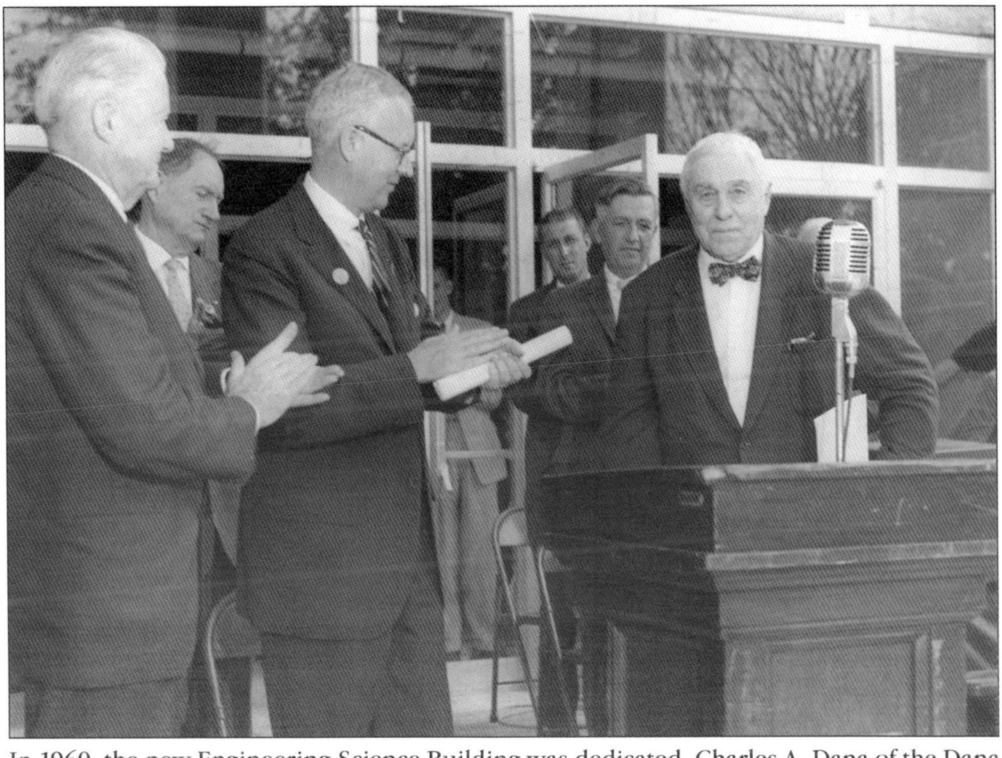

In 1960, the new Engineering-Science Building was dedicated. Charles A. Dana of the Dana Corporation (at the microphone), the largest private donor to the project, was honored at the dedication.

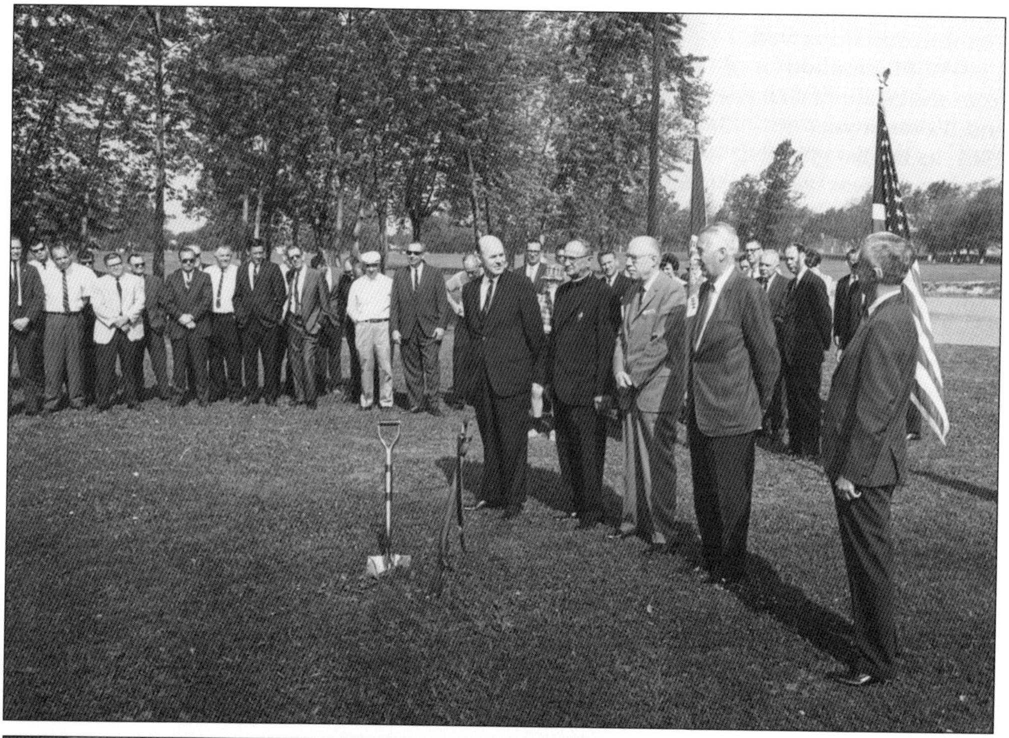

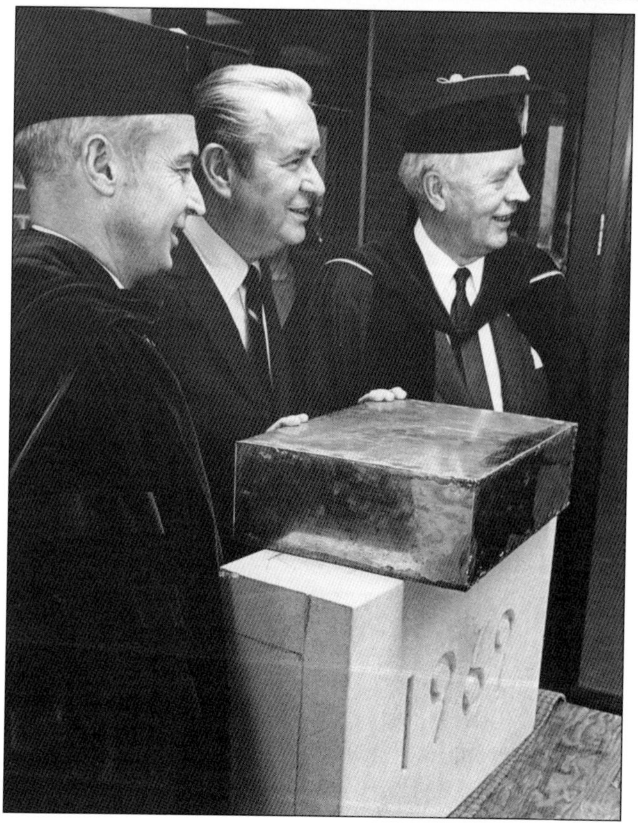

The Rossford Ordnance Depot was deactivated in 1962, and Congressman Thomas Ludlow Ashley tried to negotiate a deal to sell the site to UT for a community college, but the deal fell through. Dr. Carlson then proposed building the college on the original Scott trust land on Nebraska Avenue. This, too, was met with opposition, particularly by the local newspaper, which questioned whether the land was owned by the university or the city. A court case settled the ownership question, and the ground breaking took place on June 9, 1967. Gov. James Rhodes (left, at center) attended the dedication in 1969, along with community and technical college dean Newton Rochte (left) and President Carlson.

Dr. Carlson also continued to work with the University of Akron and the University of Cincinnati to get state financial assistance for UT. The ACT group (named for Akron, Cincinnati, and Toledo) pressed Governor Rhodes for funding, and in 1965, a subsidy of $200 per student was approved.

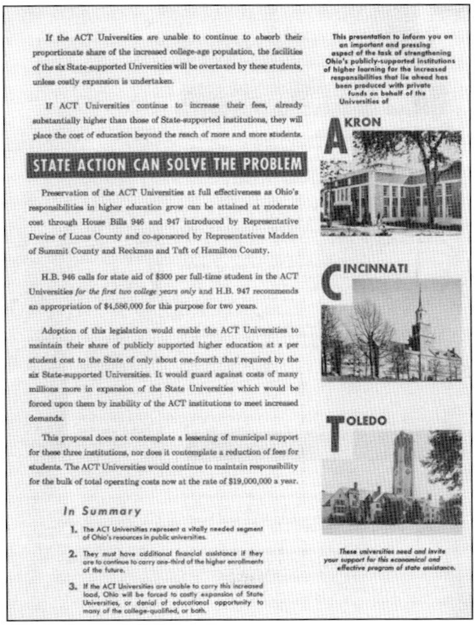

If the ACT Universities are unable to continue to absorb their proportionate share of the increased college-age population, the facilities of the six State-supported Universities will be overtaxed by these students, unless costly expansion is undertaken.

If ACT Universities continue to increase their fees, already substantially higher than those of State-supported institutions, they will place the cost of education beyond the reach of more and more students.

STATE ACTION CAN SOLVE THE PROBLEM

Preservation of the ACT Universities at full effectiveness as Ohio's responsibilities in higher education grow can be attained at moderate cost through House Bills 946 and 947 introduced by Representative Devine of Lucas County and co-sponsored by Representatives Madden of Summit County and Reckman and Taft of Hamilton County.

H.B. 946 calls for state aid of $300 per full-time student in the ACT Universities *for the first two college years only* and H.B. 947 recommends an appropriation of $4,586,000 for this purpose for two years.

Adoption of this legislation would enable the ACT Universities to maintain their share of publicly supported higher education at a per student cost to the State of only about one-fourth that required by the six State-supported Universities. It would guard against costs of many millions more in expansion of the State Universities which would be forced upon them by inability of the ACT institutions to meet increased demands.

This proposal does not contemplate a lessening of municipal support for these three institutions, nor does it contemplate a reduction of fees for students. The ACT Universities would continue to maintain responsibility for the bulk of total operating costs now at the rate of $19,000,000 a year.

In Summary

1. The ACT Universities represent a vitally needed segment of Ohio's resources in public universities.
2. They must have additional financial assistance if they are to continue to carry one-third of the higher enrollments of the future.
3. If the ACT Universities are unable to carry this increased load, Ohio will be forced to costly expansion of State Universities, or denial of educational opportunity to many of the college-qualified, or both.

This presentation to inform you on an important and pressing aspect of the task of strengthening Ohio's publicly-supported institutions of higher learning for the increased responsibilities that lie ahead has been produced with private funds on behalf of the Universities of

AKRON

CINCINNATI

TOLEDO

These universities need and invite your support for this economical and effective program of state assistance.

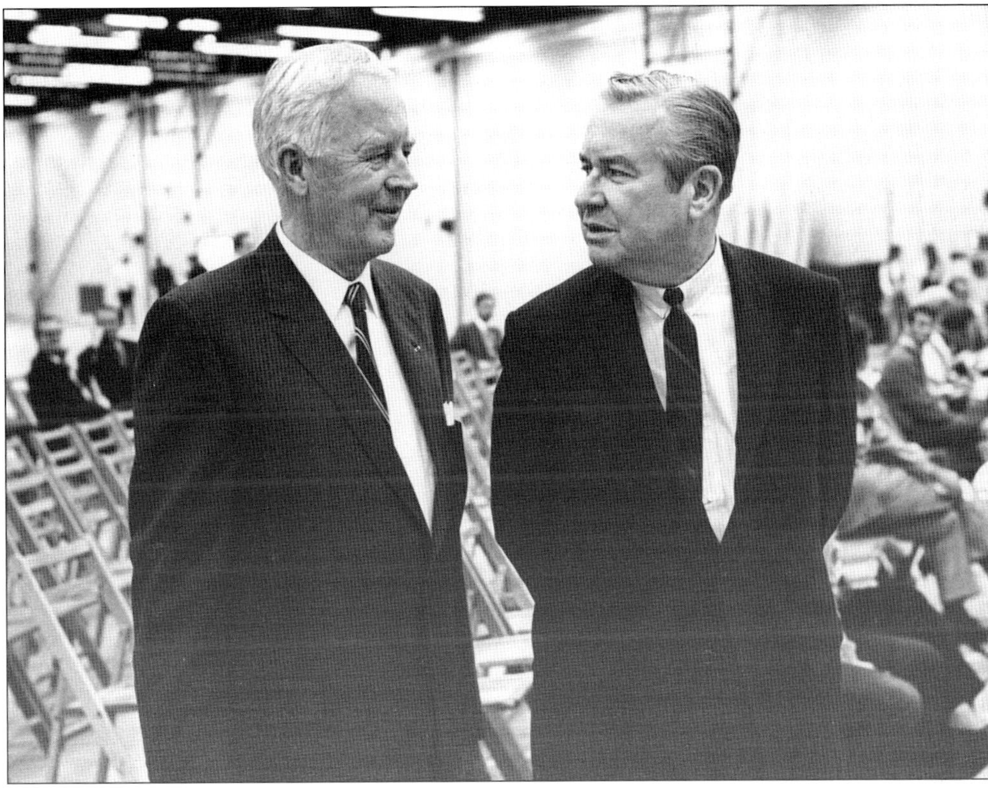

But this was only the beginning. On July 3, 1965, the Ohio General Assembly passed a bill that incorporated the University of Toledo into the state's system of higher education. In 1966, Toledo voters gave their blessing to state status with the passage of Issues 2 and 3. Effective July 1, 1967, the university became a state university after 95 years of local control. Governor Rhodes attended the ceremony officially marking the transition to state university status.

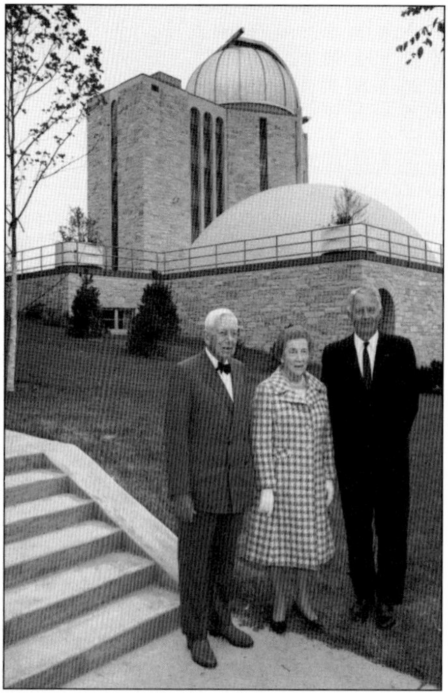

State funding provided not only operational support, but also capital investment funding. This allowed for a major building boom on campus. State funds provided for the construction of the Health Education Center, the Ritter Planetarium, an addition to the Engineering-Science Building, and the Law Center. Ritter Planetarium and Observatory was completed in 1967. George Ritter (shown here on the left with his wife and President Carlson), a Toledo lawyer, donated $400,000 for the building to house an important new academic program in astronomy. The program was the brainchild of Dr. John Turin, and it attracted many outstanding scholars to the university's faculty.

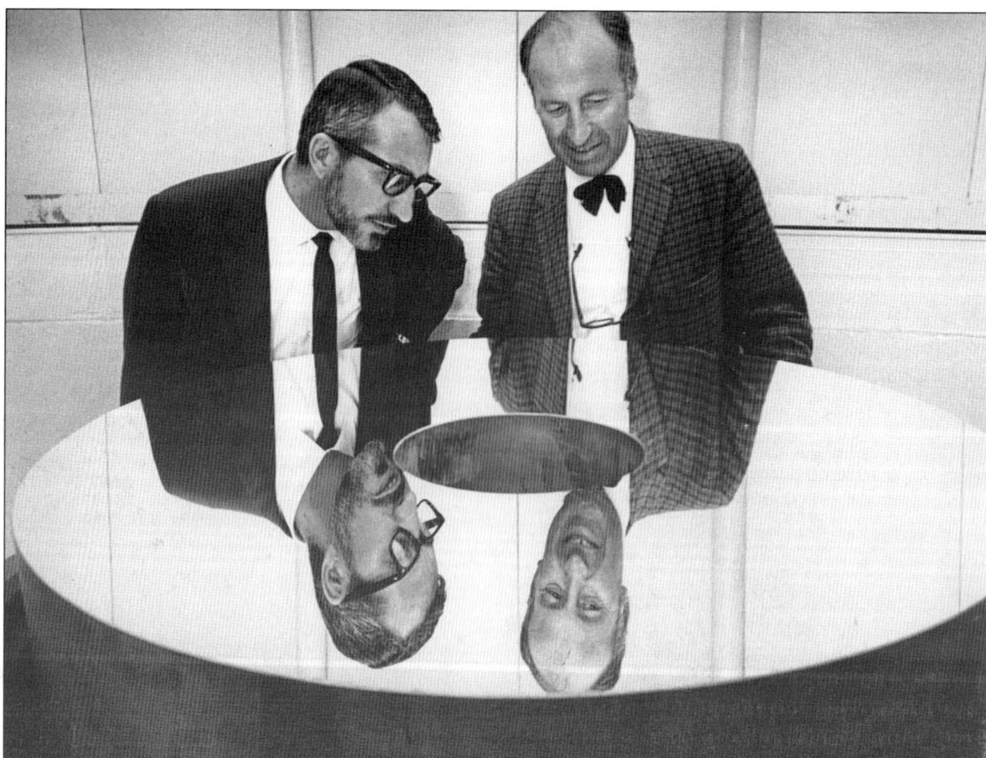

The mirror for the telescope in Ritter Observatory was the gift of Toledo corporation Owens-Illinois (O-I). The 40-inch reflecting telescope was made from a new product developed by O-I called CerVit.

In January 1966, the faculty voted to create a representative governance body due to the increasing number of faculty who could no longer govern as a body of the whole. The faculty senate became an important voice for faculty concerns.

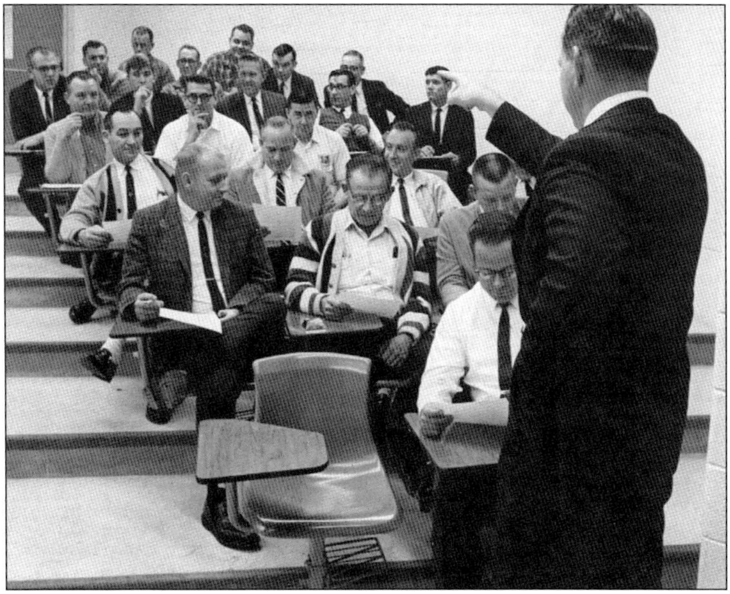

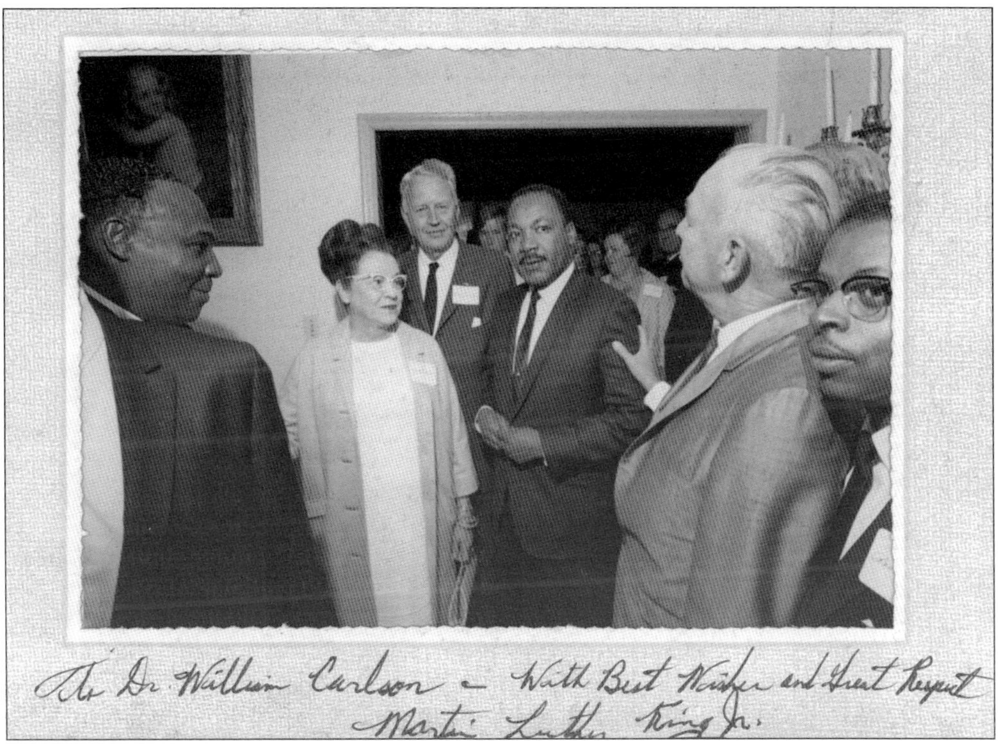

In 1967, civil rights leader Dr. Martin Luther King Jr. visited Toledo and spoke at Scott High School. After the speech, he attended a reception at the home of lawyer and businessman Edward Lamb. Dr. Carlson attended. After he received this photograph of the event, Dr. Carlson wrote to Dr. King and asked him to autograph it.

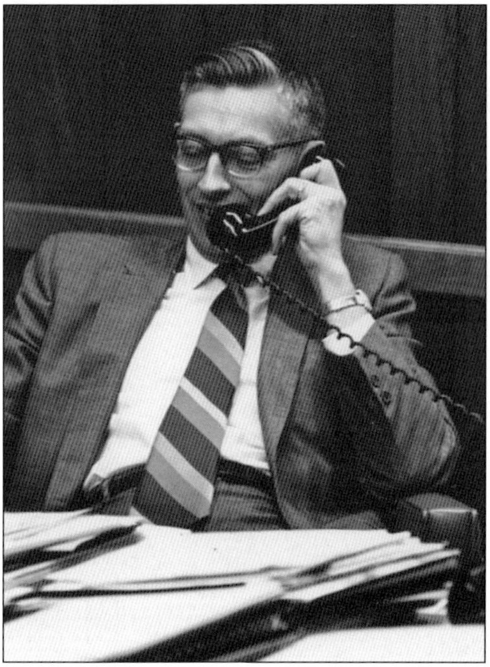

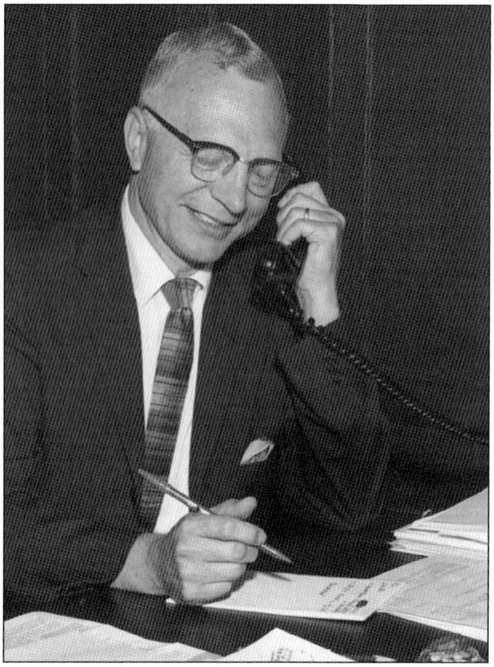

State status and rapid growth led Dr. Carlson to hire several new vice presidents, including Willard W. Smith (above, left) as vice president for business affairs, Jesse R. Long (above, right), promoted to executive vice president; and Dr. Lancelot C.A. Thompson (below) as vice president for student affairs. Thompson had been a faculty member in the chemistry department since 1958.

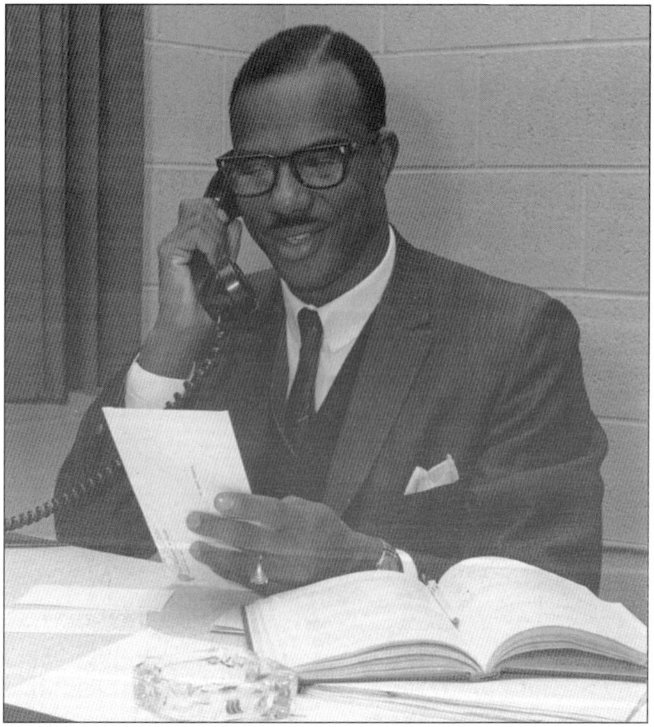

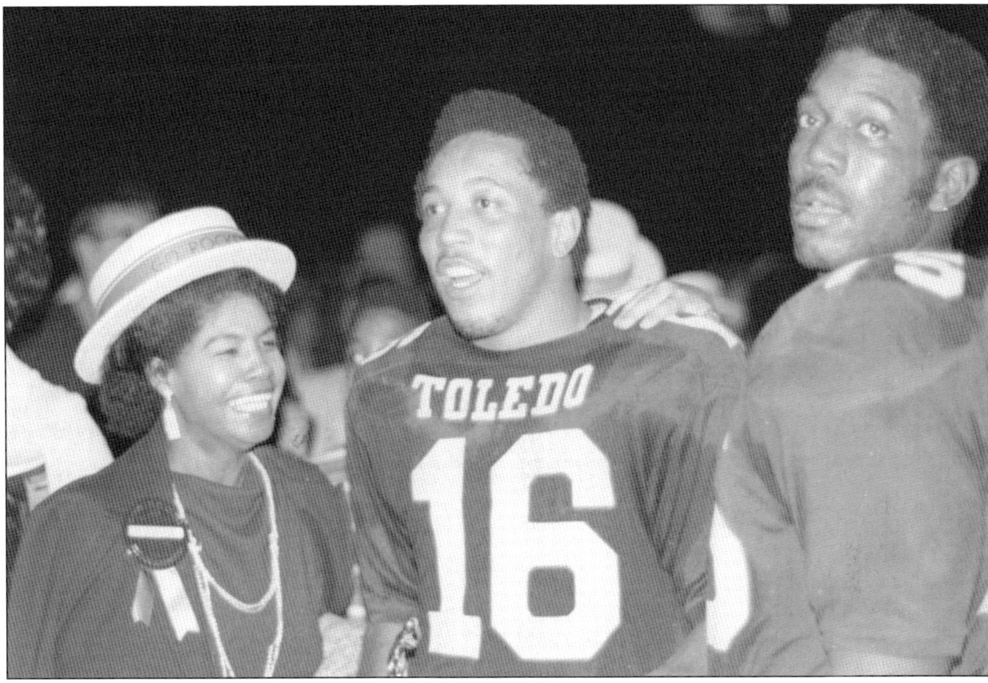

UT's long-suffering football team saw a turnaround in its fortunes under Coach Lauterbur. Lauterbur recruited Chuck Ealey from Portsmouth, Ohio, as the quarterback for the team, an unusual position for an African American at the time. With Ealey at the helm, UT won 35 consecutive games between 1969 and 1972. This remains the second longest winning streak in college football history.

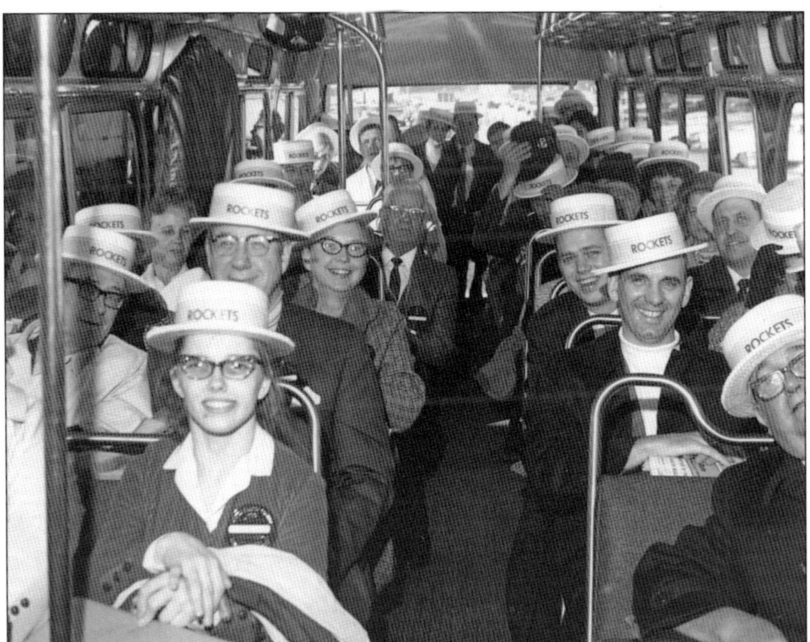

Fans of the Rockets football team traveled to the Tangerine Bowl in 1969 to see their team win its first post-season tournament game.

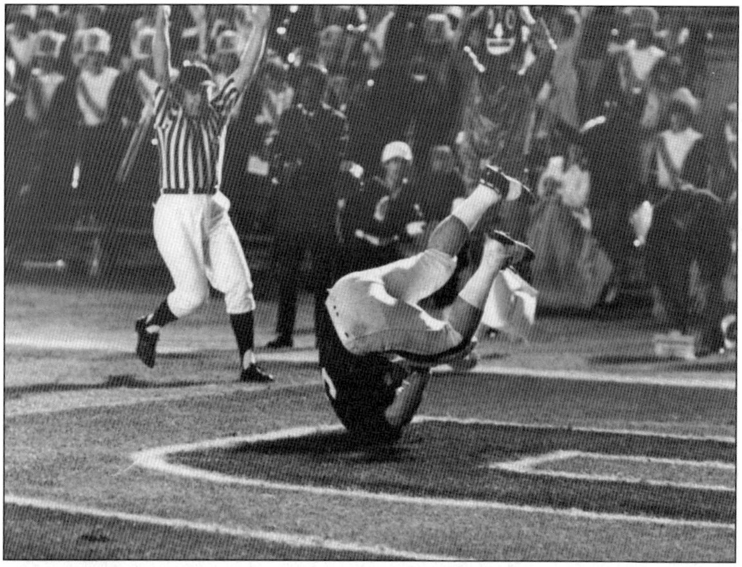

Dick Seymour scores a touchdown during the Tangerine Bowl, which UT won in 1969 by a score of 56 to 33 against Davidson College.

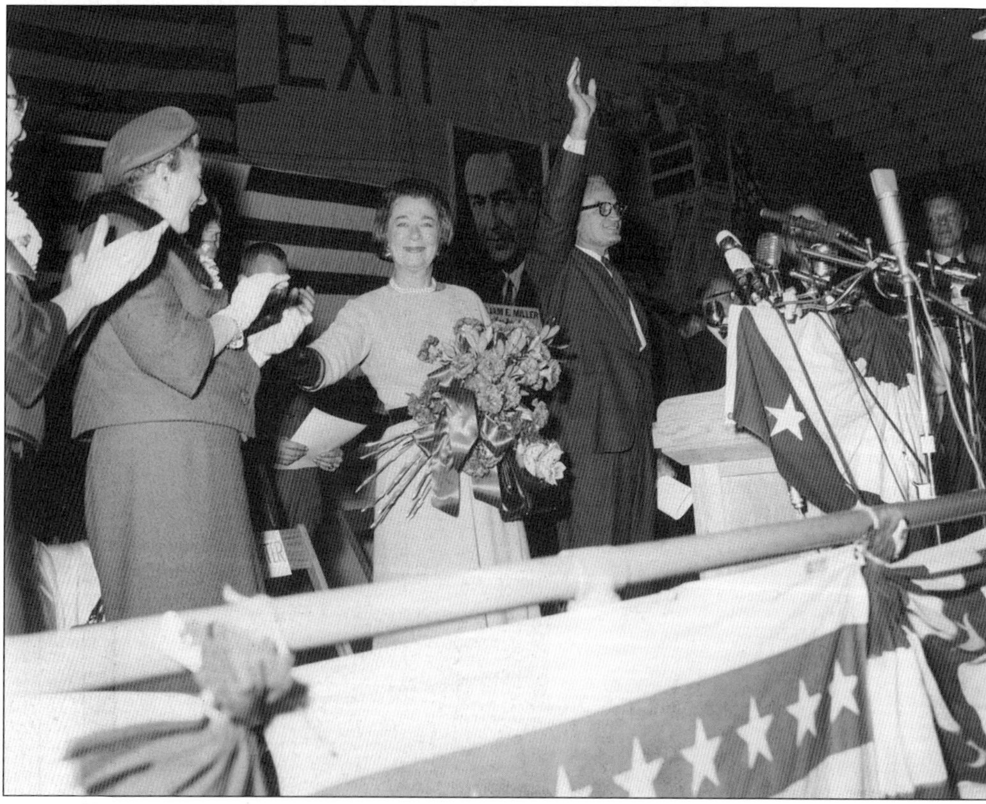

Inspired by the election of Pres. John F. Kennedy in 1960, college students around the country awakened from the political slumber of the Silent Generation. What began as the Free Speech Movement in Berkeley, California, spread to many campuses, including UT. In 1964, UT was embarrassed when Republican presidential candidate Barry Goldwater was drowned out by supporters of his opponent, Lyndon Johnson, when he attempted to address students in the Field House.

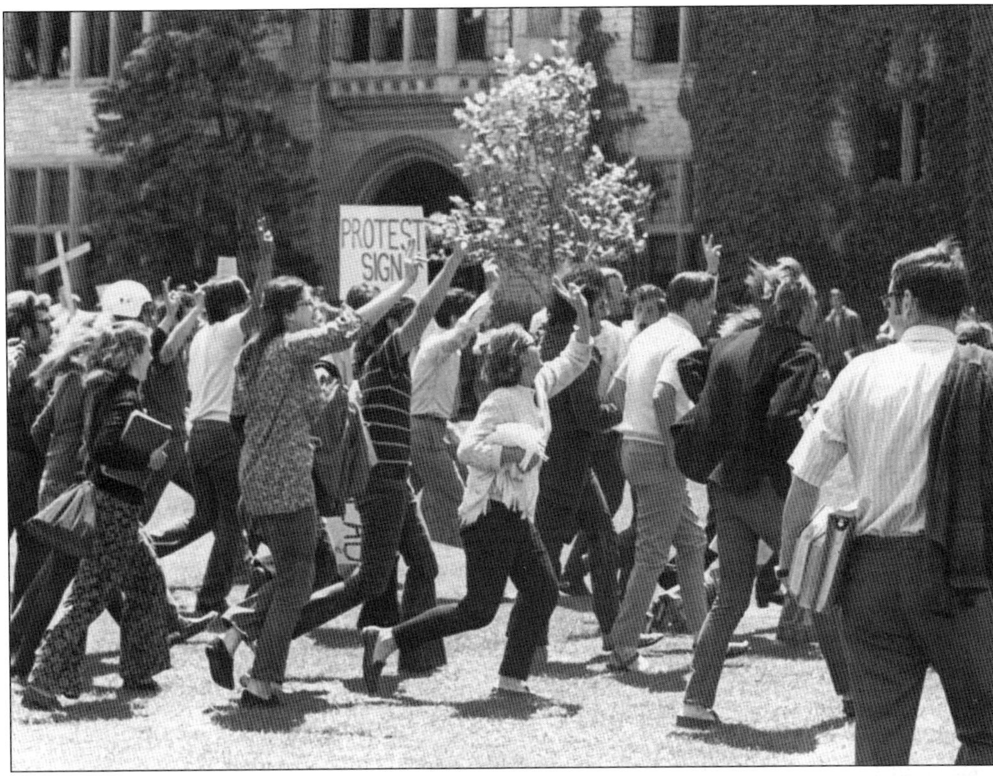

On May 5, 1966, local members of the Students for a Democratic Society protested the Vietnam draft outside Dana Auditorium. A few days later, they disrupted an ROTC Honors Day review. Other notable protests included opposition to the allocation of space in Doermann Theatre to the student records office in 1967 and a dormitory food riot in April 1968.

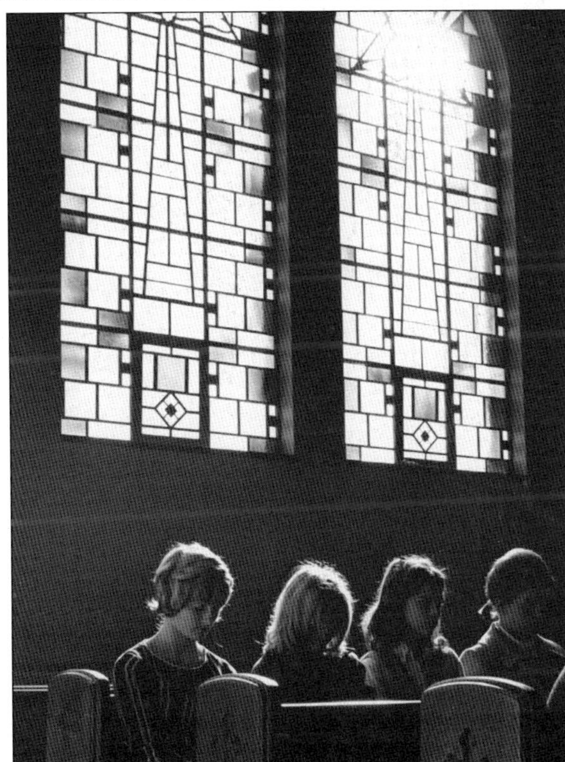

On October 15, 1969, over 1,000 UT students and faculty participated in the national Vietnam War moratorium observance. Protestors marched from the UT campus to Gesu Church for a memorial service dedicated to those who had died in the war.

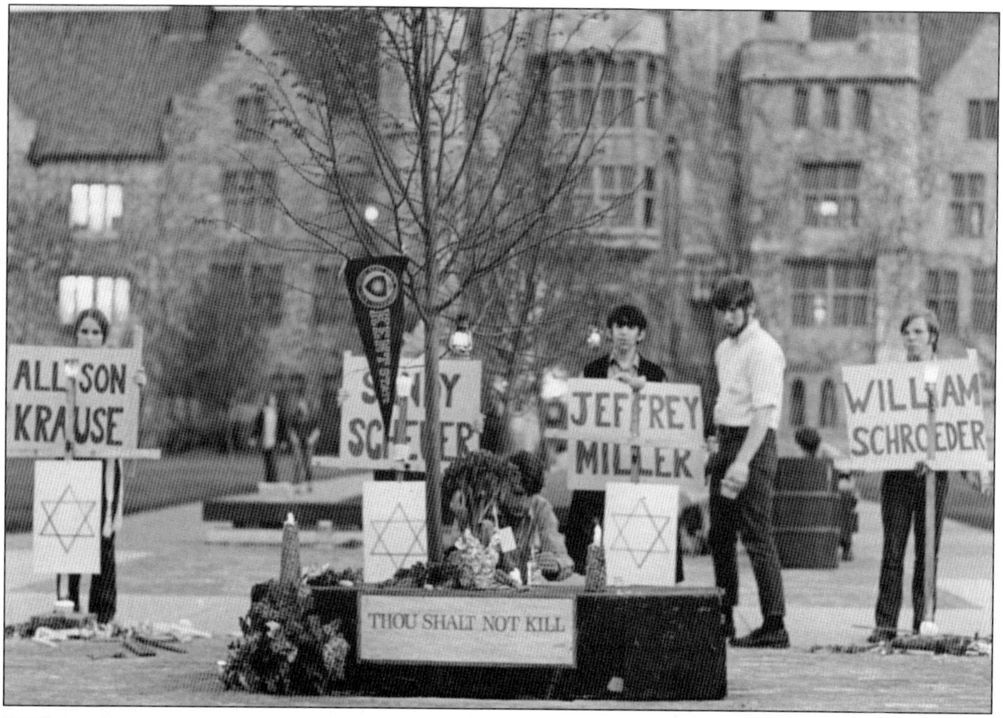

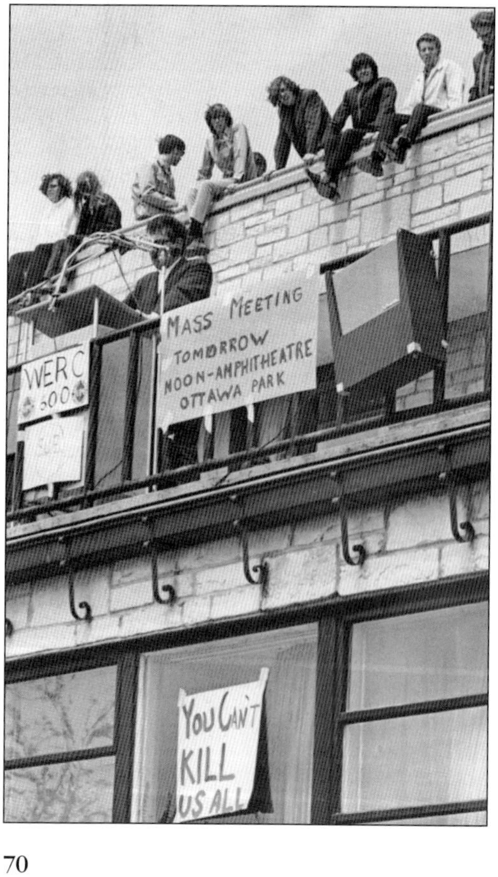

Student protests reached a crisis on May 4, 1970, when members of the Ohio National Guard killed four students on the campus of Kent State University in northeast Ohio. That afternoon, the UT Student Senate met and requested a moratorium on classes as a memorial to the students. Rallies continued throughout the week.

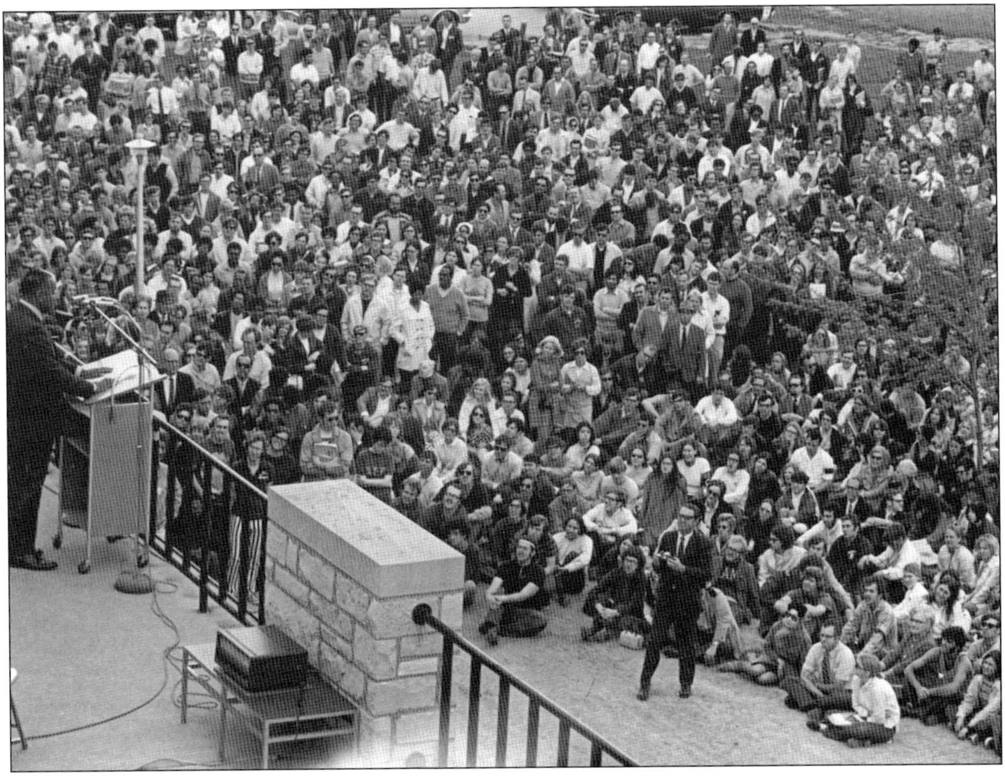

On May 5, newspaper columnist Carl Rowan (at podium), who had been scheduled to speak as part of the University Convocation series, spoke outside to a large crowd that included Dr. Carlson. The faculty senate passed a resolution deploring the violence at Kent State, and asked that the university classes remain cancelled for the remainder of the week. A petition was signed by thousands of students expressing their outrage at the violence at Kent State. The week ended with a peaceful candlelight procession.

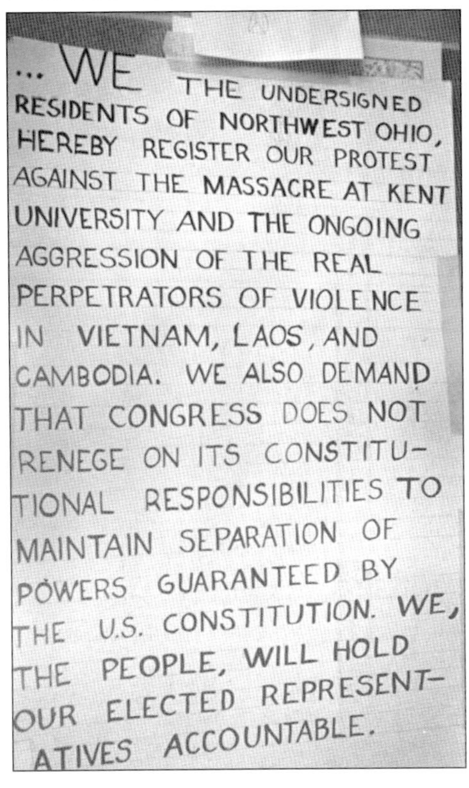

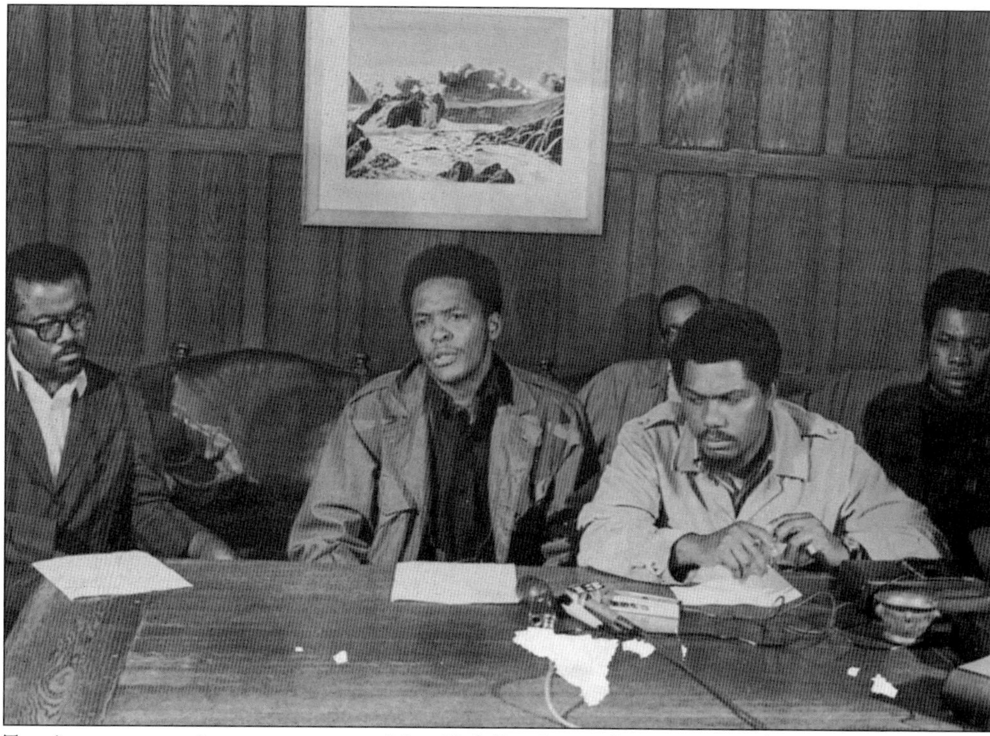

Tensions rose again on campus on May 15 following a shooting at Jackson State University in Mississippi that killed two African American students there. To protest what seemed like a lack of sympathy by Dr. Carlson for these deaths, black students blocked the entrance to University Hall on Monday, May 18. Leaders of the protest met with the president in his office and presented him with a set of demands that included hiring more black faculty and graduate assistants and implementing a black studies academic program.

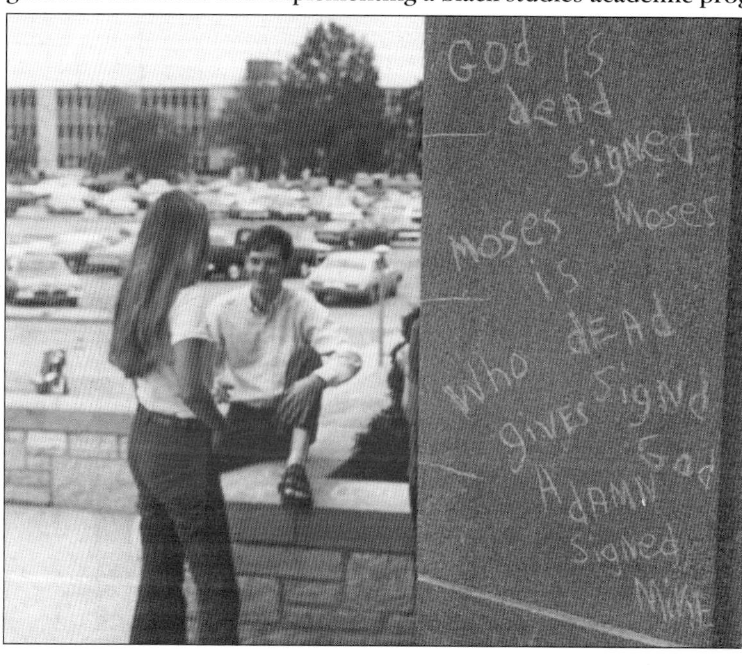

University students continued to protest the war and be politically active. A message written in chalk on the outside of the student union in 1971 expressed the cynicism of many about political events of the time. The defeat of antiwar presidential candidate George McGovern in 1972 added to these feelings.

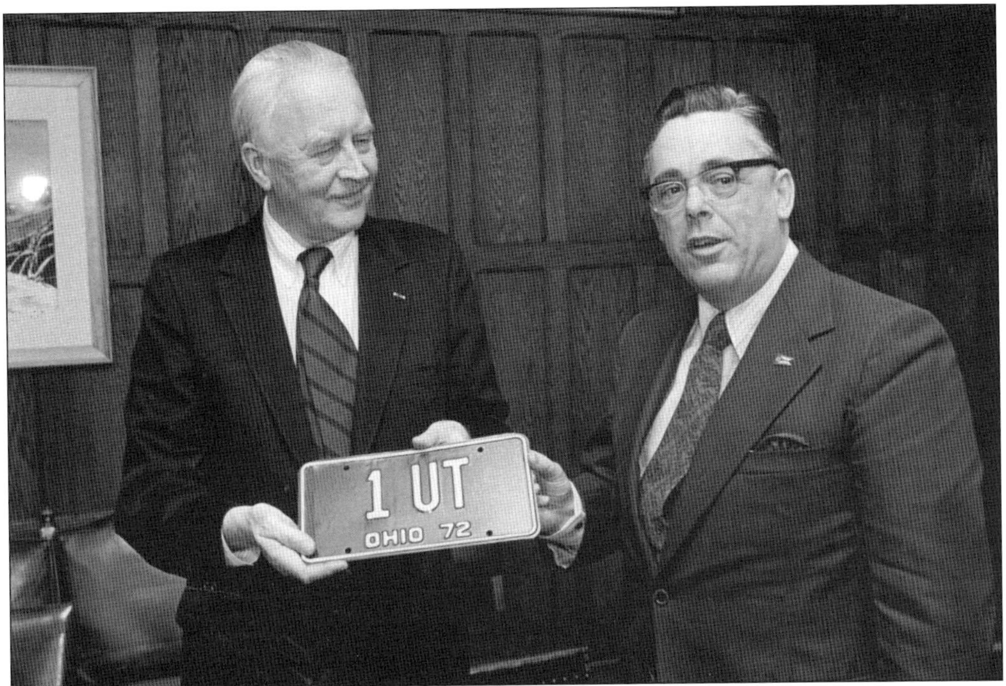

The year 1972 was important in the university's history, as UT marked its centennial with a series of events. Ohio license plates that year were issued in blue and gold to commemorate the centennial. Here, Dr. Carlson receives his "1 UT" plates from Donald Curry.

A major fundraising campaign was undertaken to mark the 100-year anniversary. Called the Centennial Fund Drive, it was to be a lasting legacy to the year. Also, the university published *The Tower Builders*, an institutional history by Dr. Frank Hickerson. Hickerson died before the book was published. Jesse Long presents Hickerson's widow with a copy of the book.

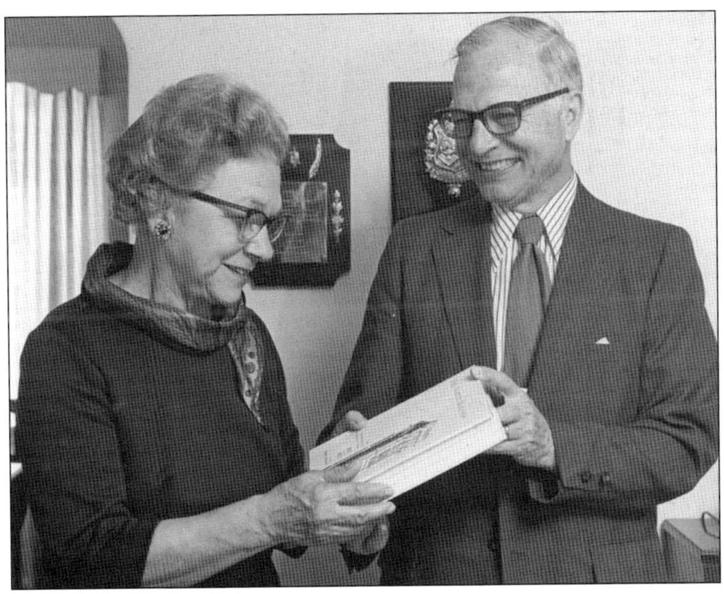

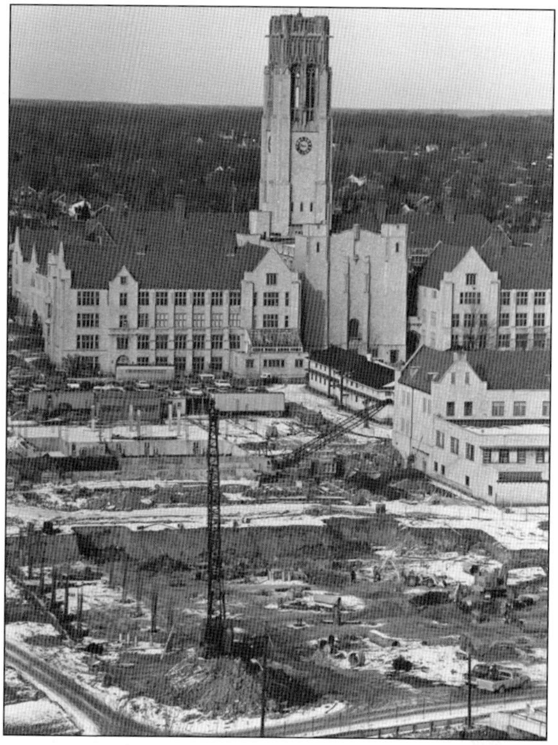

One of the largest building projects in the university's history began in 1971. UT had outgrown its library that had been constructed in 1952, and a new five-story library was built to replace it. It took over two years to complete and was located in the center of campus. It was named in honor of Dr. William S. Carlson, who announced his retirement in 1972.

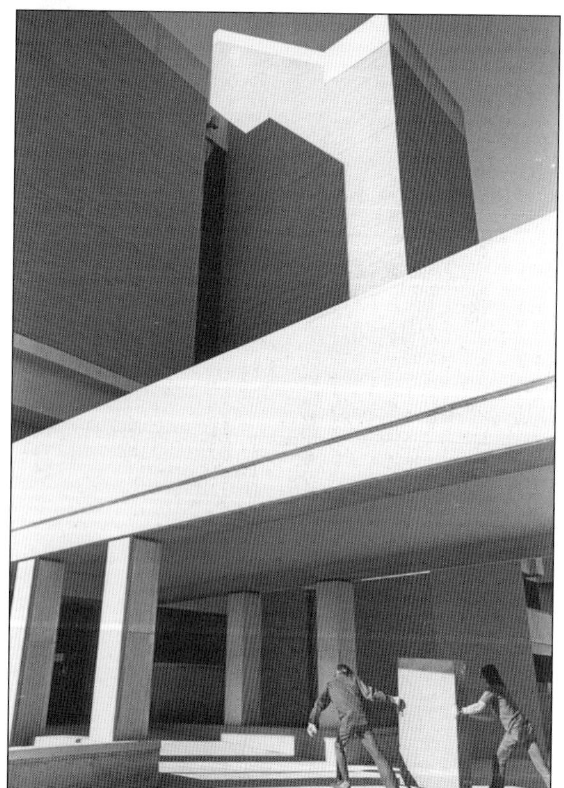

All of the library's holdings had to be moved from the old library. The materials were transferred cart by cart and placed in the stacks of the new library.

Dr. Carlson was succeeded by Dr. Glen R. Driscoll, a historian who came to UT from the University of Missouri. Dr. Driscoll oversaw a major expansion of the campus, including additions to the Student Union in 1972 and the Law Center in 1978, as well as the construction of several new buildings, including the Center for the Performing Arts in 1976.

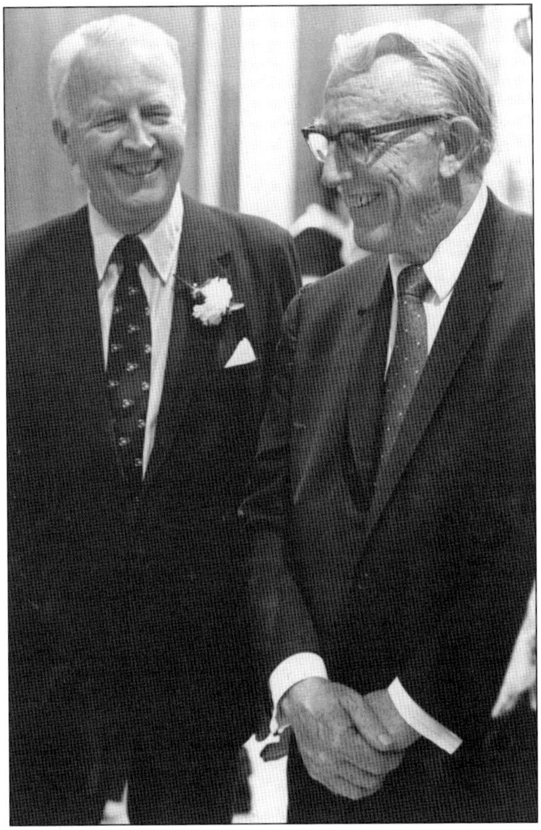

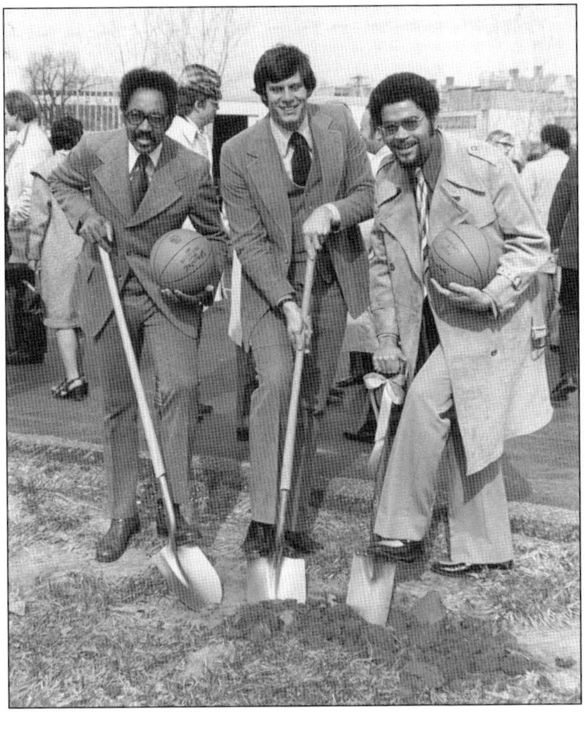

Also in 1976, Centennial Hall was constructed as a new basketball arena, replacing the aged Field House. Here, basketball stars Ralph Lewis (who played in 1960–1962), Steve Mix (1967–1969), and Ray Wolford (1962–1964) help with the ground breaking for the new arena.

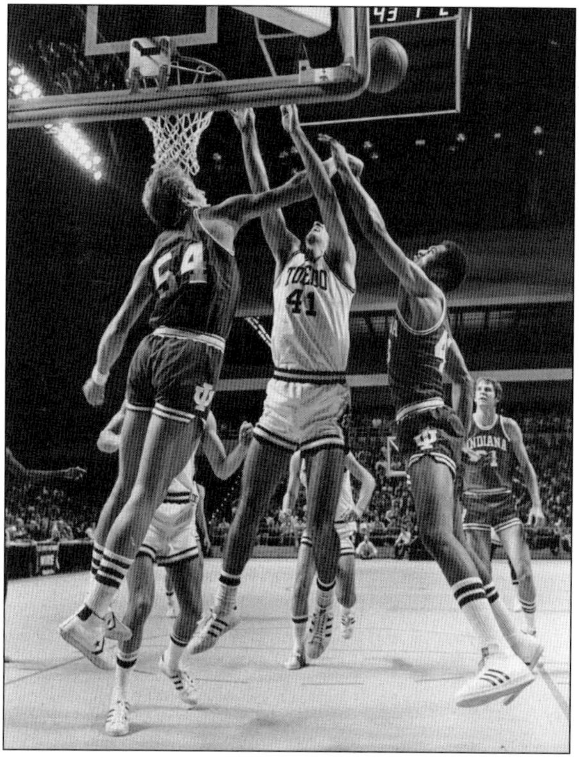

UT's basketball team was coached for 22 years by Bob Nichols, and became a national powerhouse. Nichols led the team to MAC championships in 1966–1967, 1971–1972, 1978–1979, and 1980–1981. The inaugural game in Centennial Hall was particularly thrilling. UT's team beat undefeated Indiana University by a score of 59 to 57 at the buzzer. The win ended Indiana's 33-game winning streak.

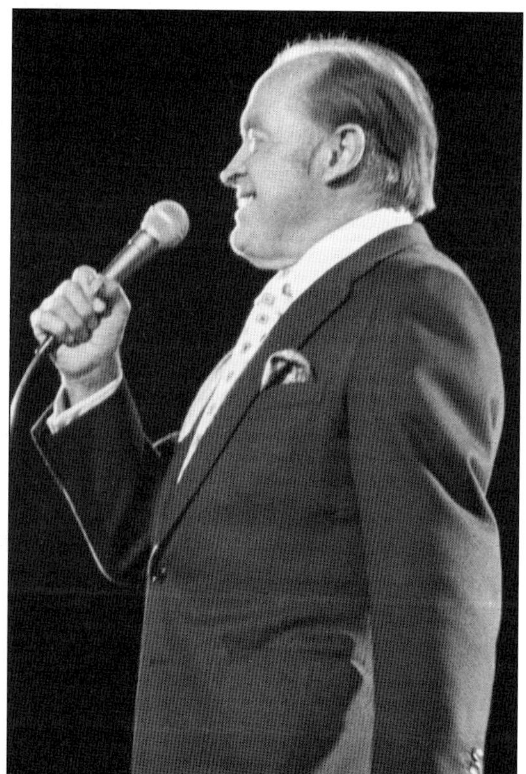

Centennial Hall was not just used for basketball, however. It became a major concert venue. Comedian Bob Hope performed in the hall as part of the opening celebrations in 1976. In 1988, the building's name was changed to Savage Hall in honor of longtime UT trustee and supporter John F. Savage.

Another project inspired by the centennial celebration and funded by the fund drive of that year was the beautification of the central core of the campus. A parking lot between University Hall and the student union, along with the remaining "temporary" barracks that had been moved to campus following World War II, were demolished to make way for a green space named Centennial Mall.

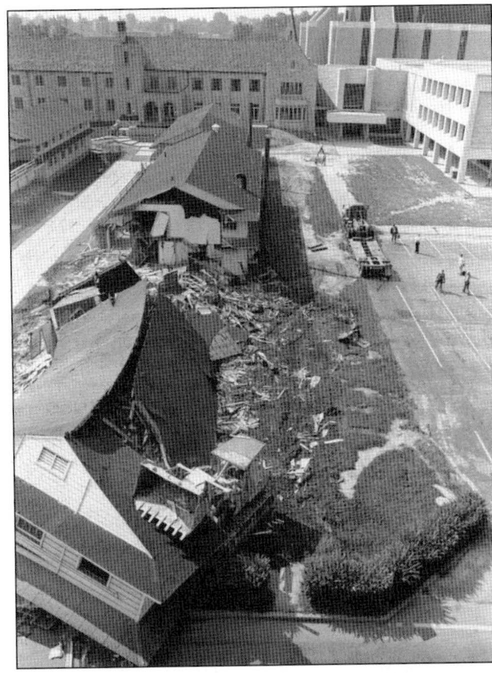

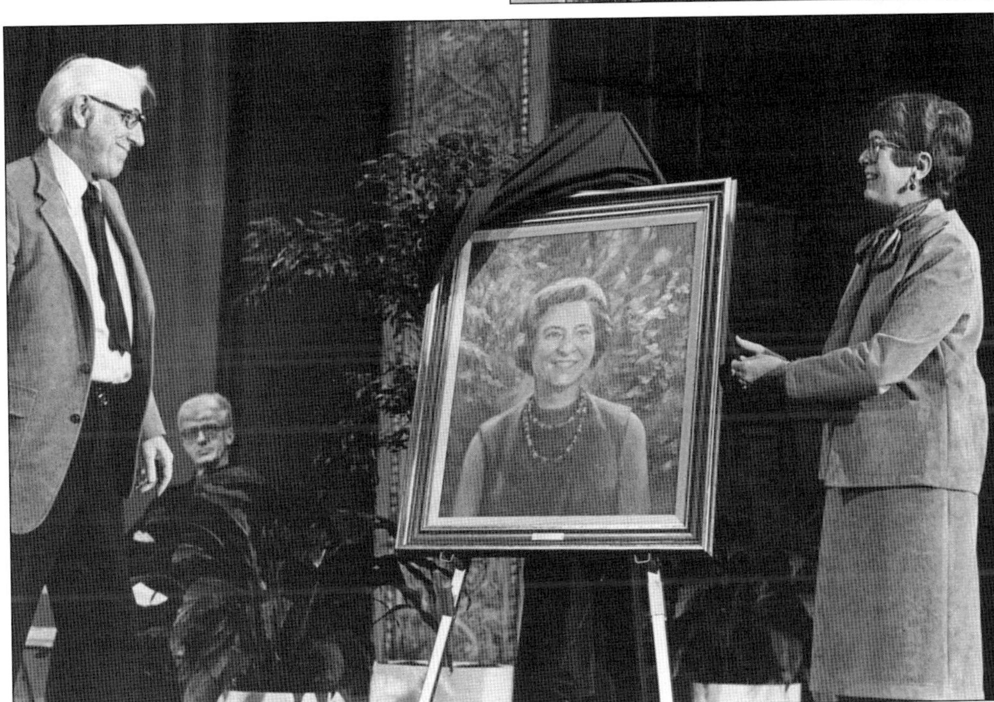

Between 1979 and 1989, the University of Toledo was the fastest growing university in Ohio. The population increased from 18,000 students to 24,000 students. Dr. Driscoll sought ways the university could embrace its urban mission. He founded the Urban Affairs Center and the Catharine S. Eberly Center for Women, which was dedicated in December 1980 in honor of the late board of trustee member. Here, a portrait of Eberly is unveiled by President Driscoll and trustee Lois Kennedy.

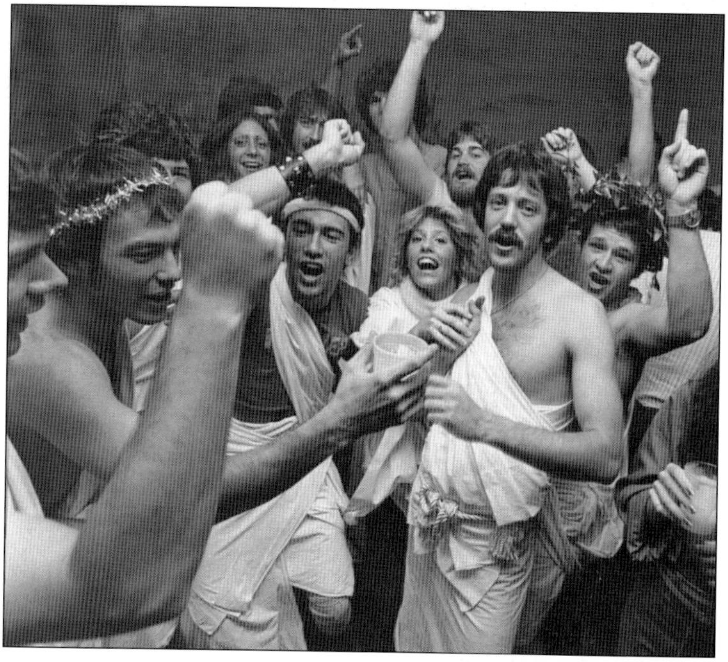

The 1978 movie *National Lampoon's Animal House* is generally credited with reviving fraternities on campuses across the country. Starring John Belushi, the movie popularized toga-themed drinking parties. UT fraternities joined in the craze.

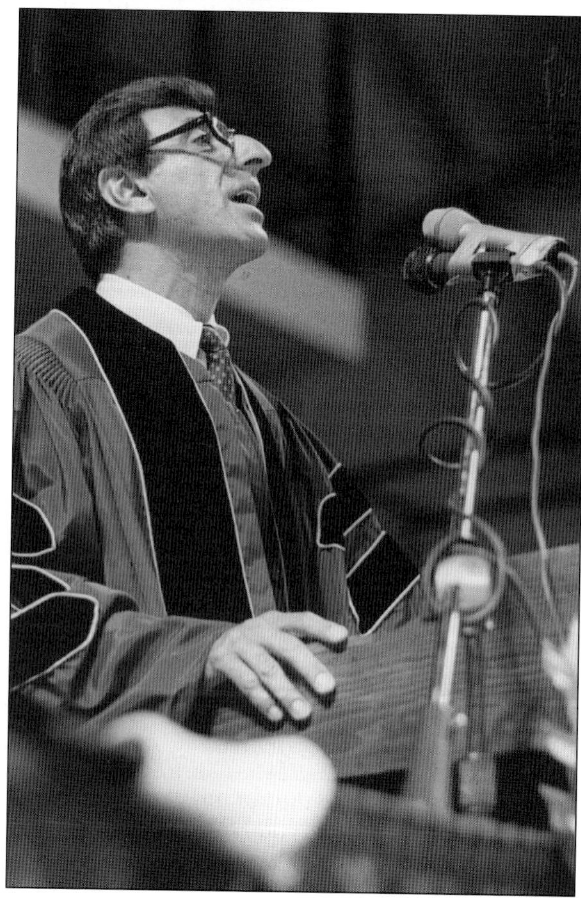

Toledo native Jamie Farr became a national celebrity in the late 1970s due to his recurring role as Corporal Klinger on the popular television series *M*A*S*H*. In 1983, the university gave Farr an honorary degree. Farr donated his scripts from the series to the Ward M. Canaday Center for Special Collections in UT's library.

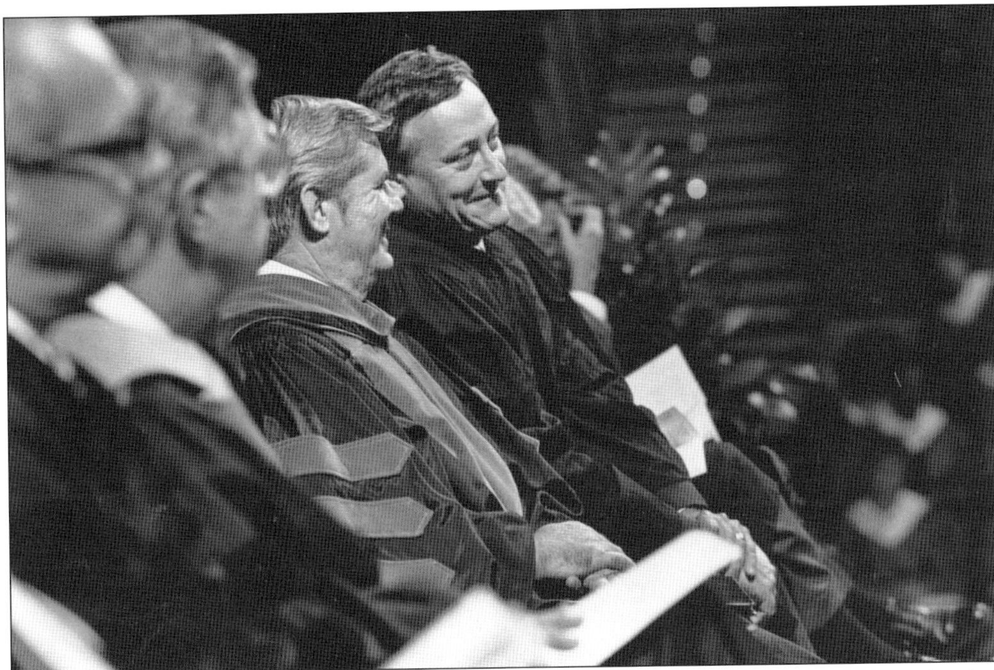

After serving 12 years as president, Dr. Driscoll announced his retirement in 1984. After a national search, Dr. James D. McComas, president of Mississippi State University, was selected as his replacement. Dr. McComas confers with Ohio governor Richard Celeste at his inauguration ceremony.

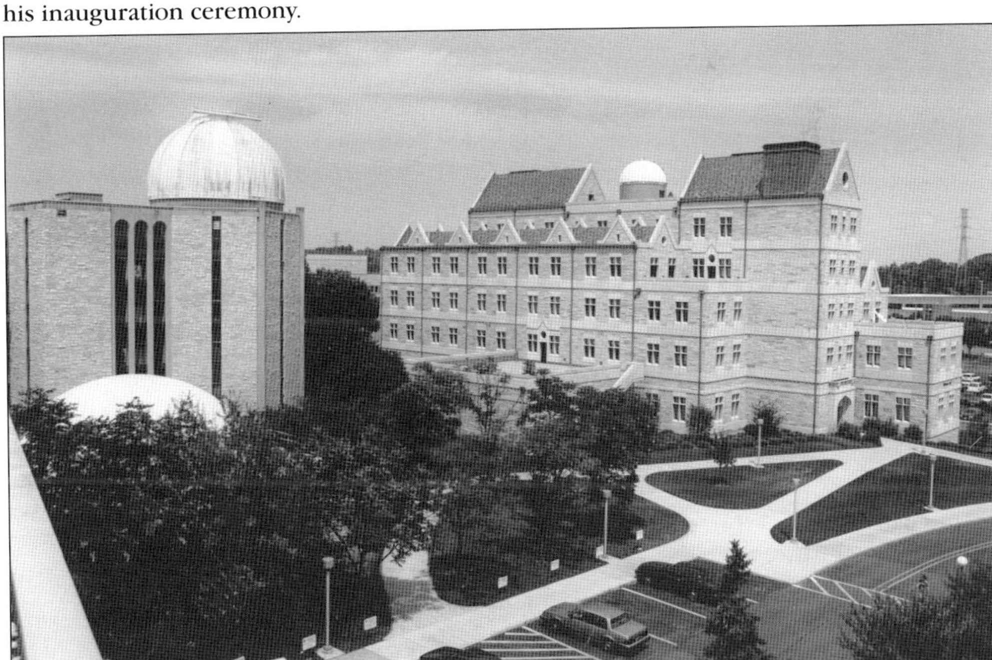

Dr. McComas continued the building boom. McMaster Hall, which expanded the physics and astronomy program, was completed in 1987. It was named for Helen and Harold McMaster, who donated the funds to help complete construction.

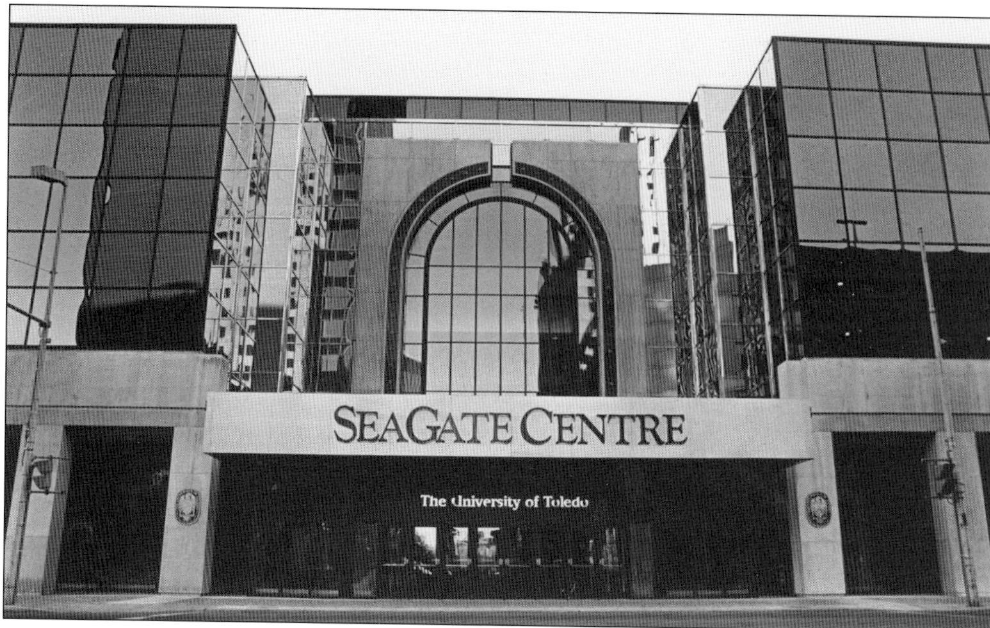

Also in 1987, the university expanded its academic offerings downtown. The SeaGate Centre was envisioned as a way to attract Toledo office workers to enroll in the university.

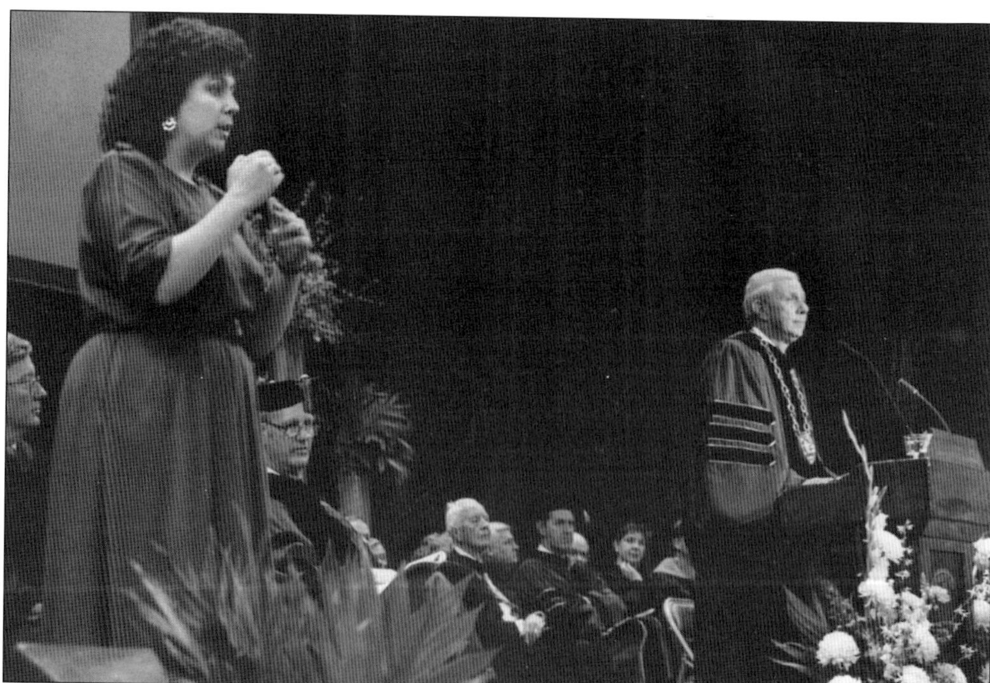
Dr. McComas retired in 1988 to become president of Virginia Polytechnic University. College of Law dean John Stoepler served as interim president until Dr. Frank Horton was appointed 13th president in 1988. He was inaugurated on April 13, 1989.

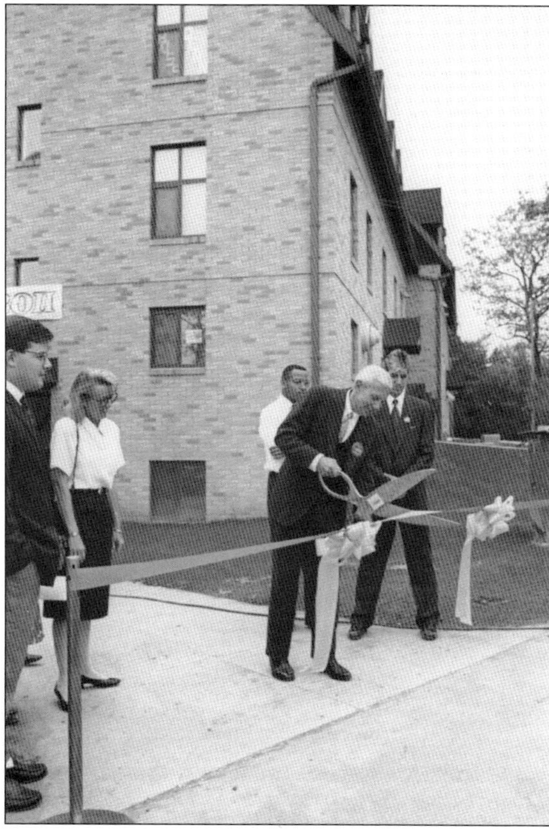

During Dr. Horton's tenure, several more building projects were completed, including the Student Recreation Center in 1990, Greek Village in 1990 (which was later named for Dr. McComas), and a major renovation of the Glass Bowl Stadium (below).

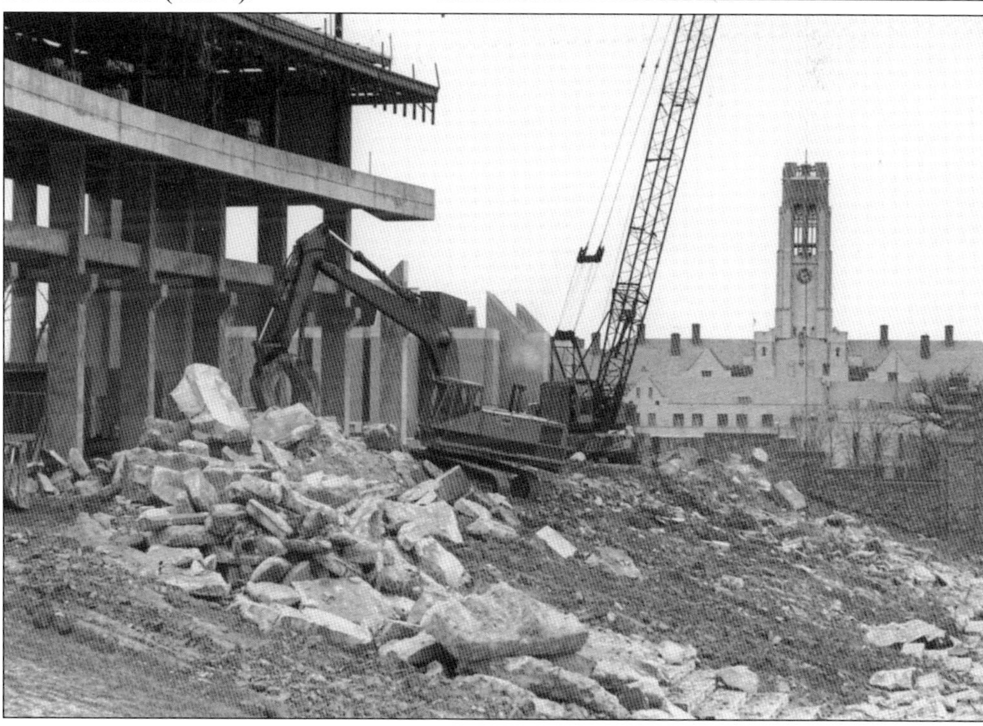

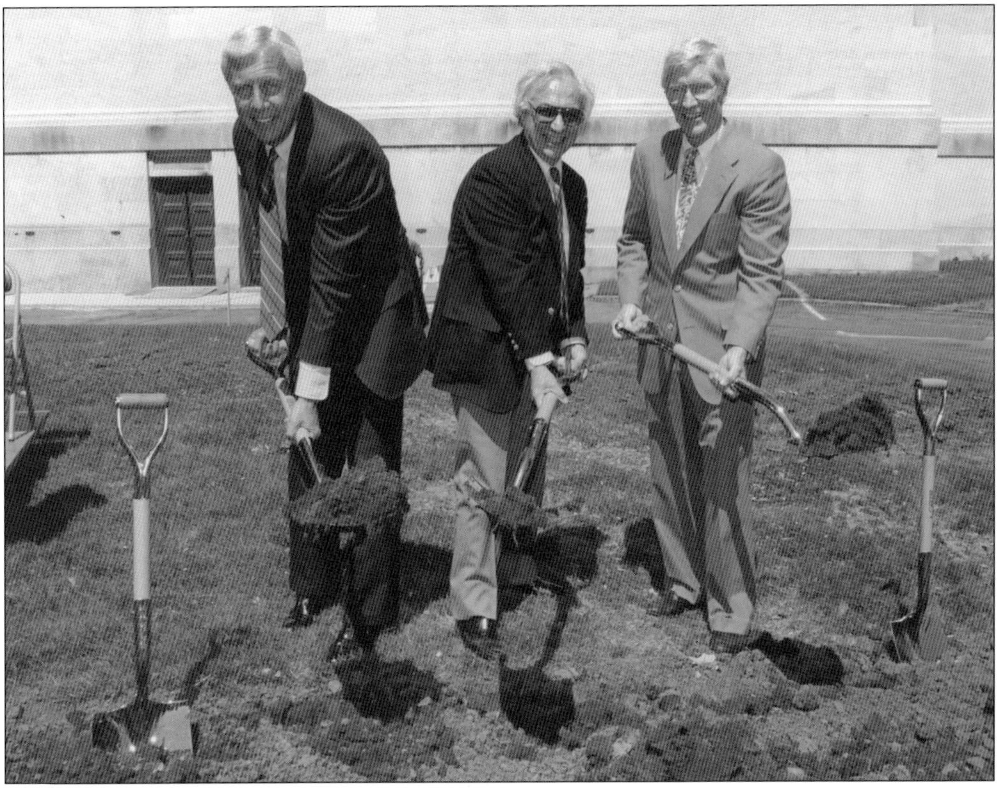

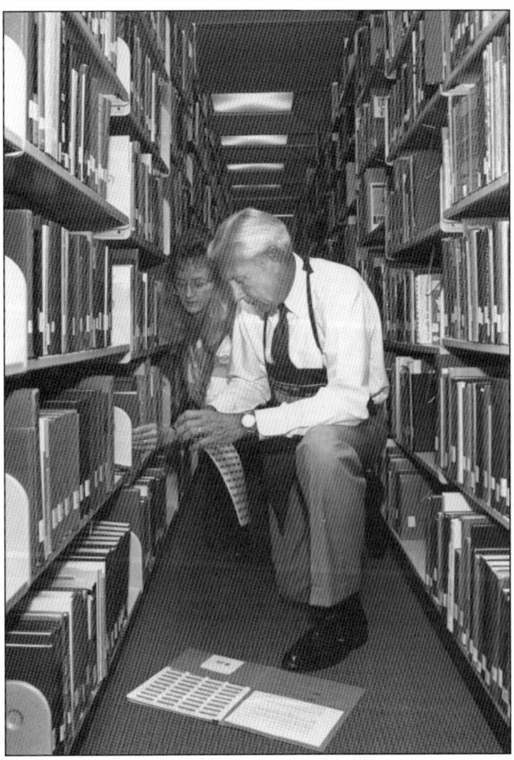

In 1991, UT and the Toledo Museum of Art approved the construction of the Center for the Visual Arts, to be designed by internationally known architect Frank Gehry. The building was jointly owned by UT and the museum, and built next to the Toledo Museum of Art. Gehry (center) joined Dr. Frank Horton and Toledo Museum of Art director David Steadman at the ground-breaking ceremony. The building was completed in 1992.

As computer technology became an essential component of higher education, libraries began to replace their card catalogs with online systems that allowed for fast searching. William S. Carlson Library automated its catalog in 1991. President Horton showed his support by volunteering to help with the arduous task of placing a barcode in each volume in the library's collection. UT joined OhioLINK, the state academic library consortium, in 1994.

As Ohio became a battleground state in presidential elections, UT saw more visits from presidential candidates, including Bill Clinton, shown here on the campaign trail in 1992.

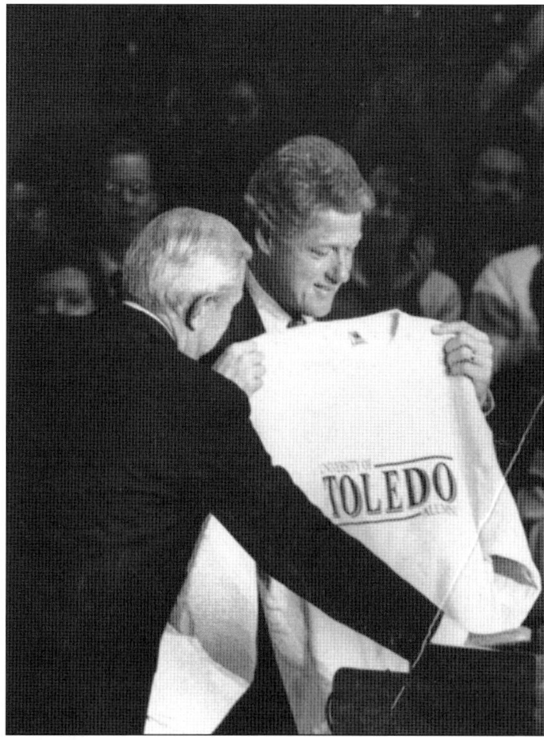

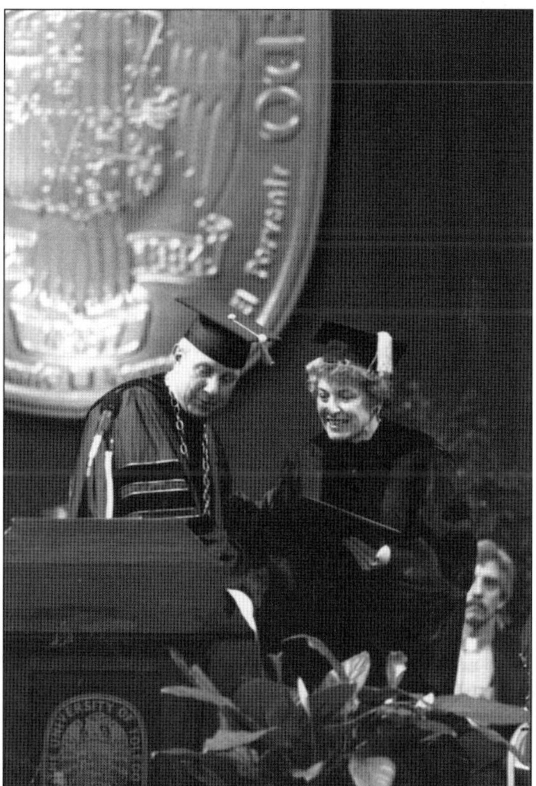

US representative Marcy Kaptur received an honorary degree from UT at the commencement ceremony in December 1993. Representative Kaptur is the longest serving woman in the US House of Representatives.

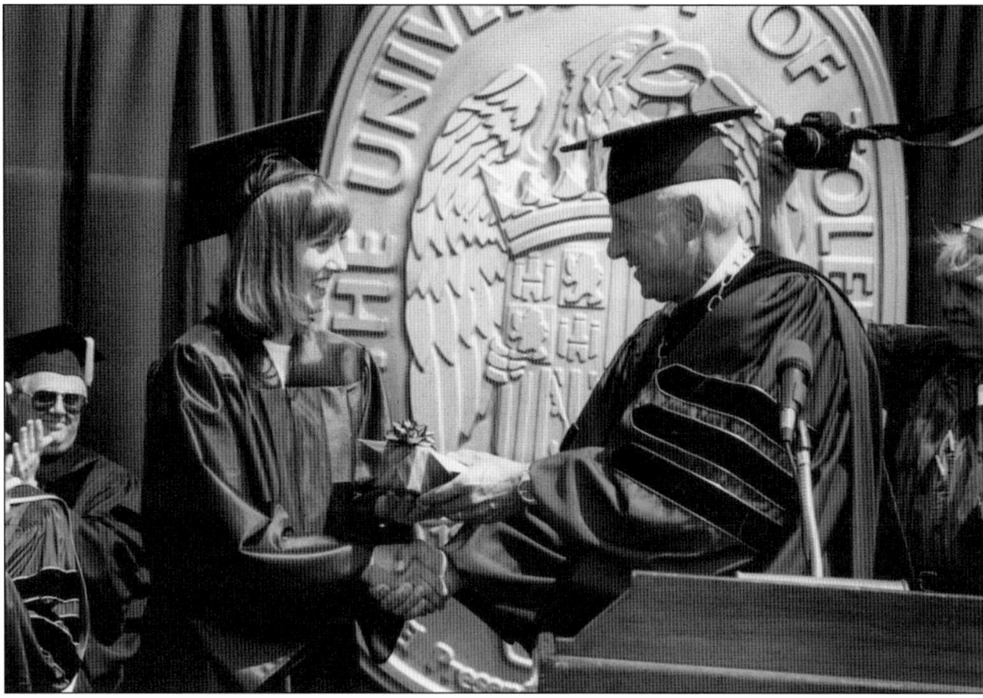

President Horton handed out the 100,000th University of Toledo diploma to Kimberly Urban at the June 11, 1994, commencement ceremony. He also personally signed each diploma awarded during his tenure.

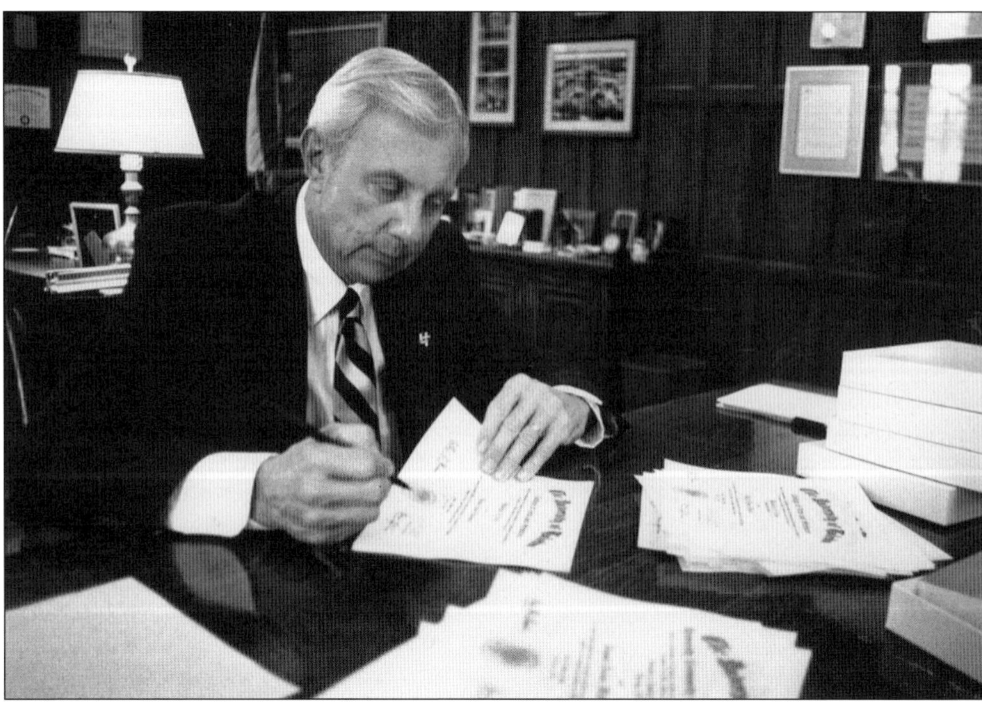

Five

A New Medical College for Toledo

In 1910, the Carnegie Foundation published a report by Abraham Flexner that reviewed the state of medical education in the country. In that report, Flexner contended that there were too many inadequately trained physicians being turned out by too many inadequate medical schools. Among the schools cited for poor quality of education and facilities was the Toledo Medical College. As a result of that report, the school was closed by the Toledo University Board of Directors in 1918. The only medical schools that survived in Ohio were Western Reserve University, Ohio State University, and the University of Cincinnati.

Not only did the report close schools, it also affected the creation of new medical schools. Between 1910 and 1950, only 10 new medical schools were created in the entire country. By the end of the 1950s, the shortage of doctors was becoming a critical problem. A 1959 report by the Department of Health, Education, and Welfare publicized the shortage and brought the issue onto the legislative agenda. By 1963, the federal government passed the Health Professions Education Assistance Act, which provided one federal dollar for medical school construction for every dollar raised locally. Despite this federal assistance, between 1960 and 1980, the largest contributor by far to new medical school construction was state government, with 29 of 40 new schools funded by the states.

In Ohio, the Interim Commission on Education Beyond High School produced a report in 1962 that emphasized the state's shortage of doctors. It said all three of the existing medical schools should be expanded, and new schools should be created. At that time, four cities and one university had requested a new medical school from the state: Cleveland, Akron, Dayton, Toledo, and Kent State University. Of these, Toledo had been working on trying to establish a medical school since 1952.

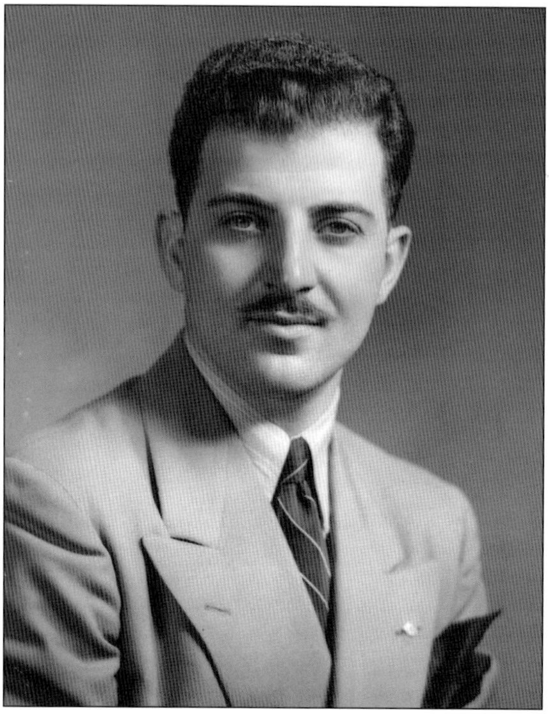

At the same time the University of Toledo was struggling with its finances in the 1950s, city council member Michael Damas (shown here) sought to reestablish the Toledo Medical College. UT president Asa Knowles agreed to a feasibility study, which was released in 1954. But the faculty were concerned about insufficient funding as the price tag was estimated at $4–5 million. Funding the school would require passage of a county-wide tax levy, so the plan was dropped. (Left, courtesy of the Toledo Lucas County Public Library.)

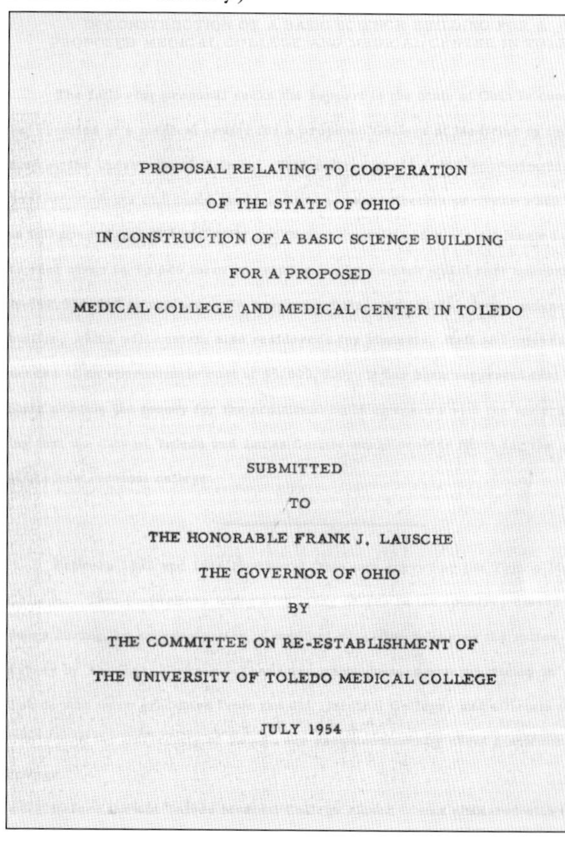

PROPOSAL RELATING TO COOPERATION

OF THE STATE OF OHIO

IN CONSTRUCTION OF A BASIC SCIENCE BUILDING

FOR A PROPOSED

MEDICAL COLLEGE AND MEDICAL CENTER IN TOLEDO

SUBMITTED

TO

THE HONORABLE FRANK J. LAUSCHE

THE GOVERNOR OF OHIO

BY

THE COMMITTEE ON RE-ESTABLISHMENT OF

THE UNIVERSITY OF TOLEDO MEDICAL COLLEGE

JULY 1954

After he was elected mayor, Damas continued to advocate for a medical college. He appointed a 13-member feasibility study committee to explore the idea. Dr. William R. Willard, dean of the College of Medicine at the University of Kentucky Medical Center, was brought in as a consultant, and in 1961, his report recommended the establishment of a state-supported medical school built on the University of Toledo campus.

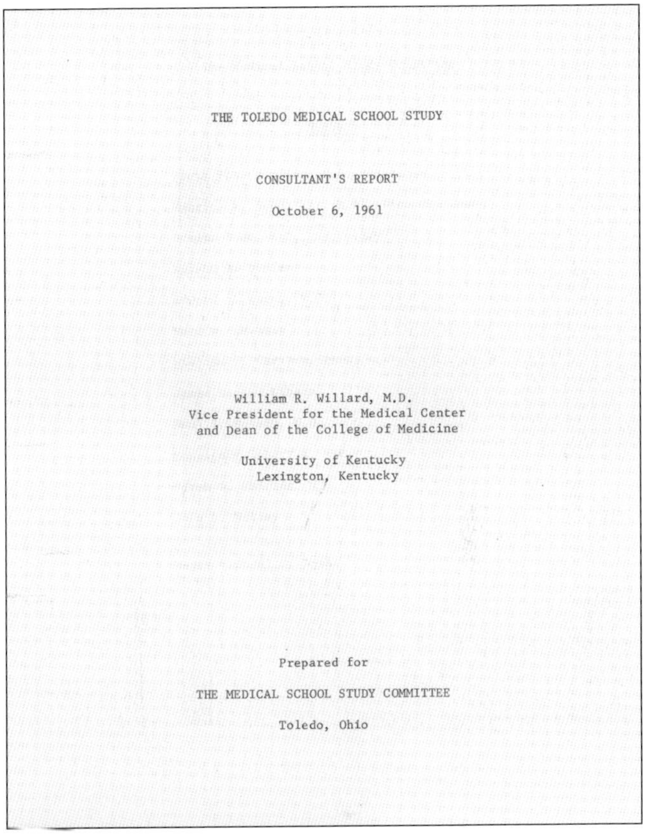

THE TOLEDO MEDICAL SCHOOL STUDY

CONSULTANT'S REPORT

October 6, 1961

William R. Willard, M.D.
Vice President for the Medical Center
and Dean of the College of Medicine

University of Kentucky
Lexington, Kentucky

Prepared for

THE MEDICAL SCHOOL STUDY COMMITTEE

Toledo, Ohio

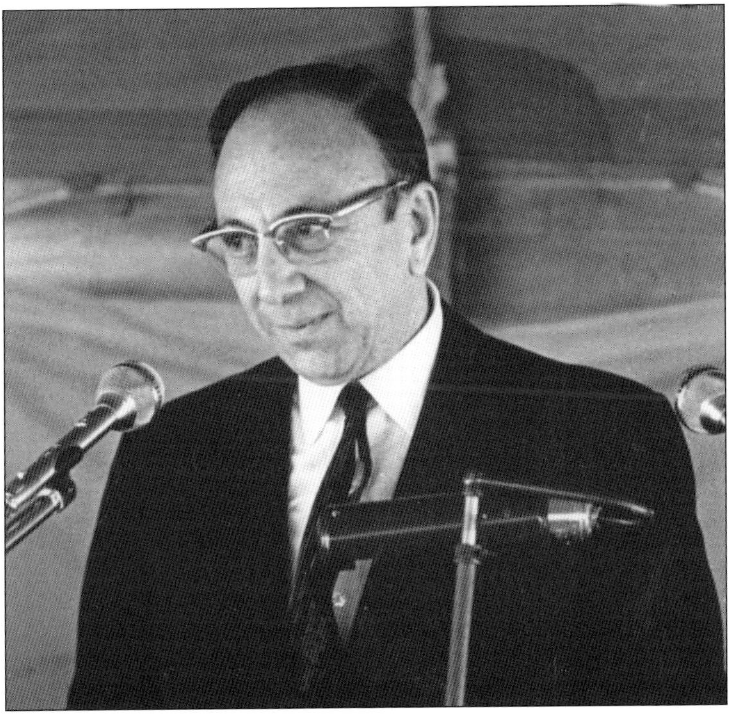

One major backer of the plan for a new medical school was Paul Block Jr., publisher of the *Toledo Blade*. But in an editorial published after the release of Willard's report, the newspaper expressed its opinion that UT was a long way from being able to administer a medical school. "A medical teaching center should be developed on its own, without encumbering TU's existing efforts to improve itself and better serve the community," the paper stated.

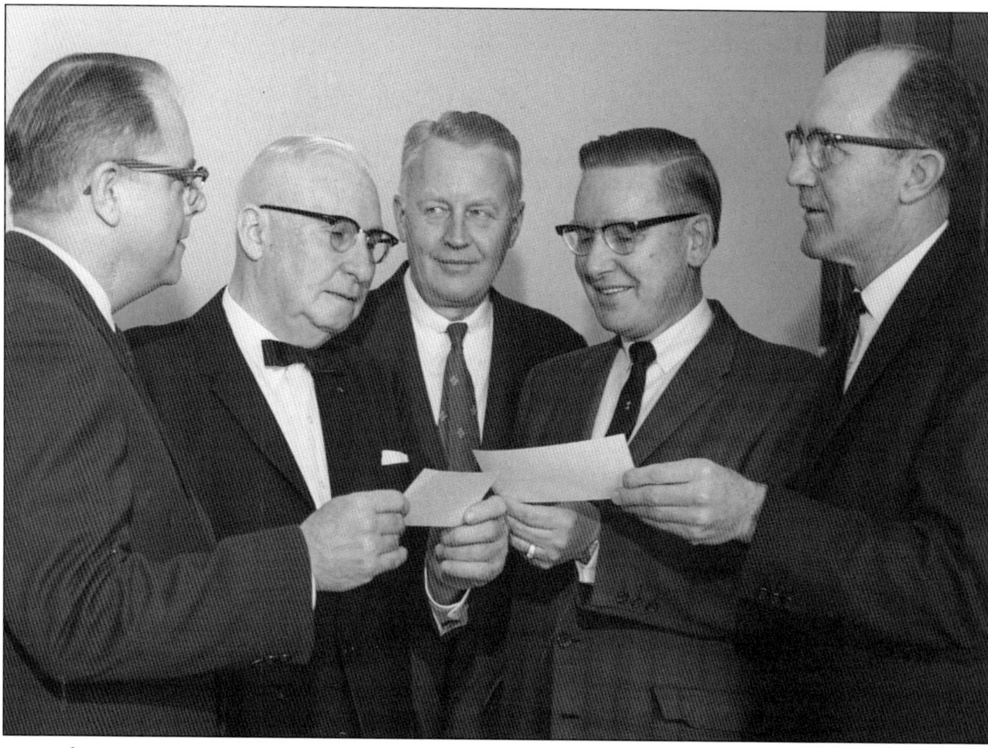

In 1962, the Academy of Medicine of Toledo and Lucas County contributed $38,000 to the Toledo Area Medical and Education Foundation to support the work of the Damas committee. With that, the group changed its name to the Toledo Area Medical College and Education Foundation and became a major collaborator in the work to establish the school. Shown here are members of the academy presenting their contribution to UT president Dr. William Carlson.

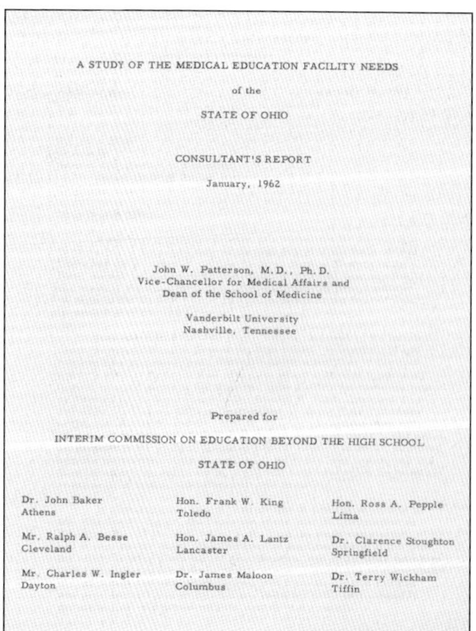

A STUDY OF THE MEDICAL EDUCATION FACILITY NEEDS

of the

STATE OF OHIO

CONSULTANT'S REPORT

January, 1962

John W. Patterson, M.D., Ph.D.
Vice-Chancellor for Medical Affairs and
Dean of the School of Medicine

Vanderbilt University
Nashville, Tennessee

Prepared for

INTERIM COMMISSION ON EDUCATION BEYOND THE HIGH SCHOOL

STATE OF OHIO

Dr. John Baker Athens	Hon. Frank W. King Toledo	Hon. Ross A. Pepple Lima
Mr. Ralph A. Besse Cleveland	Hon. James A. Lantz Lancaster	Dr. Clarence Stoughton Springfield
Mr. Charles W. Ingler Dayton	Dr. James Maloon Columbus	Dr. Terry Wickham Tiffin

At the state level, Gov. Michael DiSalle hired Dr. John W. Patterson, dean of Vanderbilt University's college of medicine, to assess the state's medical education needs. Patterson's report, issued in 1962, suggested the state should build two new medical schools, with one in the Cleveland area and another located in either Toledo, Akron, or Dayton. He did note that Toledo had a long interest and established support for a school.

Governor DiSalle followed up the report with a series of public hearings. At that time, UT president William S. Carlson noted that land had been set aside on the campus for the medical school. A report issued the week after the public hearings recommended that the new school be established on the University of Toledo campus and suggested a $1 million allocation from the General Assembly to begin work on the plans. UT quickly issued this brochure promoting the medical college.

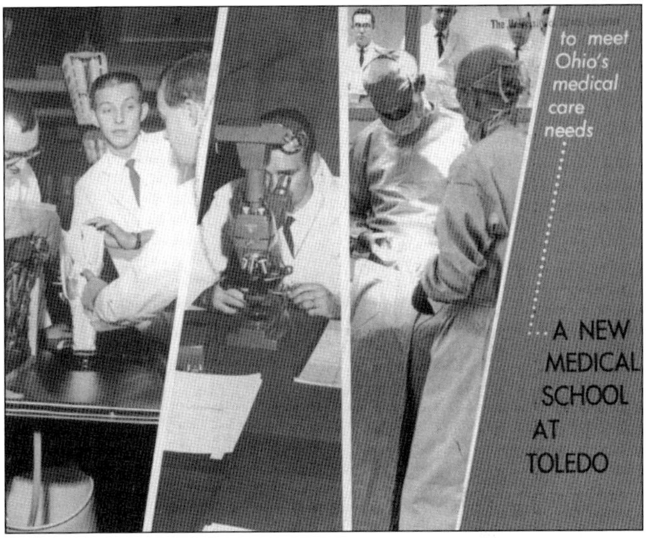

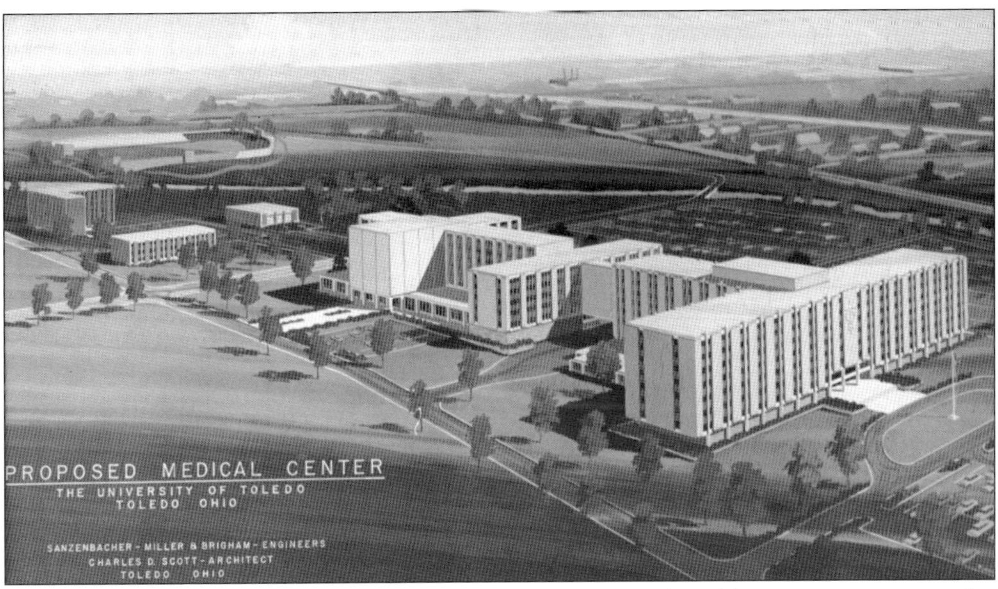

In November 1963, Ohio voters approved a $250-million bond levy to raise money for construction on state-assisted college campuses. It was assumed by President Carlson that planning money for the new Toledo medical college was included in the funding. In anticipation of the plan for the new medical school moving forward, in 1964, architectural renderings of a proposed medical center were completed.

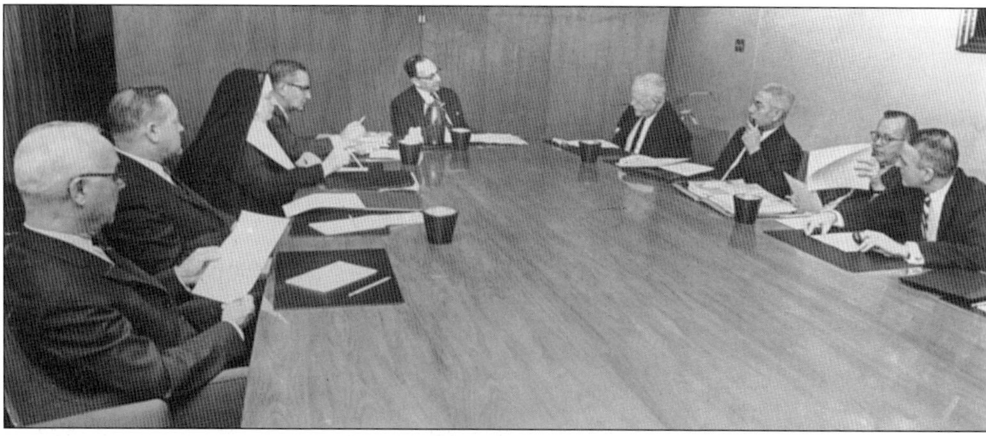

In September 1964, the Ohio Board of Regents, a higher education oversight board appointed by newly-elected governor James Rhodes, recommended Toledo as the site of a new medical school. But the board recommended the new school be separate from UT. On December 18, 1964, the Ohio General Assembly passed a bill creating the Medical College of Ohio (MCO) at Toledo. The first board of directors consisted of Paul Block Jr. (center), who served as chair, and included, from left to right, Dr. Bryon G. Shaffer, John A. Skipton, Sister Mary Lawrence, Frank F.A. Rawling, J. Preston Levis, James Slater Gibson, William W. Knight Jr., and Bernard R. Baker II.

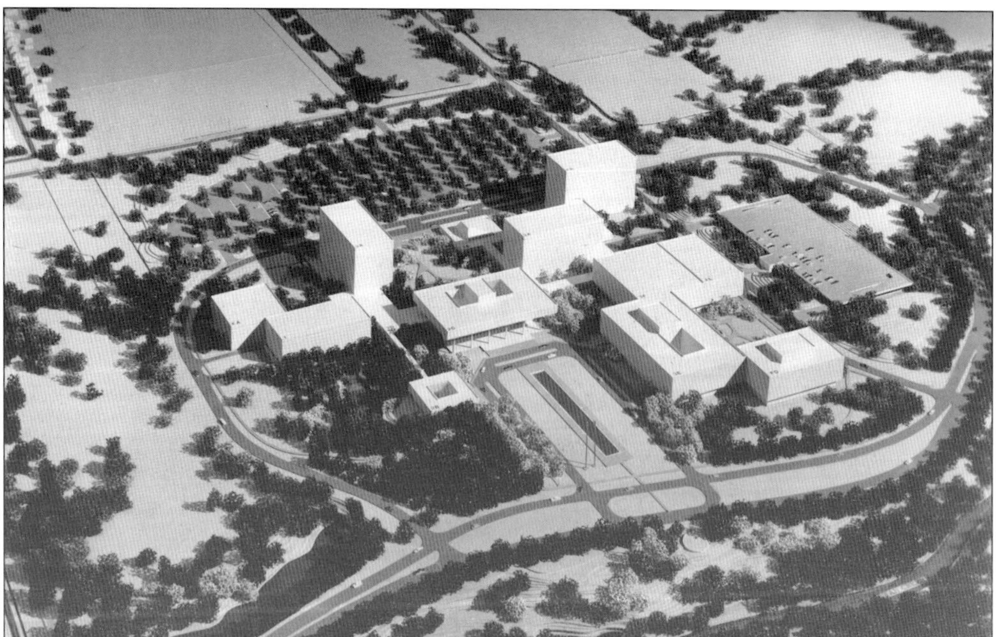

The first order of business was selection of a site for the new school. After again considering the space on the UT campus, a consultant suggested land near the Toledo State Hospital on Arlington Avenue. A few of the state hospital buildings still remained at the time of the decision, but all were eventually torn down. Yamasaki & Associates, an architectural firm in Troy, Michigan, was selected to develop a master plan. The firm had an international reputation, having previously designed the World Trade Center in New York City.

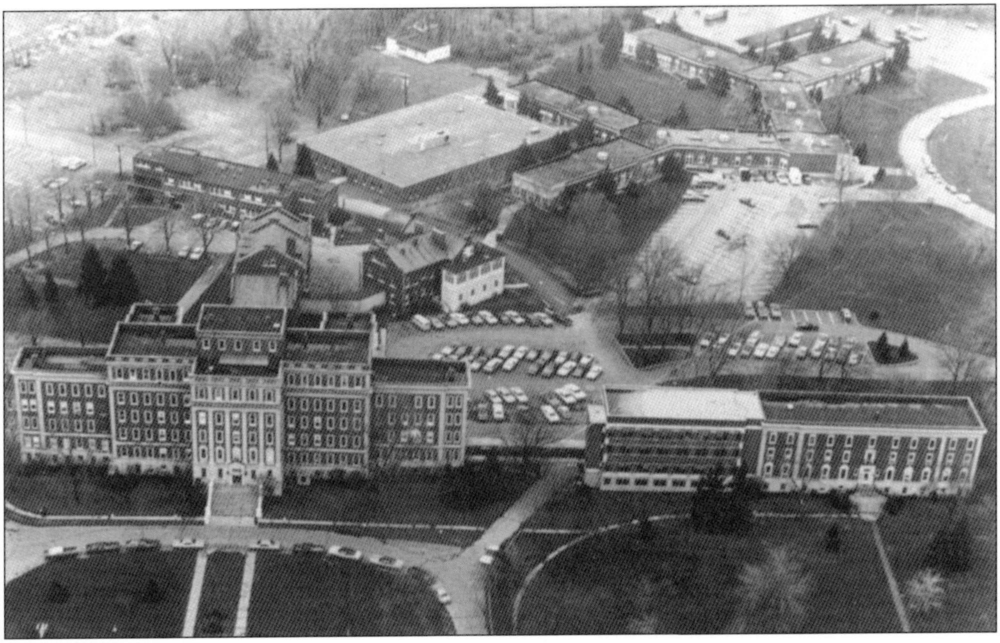

During the time the first building was under construction, the Medical College of Ohio faculty utilized work space at various locations, including the Maumee Valley Hospital (foreground) and the William Roche Memorial Hospital (background).

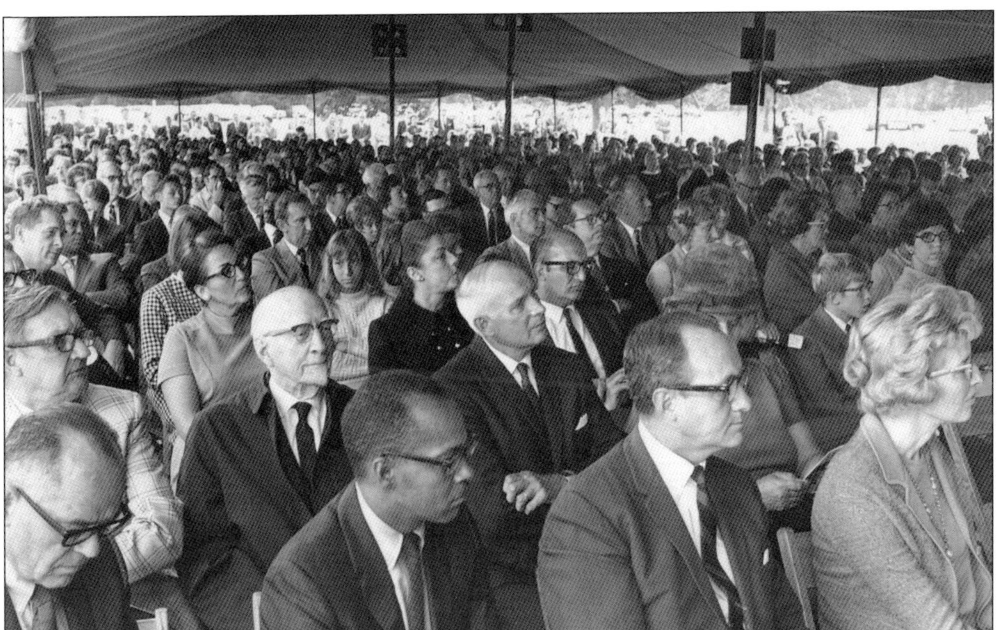

The dedication ceremony for the new medical college took place on September 21, 1969, with Gov. James Rhodes addressing the crowd. Over 600 people attended the ceremony.

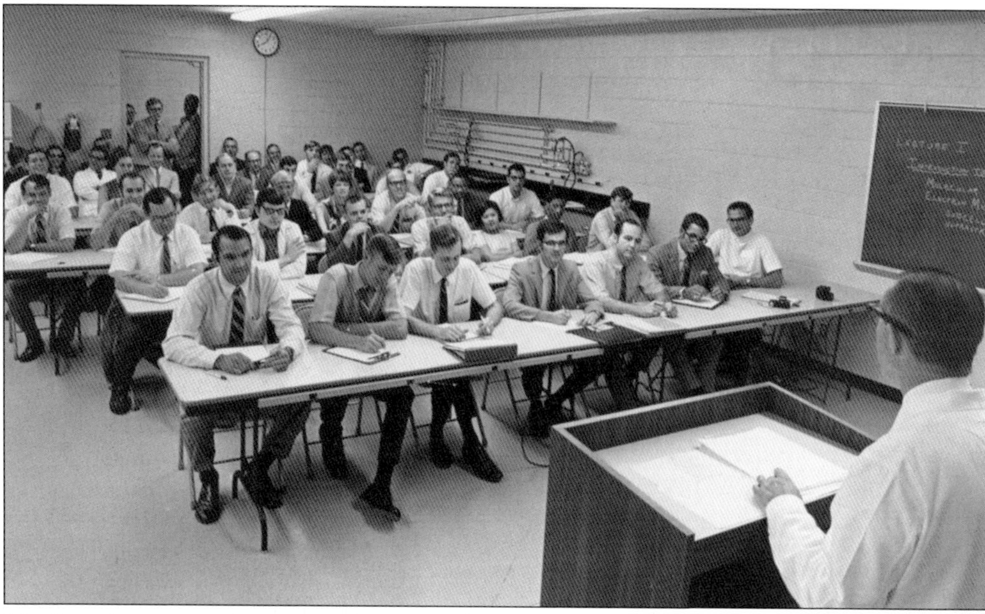

The first class entered on September 15, 1969. It consisted of 32 students, and was diverse—it included three women and two African Americans. Tuition was $900 for Ohio residents, and $1,575 for nonresidents. Nearly 150 local physicians volunteered as teachers, and others served as preceptors.

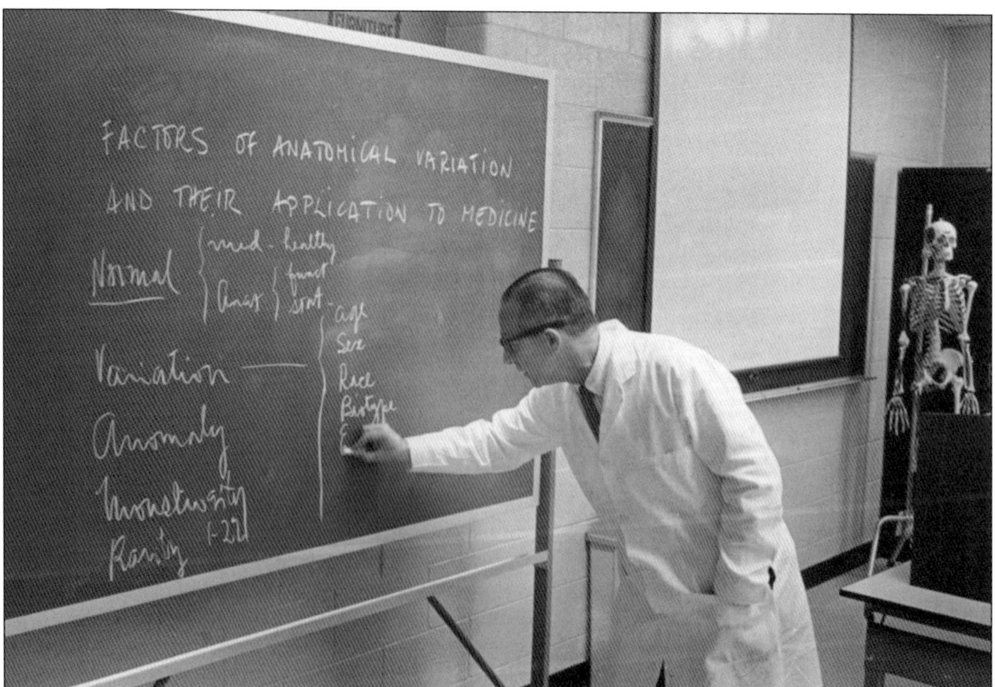

Dr. Liberato DiDio gives a lecture on anatomy to the students of the Medical College of Ohio at Toledo on the first day of class.

Dr. Glidden Brooks was named president of the college. He came to MCO after serving as vice president and director of the Institute of Health Sciences at Brown University.

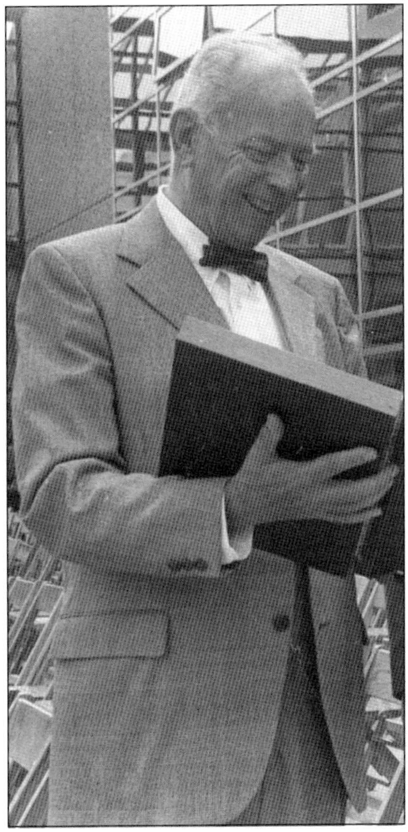

The Lucas County commissioners turned over management of Maumee Valley Hospital to MCO in 1970; it was to serve as the college's teaching hospital. Shown here are the commissioners and lawyers shortly after agreeing to the terms of the contract for the hospital. It was difficult to recruit faculty to the new college because of inadequate and antiquated facilities.

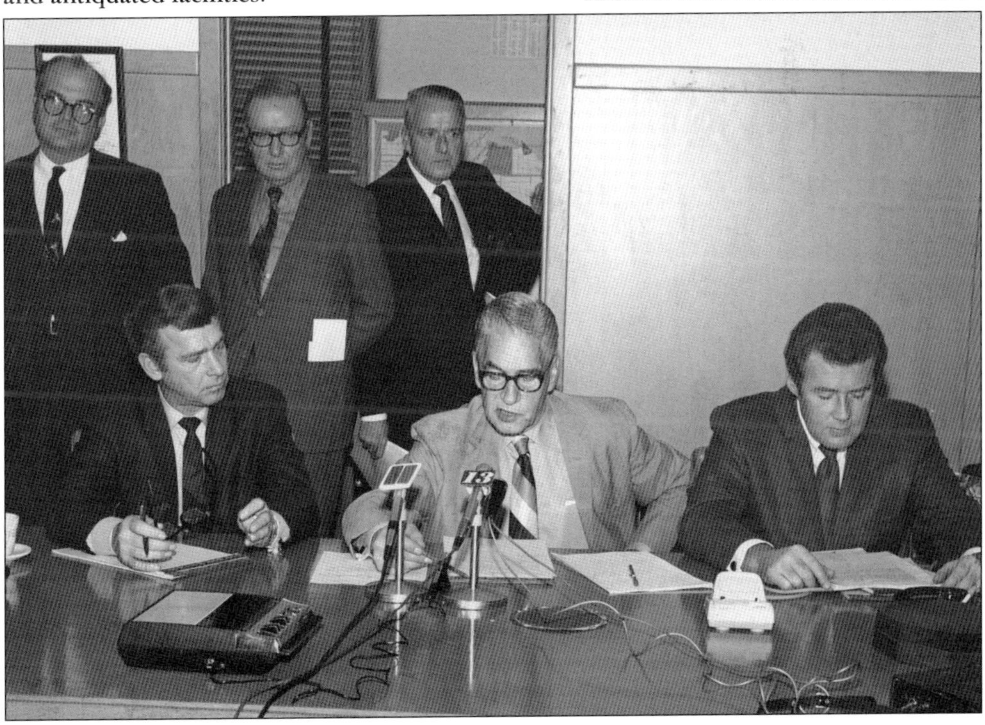

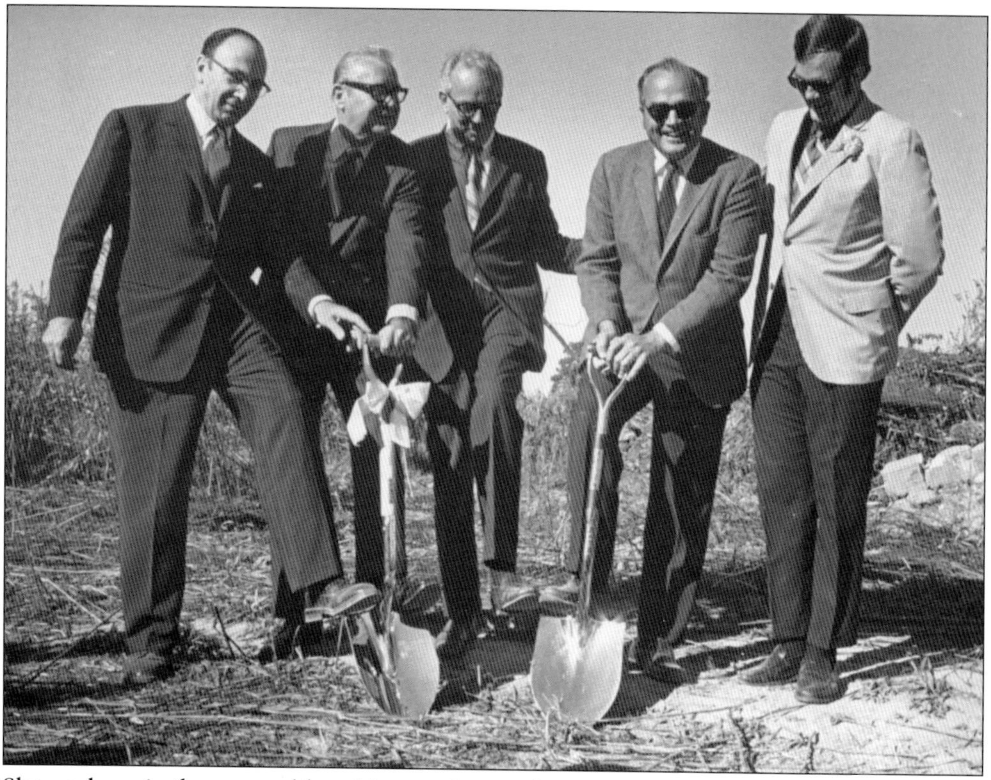

Shown here is the ground breaking on September 11, 1970, for the first building to be constructed: a basic and clinical science facility. From left to right are Paul Block Jr., Gov. James A. Rhodes, medical college president Dr. Glidden Brooks, medical college dean Dr. Robert G. Page, and president of the first class of students, Lurley Archambeau.

That building, shown here under construction, would later be named for the board's first chair and one of the forces behind the creation of the medical college: Paul Block Jr.

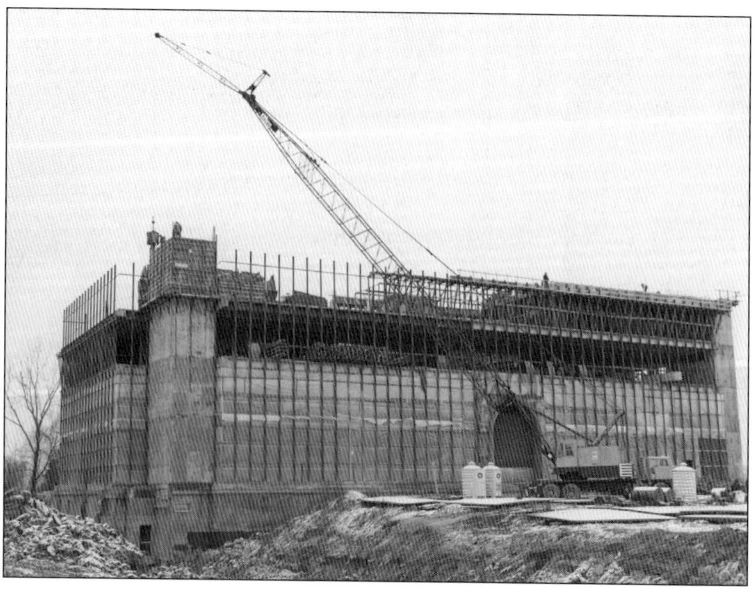

In 1971, Dr. Brooks resigned from the presidency. It took some time before Dr. Marion Anderson, professor and chairman of MCO's department of surgery, was selected to replace him in 1972.

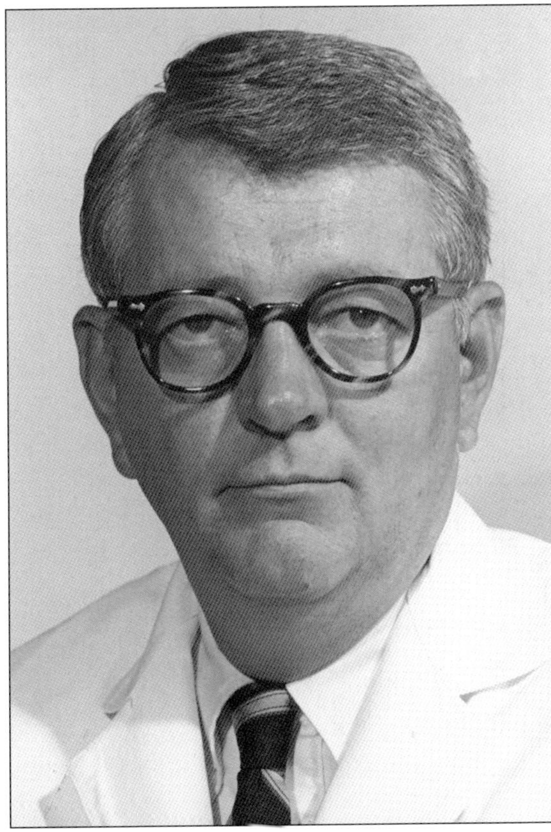

Also in 1972, the first class graduated. The ceremony took place at the Peristyle of the Toledo Museum of Art.

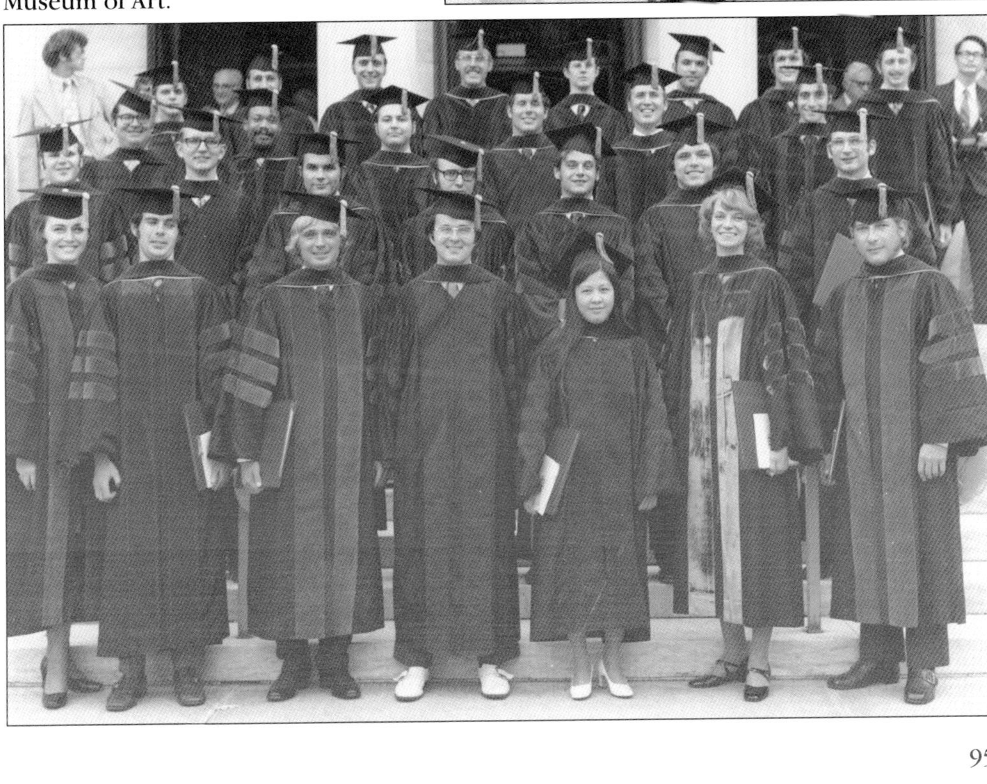

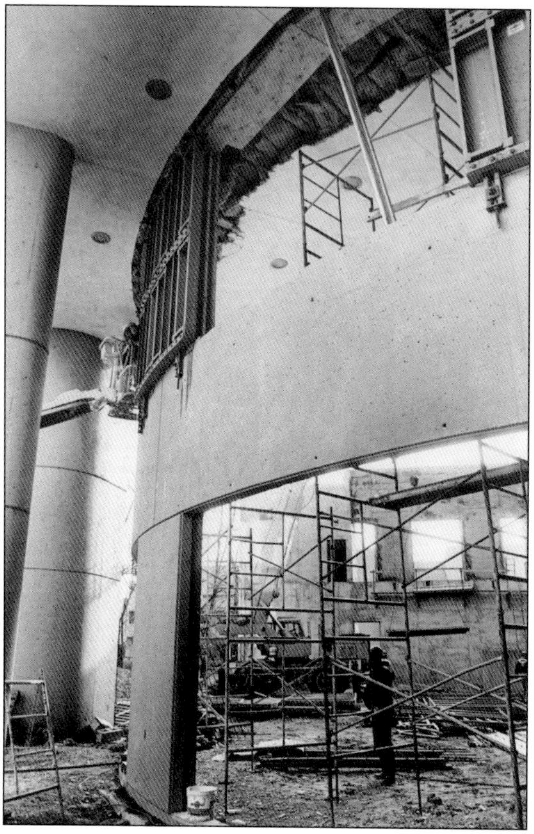

The Health Science Building was completed in the fall of 1973. Planning also began for a new teaching hospital affiliated with the medical college to replace Maumee Valley Hospital. Construction (shown here) began on the $40 million, 258-bed hospital in 1975, and took nearly four years to complete.

Another early building constructed on the campus was Raymon H. Mulford Library, named for the former president of Owens-Illinois. Ground breaking took place in 1973, and the library was completed in 1975 at a cost of $7.4 million. It was designed by internationally known architect Don Hisaka.

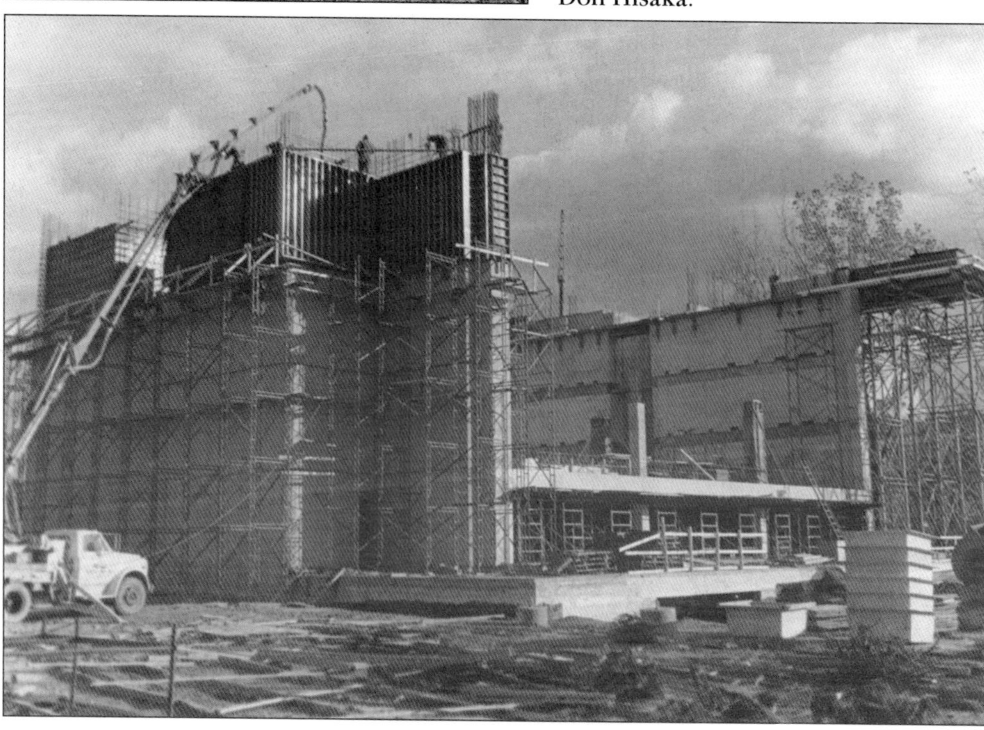

Ronald Watterson was appointed the first director of the library and would remain in that position until 1990. The stunning Mulford Library building was featured in the August 1975 issue of *Architectural Record*.

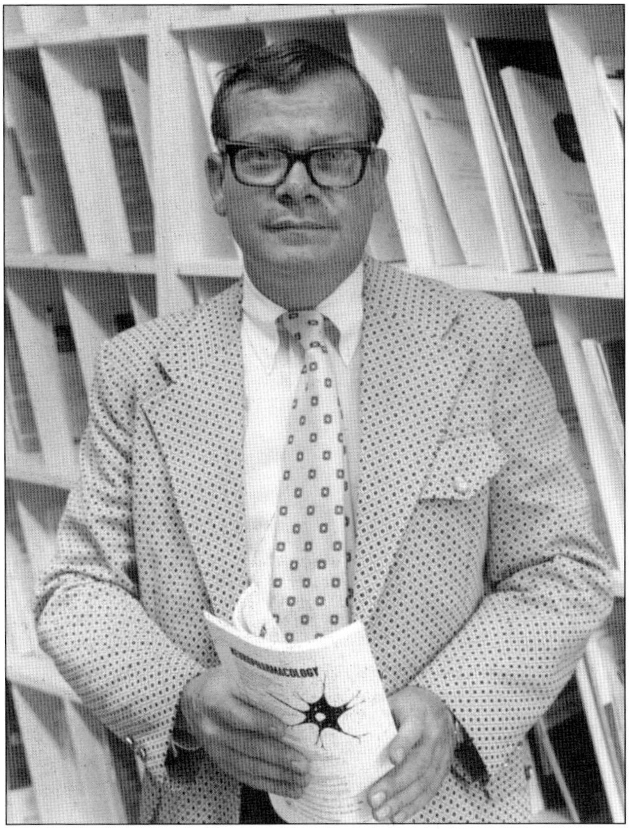

The mace for the new college was designed by renowned glass artist Dominick Labino. He is shown here (left) working on the mace, with Ronald Watterson (center) and Dr. Robert Page looking on.

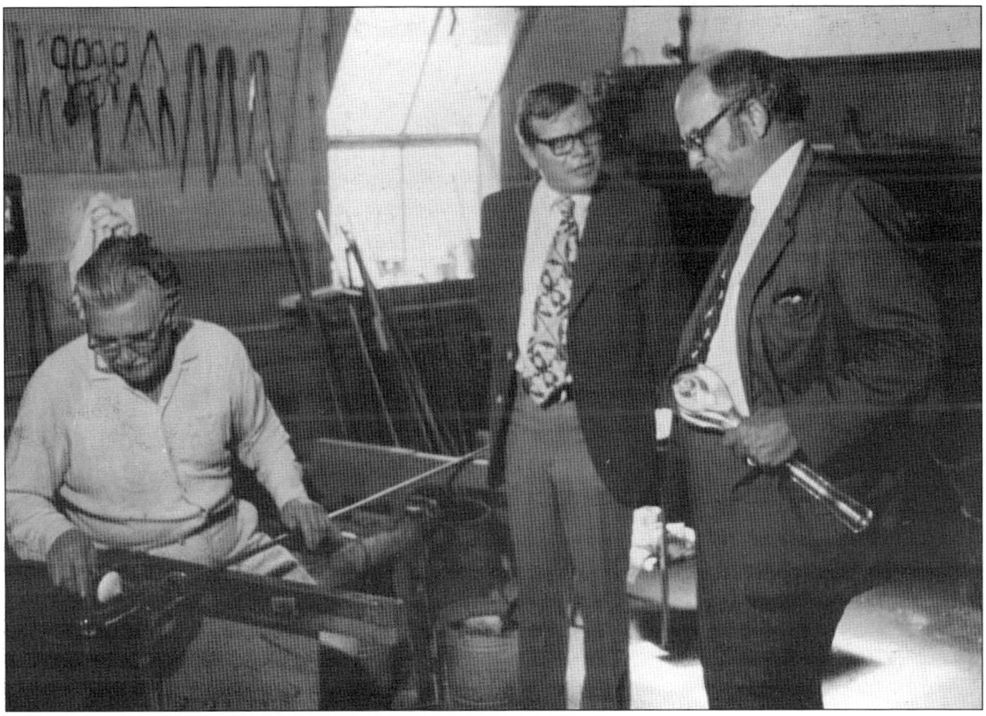

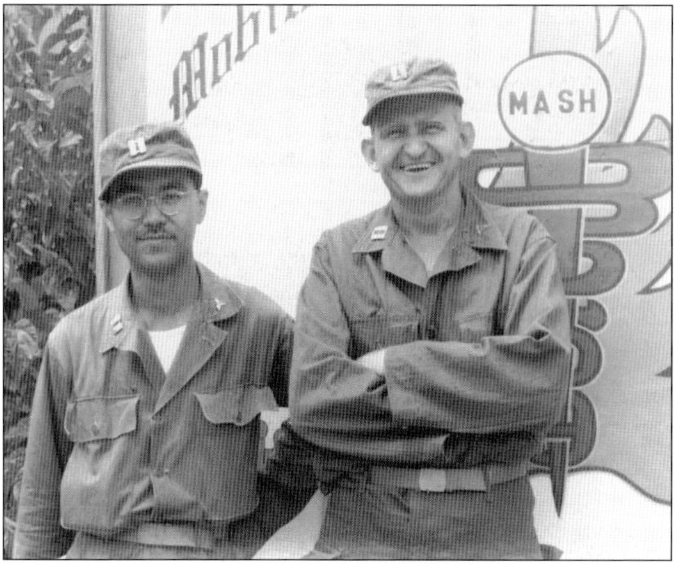

In 1974, Dr. John Howard, a world-renowned expert on pancreatic surgery and one of the founders of the American Trauma Society, was recruited to join MCO's faculty. During the Korean War, Dr. Howard, shown here on the right, had helped to develop the Mobile Army Surgical Hospital model (commonly referred to as MASH units.) His four-volume book on Korean War medicine is still important today in understanding how to treat battlefield injuries.

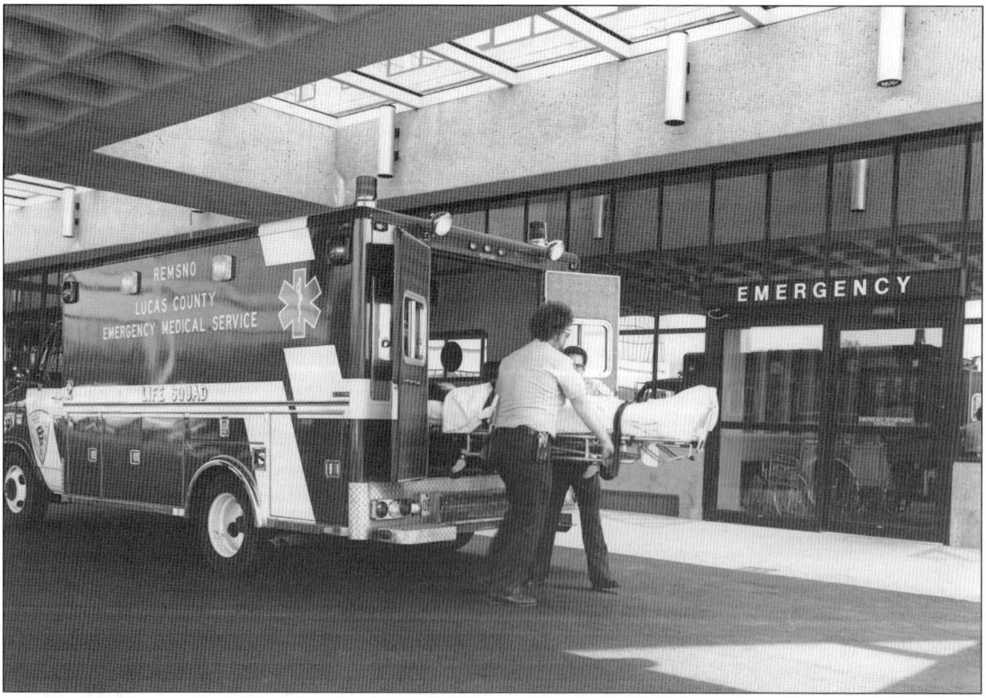

In Toledo, Dr. Howard was important in the creation of the Regional Emergency Medical Services of Northwest Ohio. The service, supported by a grant from the US Department of Health, Education, and Welfare, worked to improve trauma medicine and train ambulance drivers to provide lifesaving treatment.

Dr. Richard Ruppert became the third president of the Medical College of Ohio in 1977. He would serve in this capacity longer than any other president to date, retiring in 1993. Much of the major growth of the college occurred during his presidency.

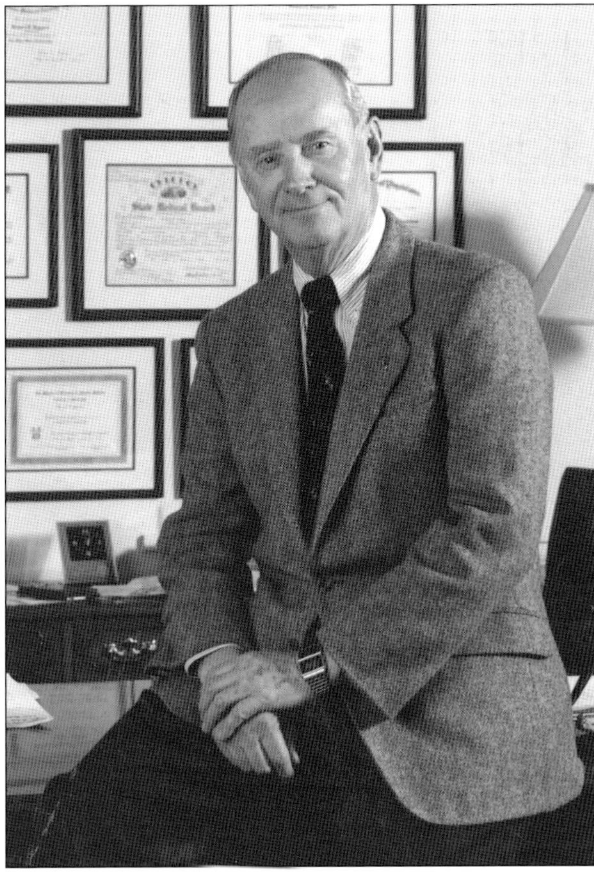

A fundraising campaign overseen by Dr. Ruppert produced significant donations from the Charles A. Dana Foundation, the Kobacker family, the Dowling Trust, and the Kresge Foundation. Shown here is Dr. Ruppert at the ground breaking for the Dana Center.

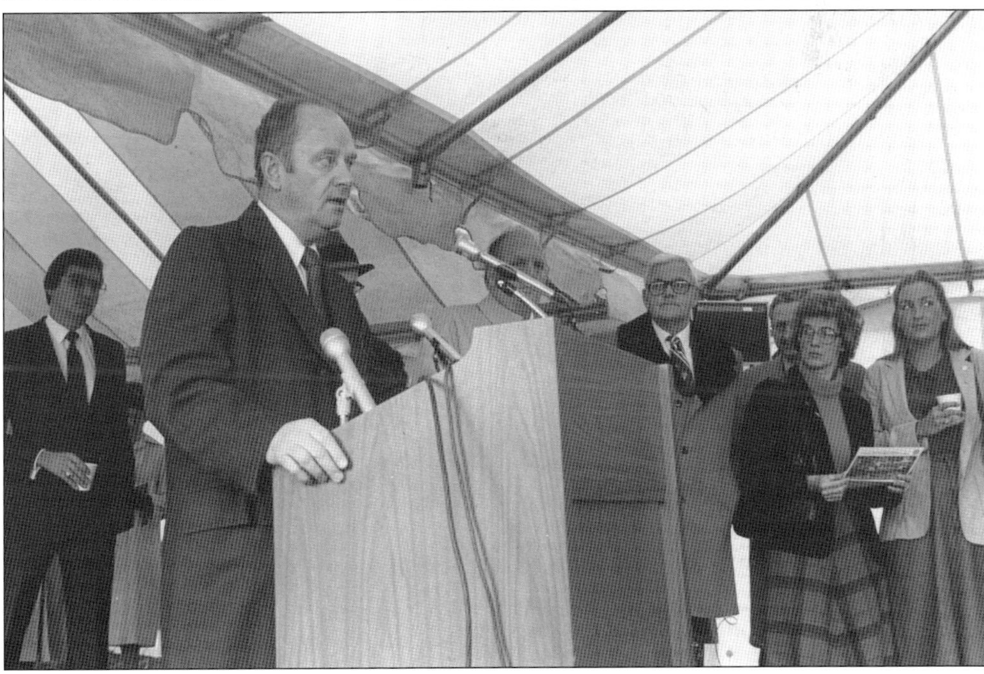

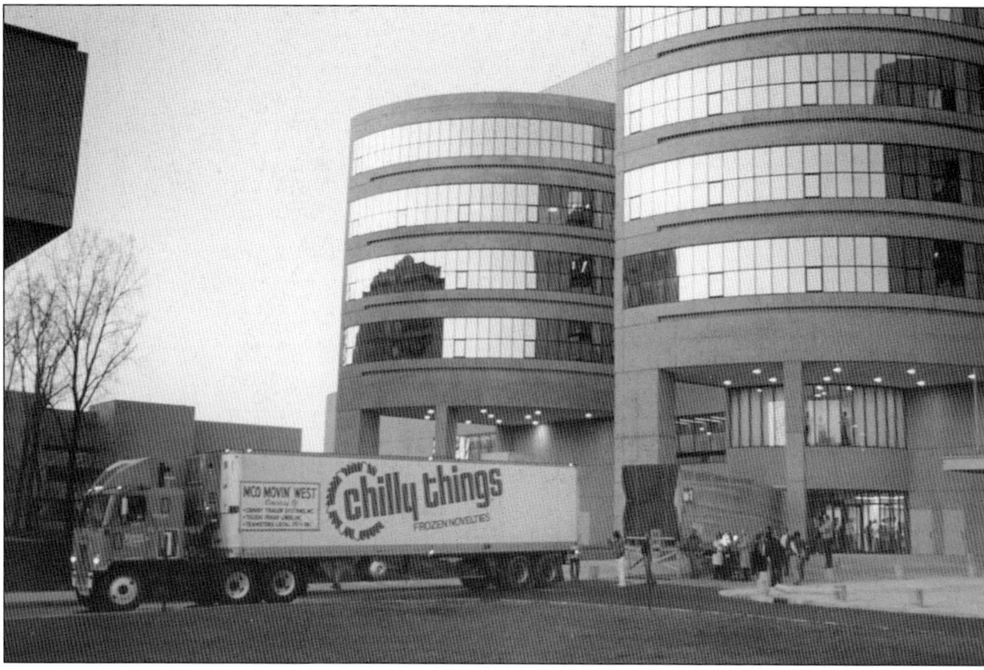

Moving day, when patients were transferred from the Maumee Valley Hospital to the new MCO Hospital, was a significant marker in the institution's history. On December 15, 1979, semi-trucks and ambulances lined up in front of the old hospital to move equipment and patients to the new building. Dr. Ruppert and his wife, Dr. Elizabeth Ruppert, professor of pediatrics, welcomed the patients, faculty, and staff to the new hospital.

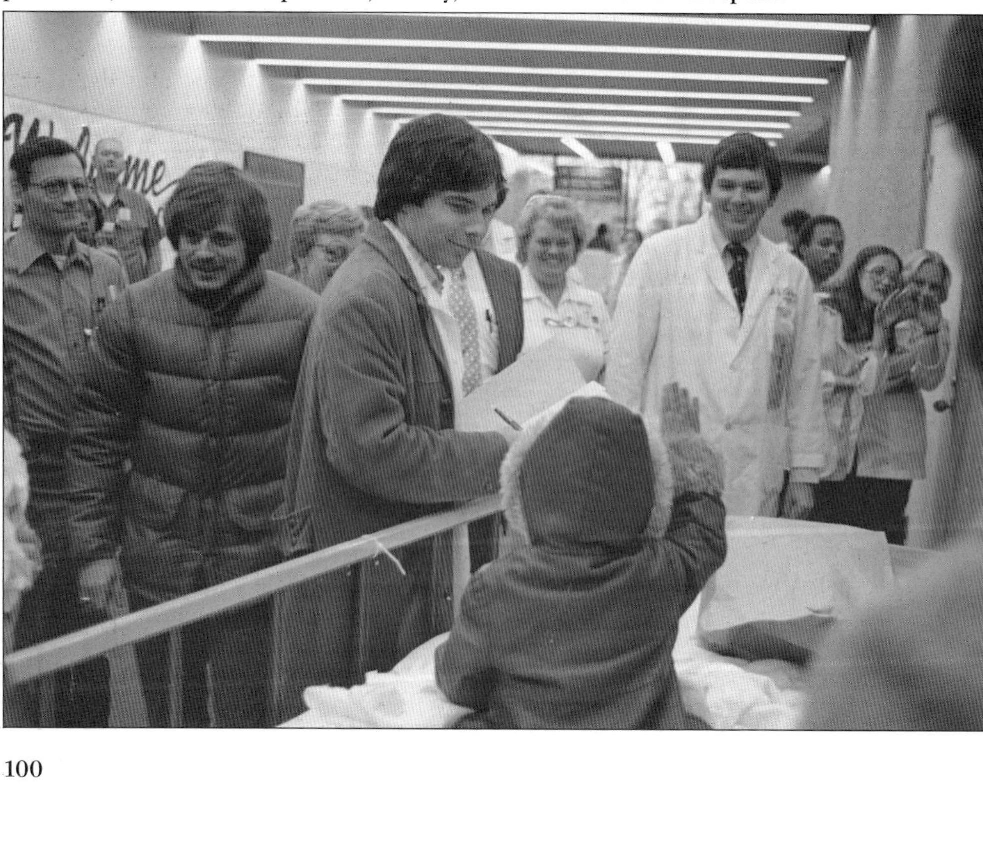

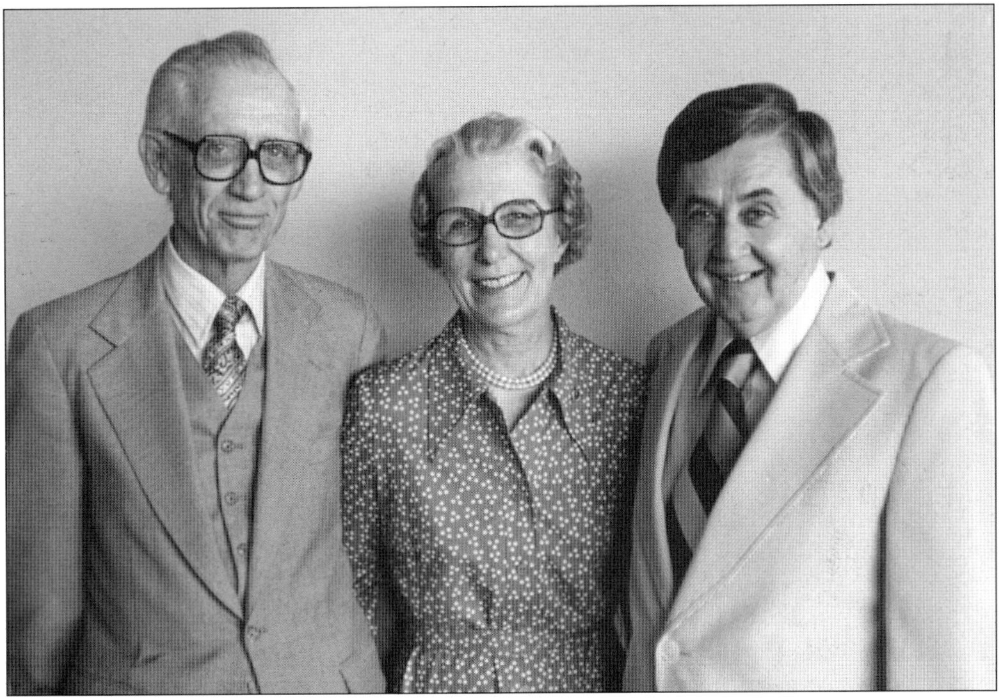

Nearly from its beginning, MCO collaborated with the University of Toledo and Bowling Green State University through the Consortium of Health Education for Northwest Ohio. Cooperative programs included physical therapy and public health. Dr. Ruth Kelly, the first dean of the College of Nursing, developed the nursing program as a cooperative program with BGSU in 1971. UT joined In 1974, and in 1978, the program to transition registered nurses to bachelor degree nurses was instituted. Shown here from left to right are Dr. William Leckie, UT vice president for academic affairs; Dr. Ruth Kelly; and Dr. Joseph Balogh, dean of the College of Health and Community Services at Bowling Green State University.

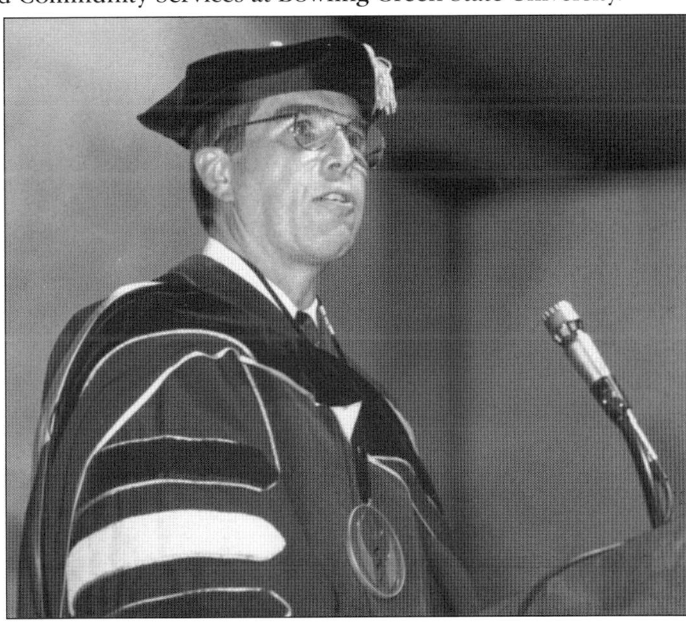

After 16 years as president, Dr. Richard Ruppert retired in 1993. Dr. Ruppert's impact on the college is hard to underestimate. Dr. Roger C. Bone became MCO's fourth president in the fall of 1993. He began a series of initiatives to prepare the college for the major changes happening in health care. Unfortunately, Dr. Bone resigned in 1996 for health reasons and died a year later.

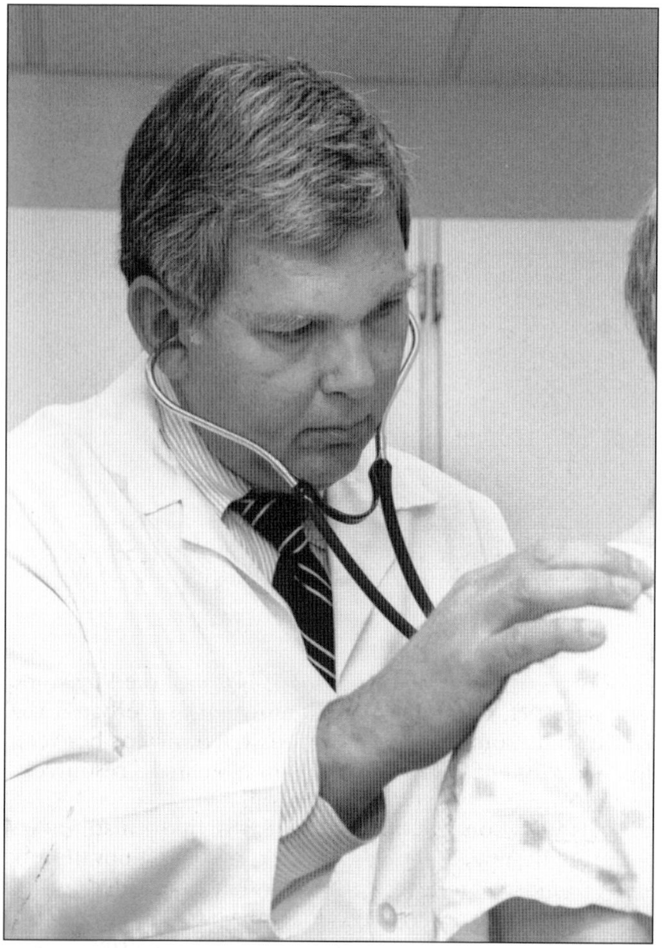

Dr. Frank McCullough, a native of Toledo, joined the College of Medicine as chief of gastroenterology in 1978. He rose through the ranks, becoming medical director in 1994, and served as the fifth president of the college from 1997 to 2003. He died in 2004.

In 2003, Dr. Amira Gohara was appointed interim president. In 2004, she was succeeded by Dr. Lloyd Jacobs (pictured). He sought to expand the reputation of the institution, and its name changed to the Medical University of Ohio to reflect this expanded influence.

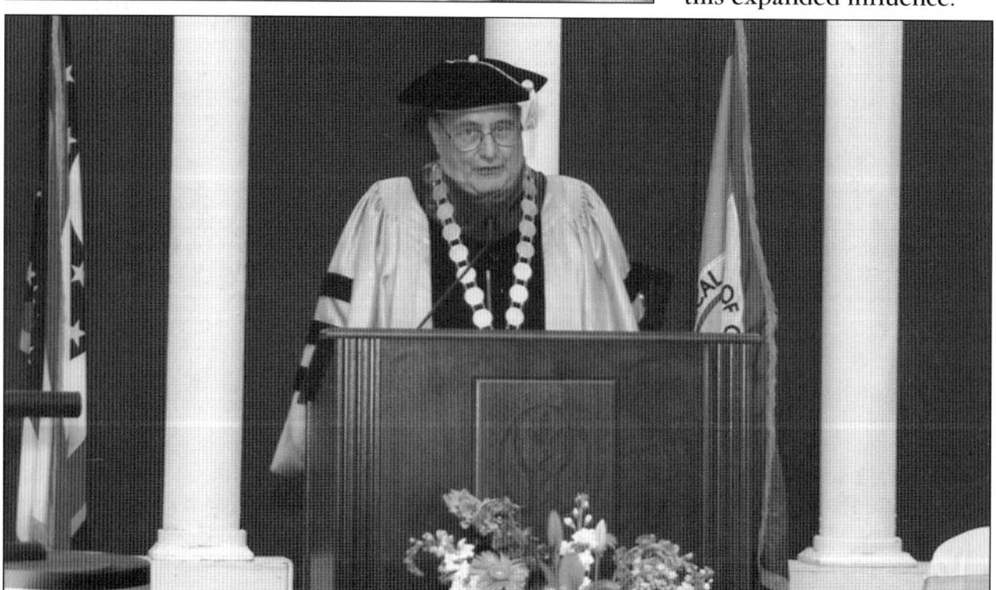

Six

A Merged, Mature University

The past two decades in the life of the University of Toledo have been marked by some consistent themes: declining state support, declining enrollment that exacerbated the financial constraints imposed by the state, sometimes contentious relationships between the administration and the faculty (no doubt made worse by declining financial resources), and changing leadership of those who oversee the academic mission.

But at the same time, the decades also saw some of the largest growth in the institution's history. A building boom not only brought new structures, but also saw the renovation of older buildings for new purposes. And most significantly, the university expanded in size and curricular offerings when UT and the Medical University of Ohio merged in 2006. UT is now one of the few schools in the country that offers degrees in medicine, pharmacy, law, engineering, education, business, nursing, and the liberal arts.

To help to make up the deficit between what the state provided and what was needed, the trustees—when permitted by the state—increased tuition during these two decades. Students took on more debt to attend, and the university provided more scholarships. The university also made a push in fundraising efforts, seeking private money to help provide necessary support.

UT also became much more involved in the economic development of the region. New initiatives partnered academic researchers with business leaders and state economic development funding in search of ways to overcome the demise of the manufacturing sector in northwest Ohio.

The decline in state support continues, as do state-imposed caps on what tuition increases the university can institute. The university has also had to deal with changing political views about the purpose of public higher education. Some political leaders have sought to "disrupt" higher education in the same way other industries and services have been disrupted with dramatically changed business models. Higher education is increasingly seen as a path to a career, and the traditional concept of a college education as a liberal education that expands the mind has been replaced with calls for achieving a degree as fast as possible at the cheapest price.

The next few decades will undoubtedly see these challenges continue—and more. Regardless of the challenges, it is certain that Jesup Scott could never have envisioned what his dream of 1872 would become.

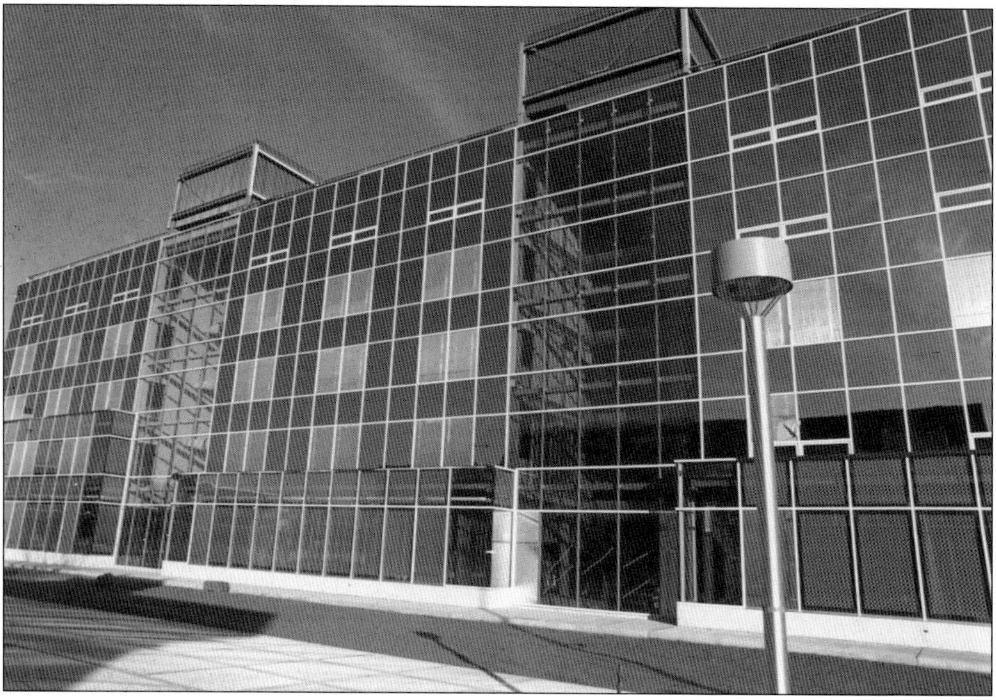

The 1990s saw several major building projects at UT. These included an $8 million expansion of a $17.8 million home for the College of Engineering named after Norman Nitschke in 1995 (above), and the International House dormitory (below).

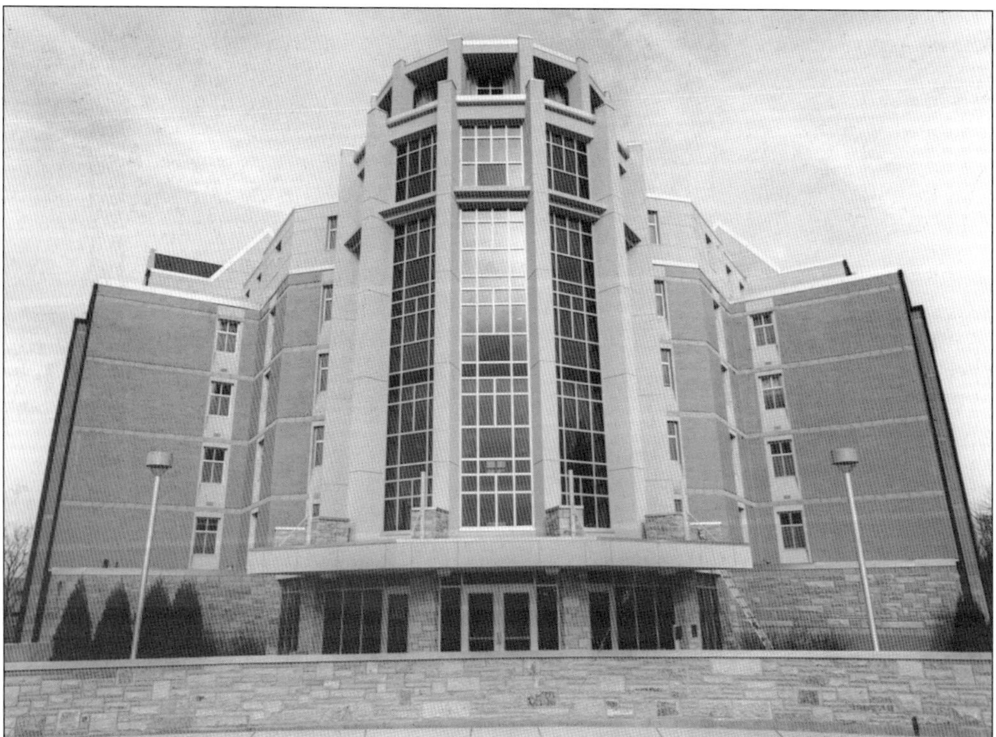

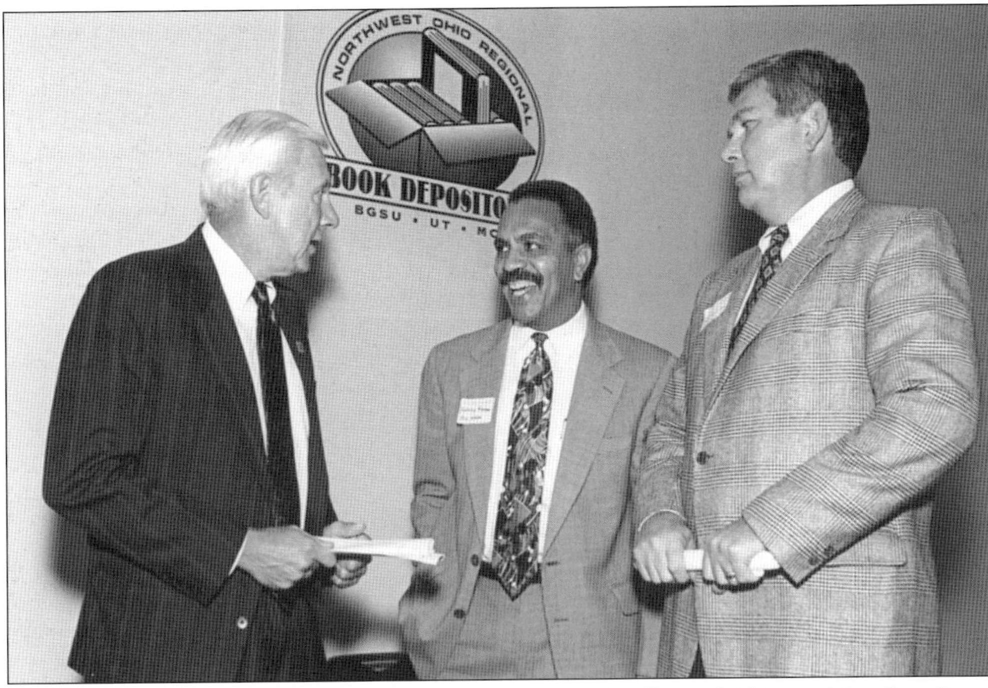

A cooperative book depository shared by UT, the Medical College of Ohio, and Bowling Green State University was completed in 1996 in Perrysburg. The $3.1 million facility allowed for the storage of little-used books in a high density, cost-effective structure. From left to right, President Horton, BGSU president Sidney Ribeau, and MCO president Frank McCullough are pictured at the dedication ceremony.

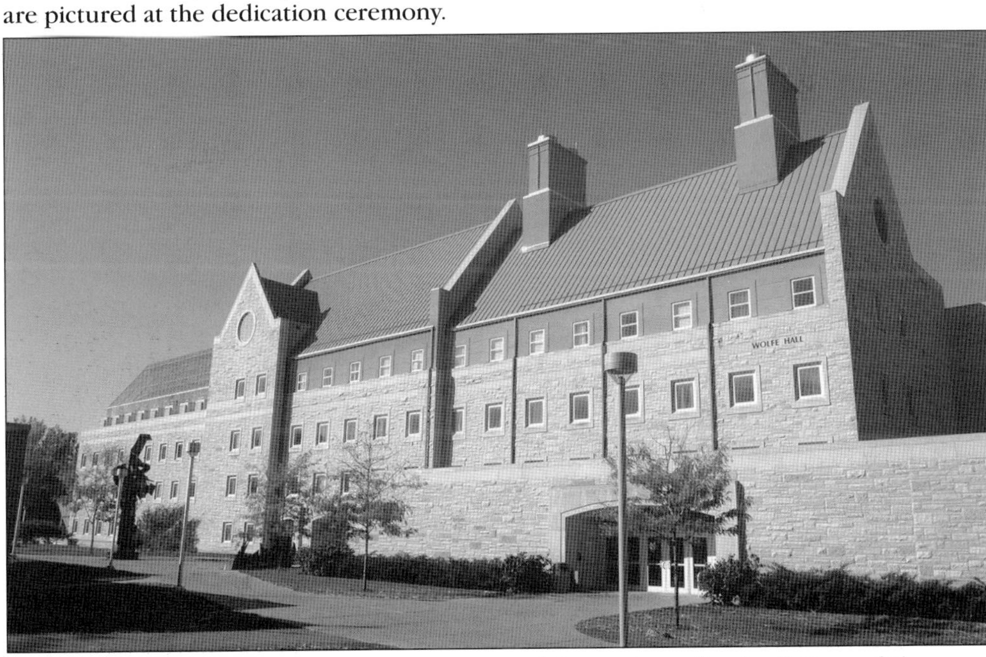

Wolfe Hall was dedicated in May 1998 as a state-of-the-art home for the College of Pharmacy. The building was constructed adjacent to Bowman-Oddy Laboratories, and was supported by a gift from Frederic Wolfe.

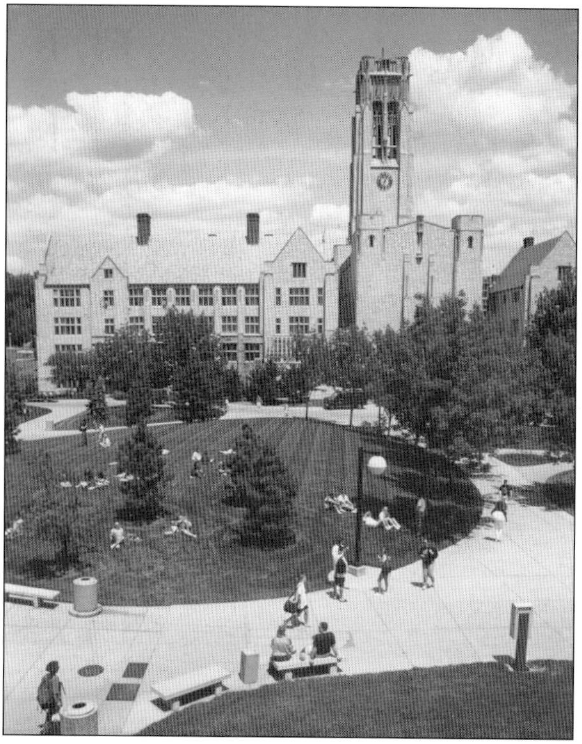

While completed in the 1980s, Centennial Mall gained new notoriety in September 1999 when the American Society of Landscape Architects named it one of the most beautifully landscaped spots in the country. "A university's architecture and grounds represent an institution's quality and stature, and the quality and appearance of Centennial Mall certainly speaks volumes about the University of Toledo's commitment to excellence," said University Beautification Committee chair Richard Eastop.

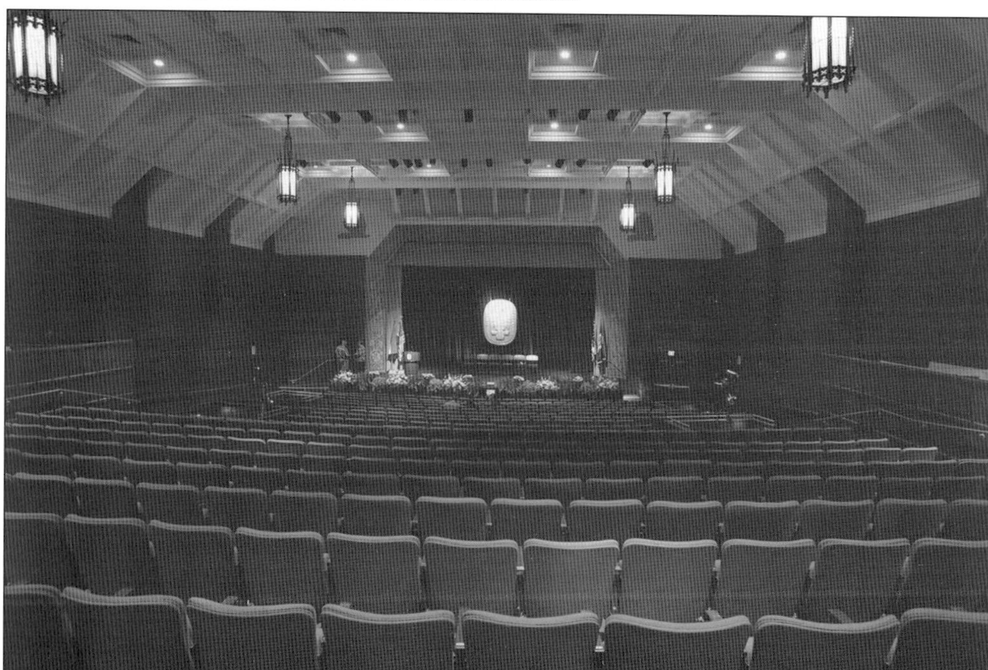

In addition to new construction, several buildings saw extensive renovation. Scott and Tucker Halls were expanded and renovated in 1995 at a cost of $3.9 million, and Doermann Theatre in University Hall underwent a $1.7 million restoration. It was rededicated in September 1995 with a series of lectures and musical performances.

An outgrowth of Toledo's glass industry, solar cells that could store energy from the sun became a major focus of research at UT, which was assisted in 1998 with the receipt of a $1.4 million grant for research in thin-film technology. This area of research would continue to expand with federal and state support and would help the university earn a reputation for its work in photovoltaics and alternative energy.

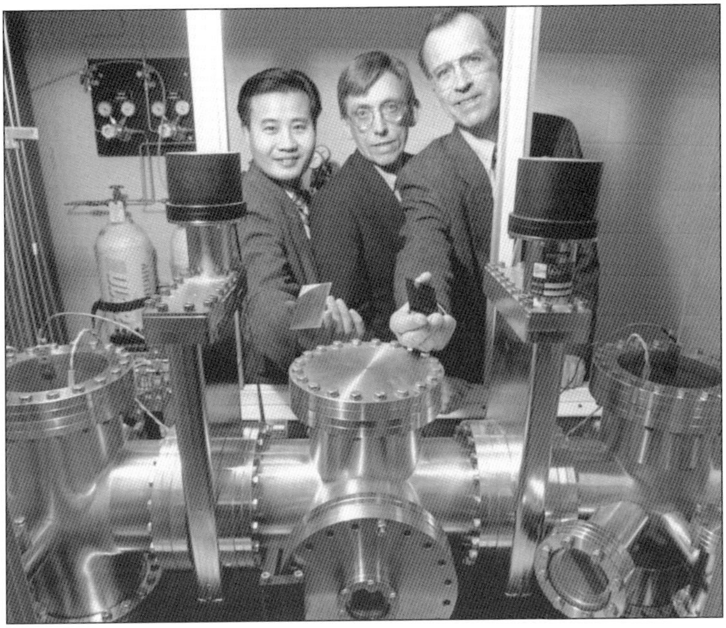

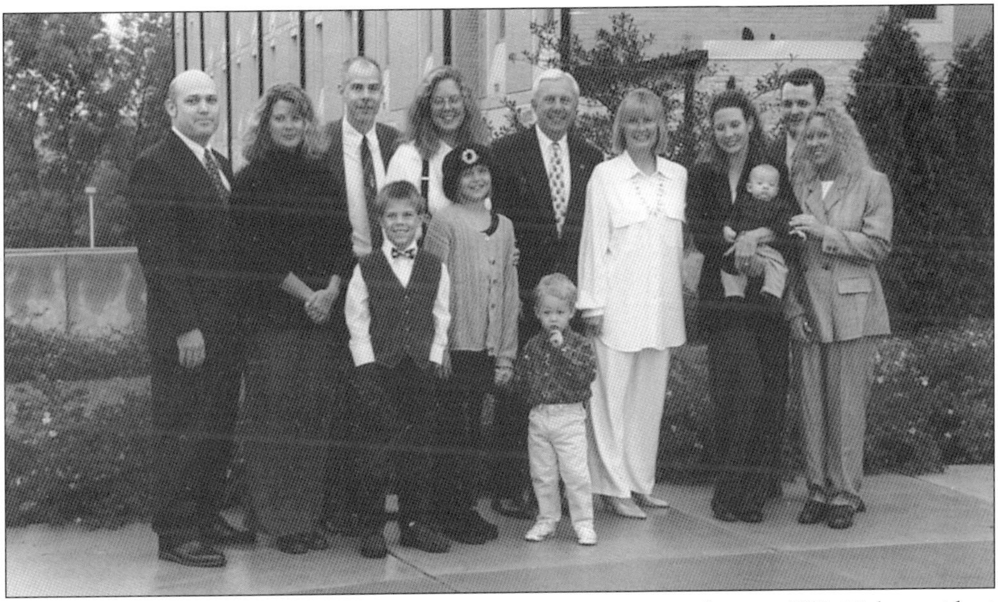

In April 1998, Dr. Frank Horton announced his intention to step down as UT's 13th president at the end of the year. Among his accomplishments were the expansion of the honors and international programs, the establishment of the Center for Teaching Excellence and the Lake Erie Center, and the successful completion of the UT 40 fundraising campaign, which exceeded its $40 million goal by $10 million. The International House was rededicated and named the Frank and Nancy Horton International House. Shown here is Dr. Horton's extended family at the event.

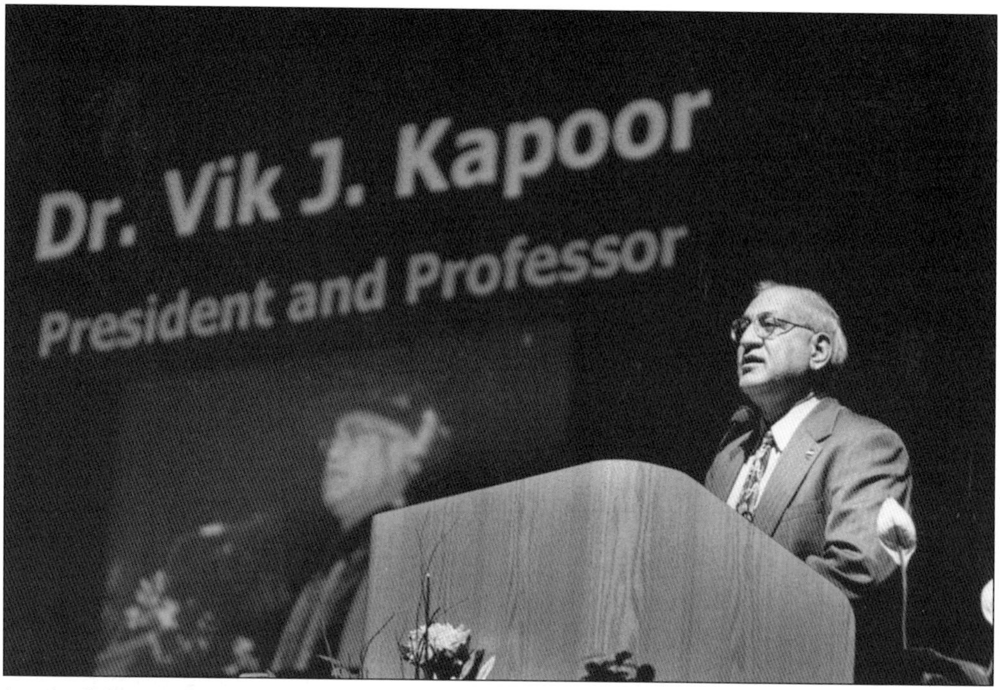

A search began for a new president, which was completed in November 1998 with the controversial selection of an in-house candidate, Dr. Vik Kapoor. Dr. Kapoor, the dean of the College of Engineering, was selected over the objection of many faculty and even a few members of the search committee.

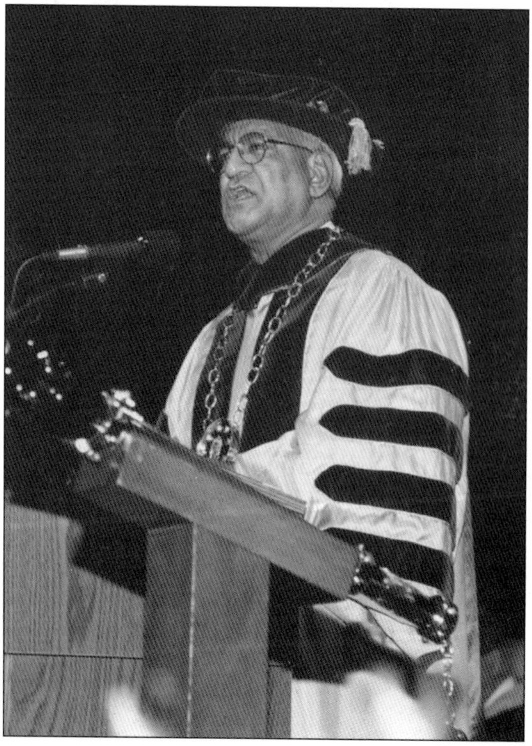

Dr. Kapoor was inaugurated in 1999. He stated as his goal the creation of a "new UT," aimed at increasing enrollment, which had declined by 5,000 students. But his leadership style was criticized as dictatorial, and many administrators of the Horton presidency were dismissed. Others, particularly faculty, resisted the rapid changes he proposed that seemed outside the norm for higher education. After 17 months, Dr. Kapoor was removed by the board of trustees. William Decatur, vice president for finance and business services, was named interim president.

Jon Hendricks, the internationally known jazz artist who developed the "vocalese" style of singing in the 1950s, was appointed to the UT faculty in 2000 as a distinguished university professor. Hendricks had popularized his style as part of an influential trio with Annie Ross and Dave Lambert. He lived much of his early life in Toledo and had attended UT but moved to New York on the advice of Charlie Parker. During his 50-plus-year career, he performed with most of the jazz greats. As a UT distinguished professor, he taught the History of Jazz course in the Department of Music.

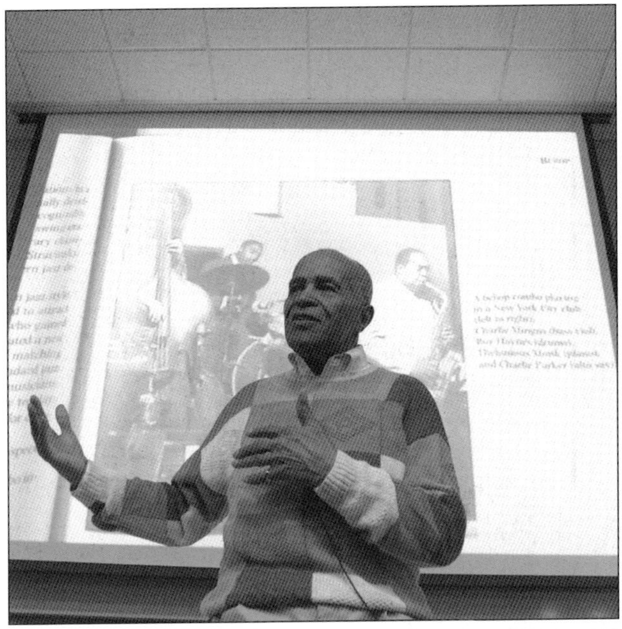

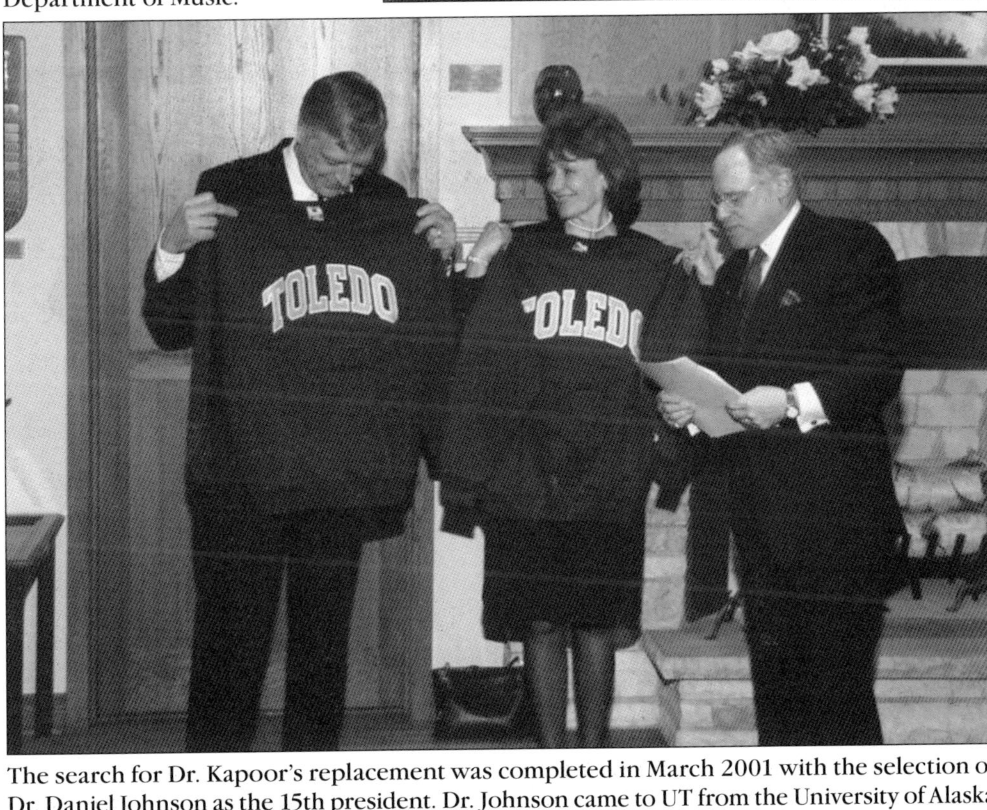

The search for Dr. Kapoor's replacement was completed in March 2001 with the selection of Dr. Daniel Johnson as the 15th president. Dr. Johnson came to UT from the University of Alaska Anchorage, where he had been provost. His focus was on establishing UT as a metropolitan research university, a reflection of his background as a sociologist. This photograph shows, from left to right, Dr. Johnson with his wife, Elaine, and board of trustees chair James Tuschman at the announcement of Dr. Johnson's selection as president.

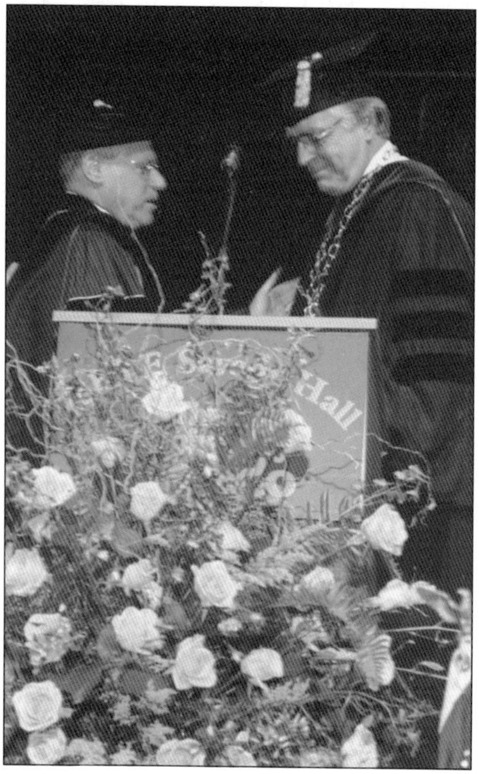

Dr. Johnson was inaugurated at a ceremony that included Adm. Vern Clark (below, right), chief of naval operations and a member of the Joint Chiefs of Staff. Dr. Johnson's inaugural address spoke of the need for the university to become more engaged in the community, a theme that remained throughout his presidency.

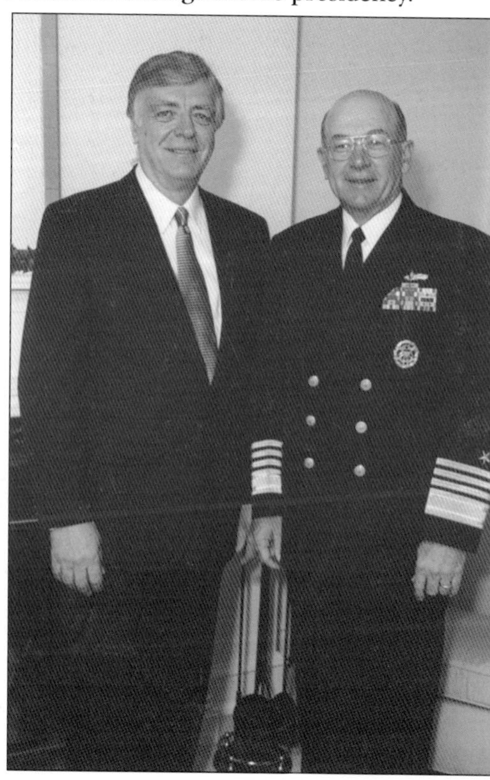

Just five days before the tragedy of the attack of September 11, 2001, US president George W. Bush visited UT along with Mexico's president Vicente Fox. The two spoke in Savage Hall and were greeted by UT president Johnson. Bush and Fox spoke of the need for cooperation between their two countries, especially in trade. "A good foreign policy starts with being friends with your neighbors," President Bush stated in his address.

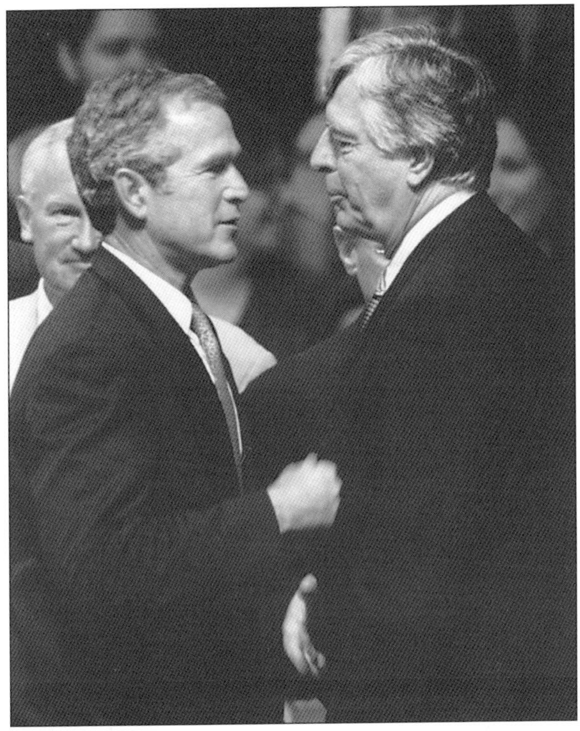

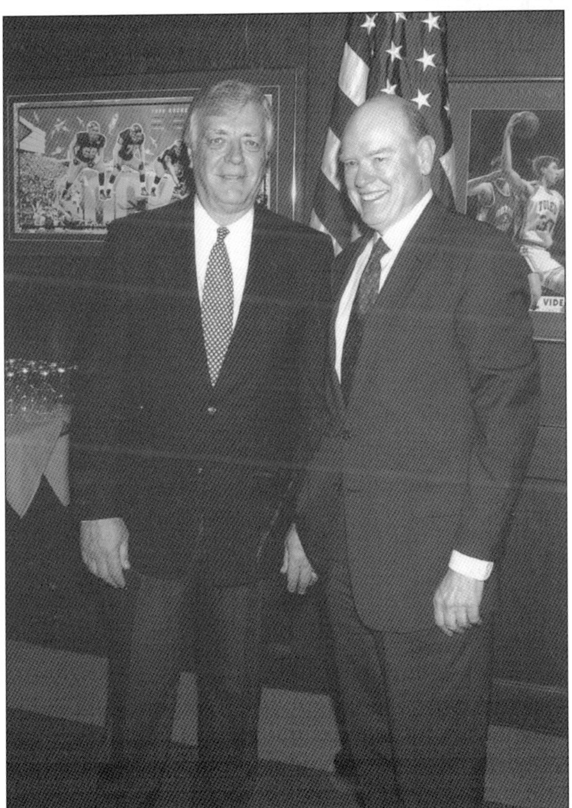

In 2002, UT alum John W. Snow, chairman of CSX Corporation, was named by President Bush to be the new secretary of the treasury. Snow was the commencement speaker and received an honorary doctorate from UT at the May 2003 ceremony. He is shown here with President Johnson.

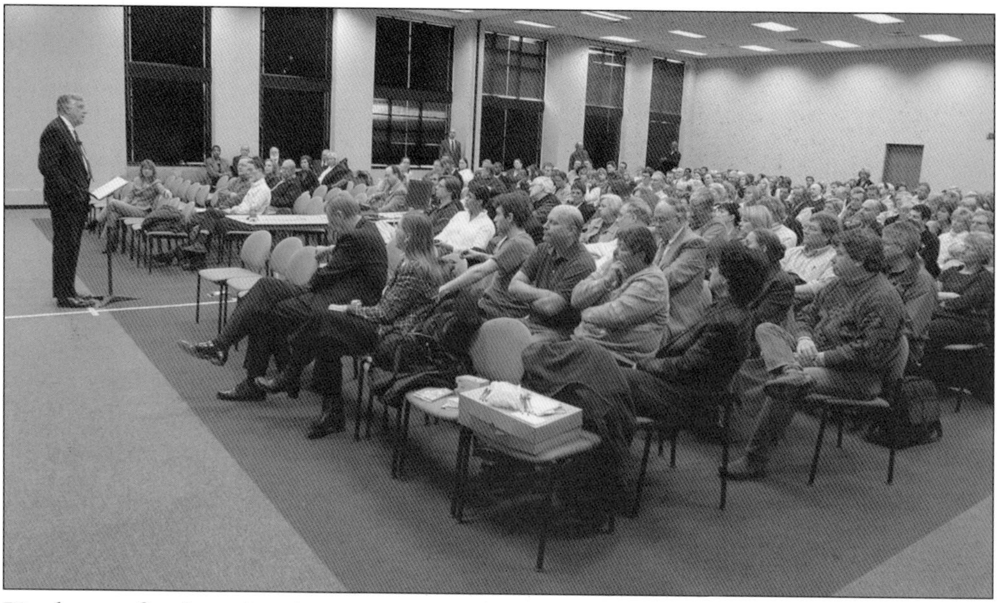

Big changes for the university were soon underway. In late 2005, it was announced that the University of Toledo and the Medical University of Ohio would merge to bring together the two institutions originally intended to be one 40 years before. The proposal was controversial on the UT campus, with MUO president Lloyd Jacobs chosen to lead the new merged university. Here, Dr. Johnson discusses the merger with the university community at a town hall meeting.

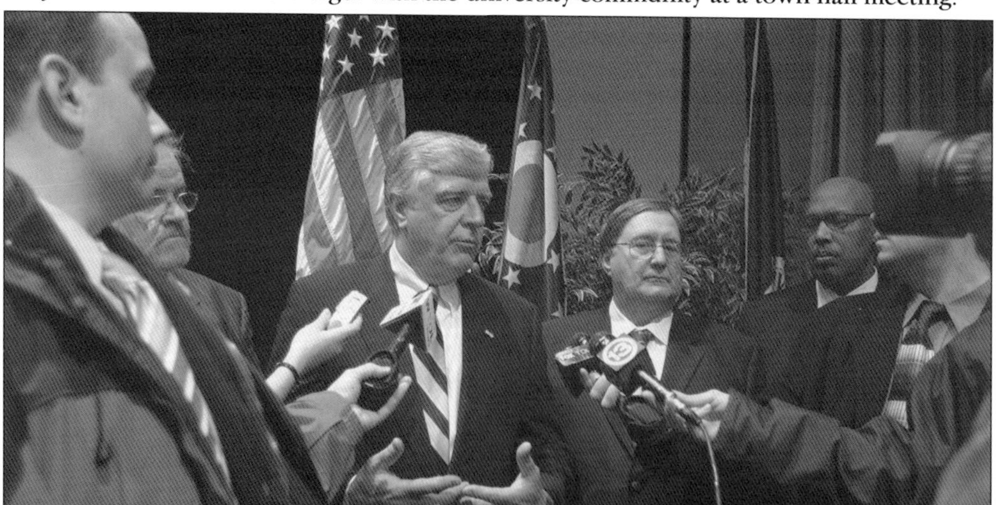

In his 2006 State of the University address, Dr. Johnson said, "We have a chance to truly transform higher education in this region and in the state if the merger is approved." He noted the merger would create new academic offerings and allow students to seamlessly enter medical programs. Many faculty in the arts and humanities remained skeptical of how the merger might affect their disciplines.

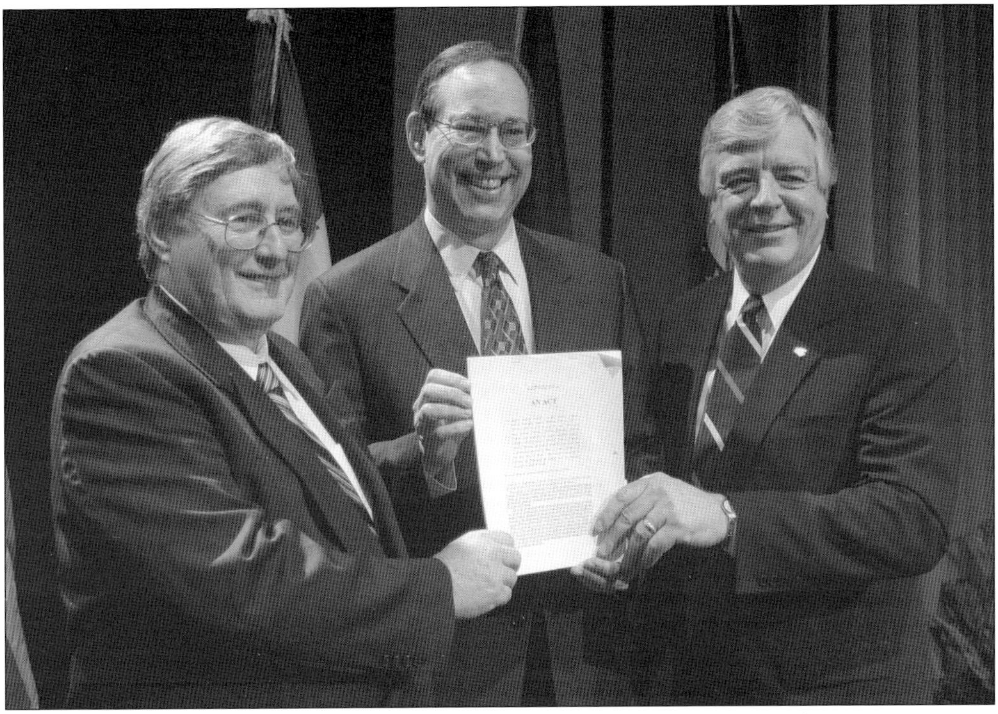

It was decided that the new university would be called the University of Toledo, and the former Medical University of Ohio would be known as the Health Science Campus. The university seal was changed to incorporate the date of the merger, and the name of MCO's hospital was changed to the University of Toledo Medical Center. A ceremony marking the merger was held in Doermann Theatre on March 31, 2006. In attendance was Ohio governor Bob Taft (center), flanked by Dr. Lloyd Jacobs (left) and Dr. Dan Johnson, who officially signed the legislation that merged the two universities.

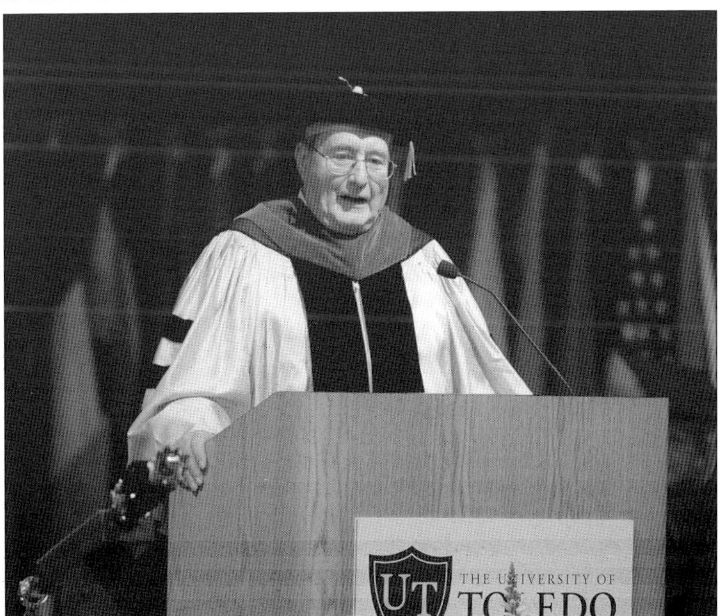

In September, an investiture ceremony officially marked the presidency of Dr. Jacobs, who became UT's 16th president. An economic study released in November 2006 stated that the new institution would have a $1.1 billion impact on Ohio's economy.

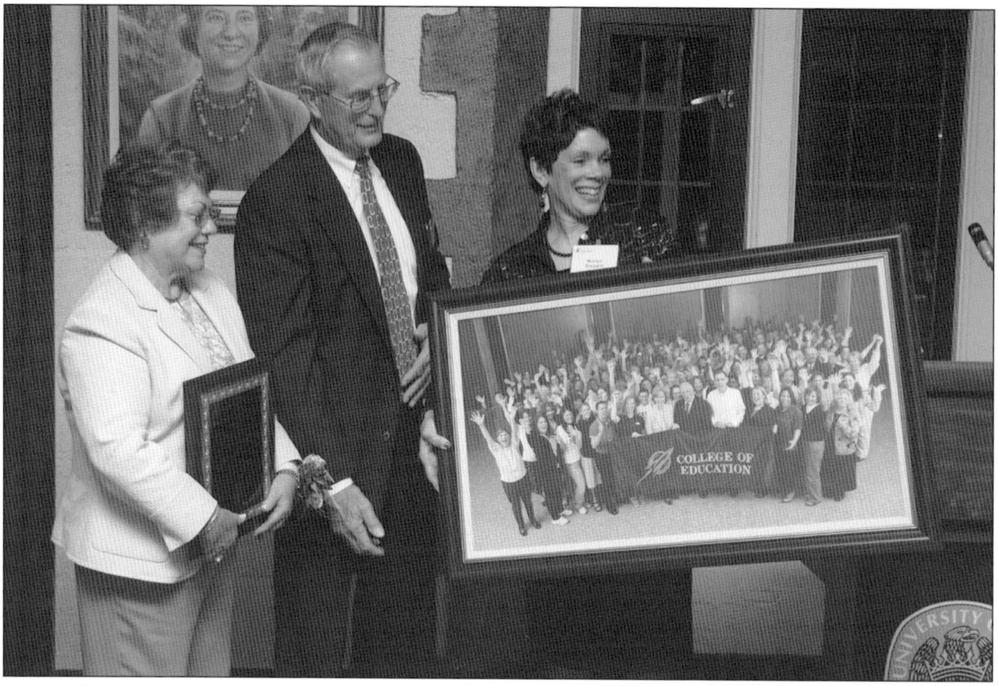

In 2006, the university received a gift of $15 million from two of its graduates, Judith and Marvin Herb (shown here on the left) and their sons Thomas and Jon. The gift was in support of the College of Education for scholarships, research support, and faculty development. In recognition of the significance of the gift, the college was renamed the Judith Herb College of Education.

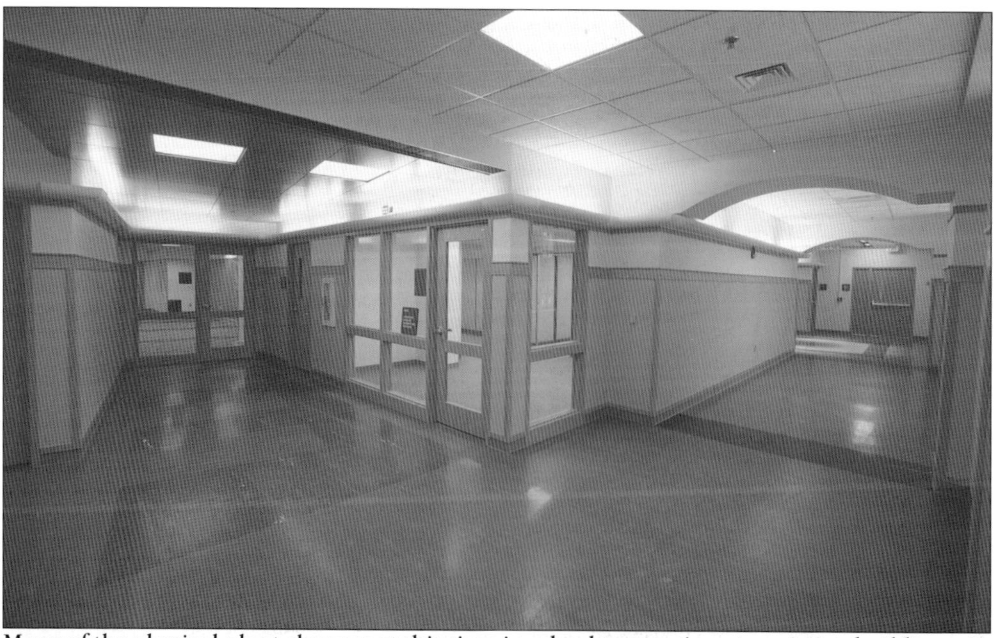

Many of the physical plant changes at this time involved renovations to existing buildings. In 2007, Gillham Hall was rededicated as the new home for the Judith Herb College of Education after a $12.4 million renovation.

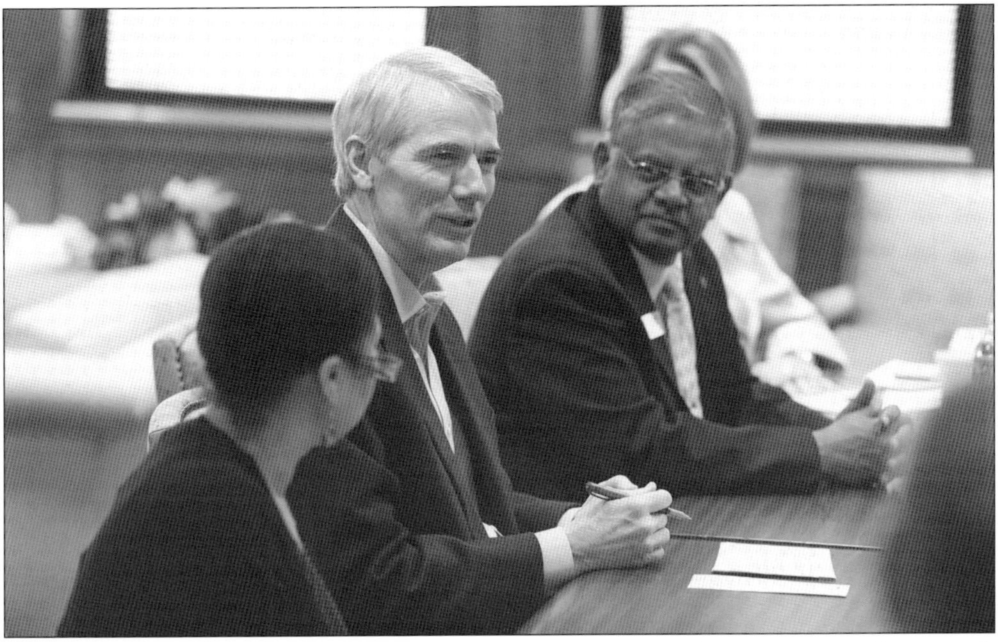

Several new and unique education programs brought national attention to UT. Research and political advocacy about the issue of human trafficking led to an annual international conference on the subject beginning in 2003 and the passage of legislation in the state that finally recognized human trafficking as a felony crime. The Human Trafficking and Social Justice Institute was created at UT in 2015. Ohio senator Rob Portman is pictured at a meeting of the group.

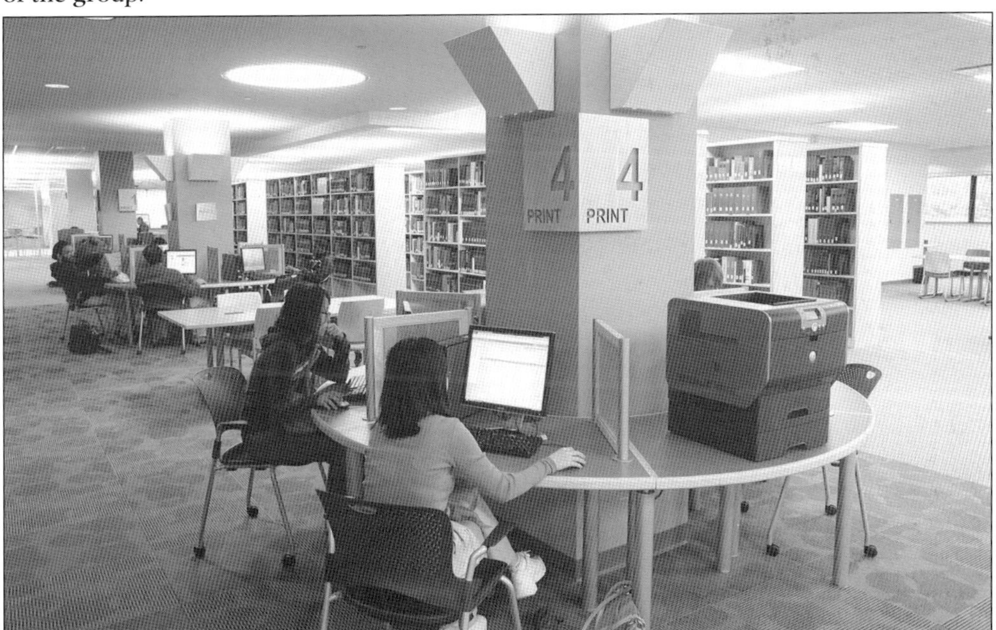

The first floor of the William S. Carlson Library was renovated in 2007 as the Information Commons. The space combined traditional library functions like the reference desk with computers and information technology support.

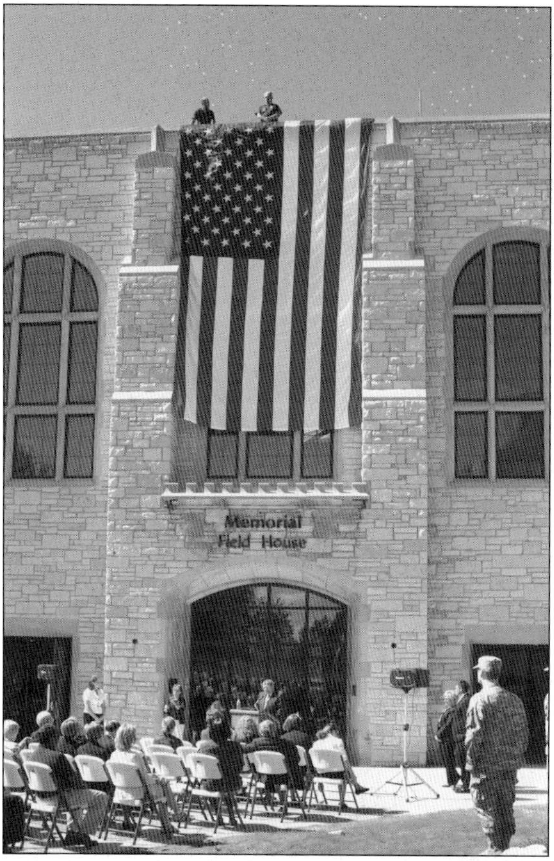

One of the most dramatic renovations was the Memorial Field House. The building, originally built as a sports facility in 1931, had been mothballed for decades. The entire interior of the building was gutted, and a new structure built within the walls as part of the $27 million renovation. It was dedicated in 2008 as the new home for the departments of English and Foreign Languages. The following year, the building received a gold rating as an environmentally friendly structure under the Leadership in Energy and Environmental Design standards.

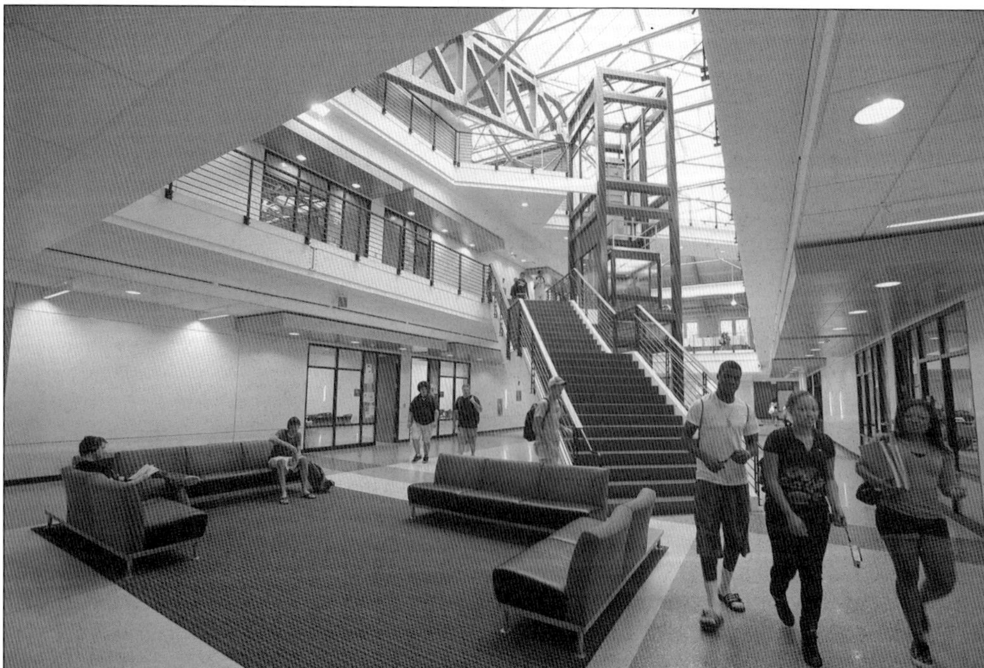

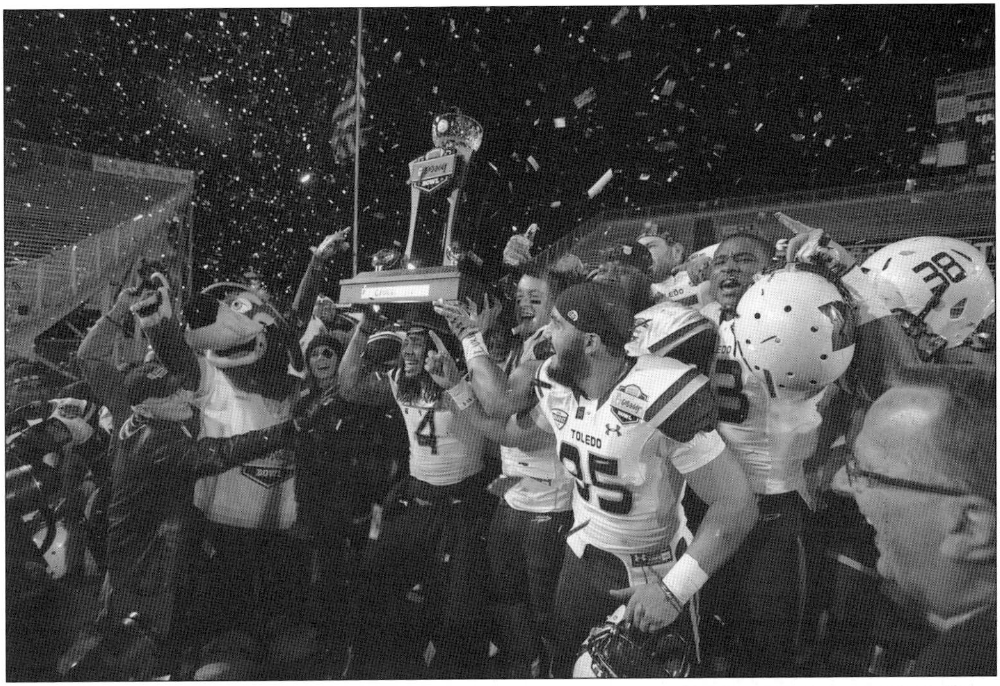

UT's athletic teams saw much success in the past two decades. The football team was named Mid-American Conference champions in 2001, 2002, 2004, and 2014, and played in several bowl games including winning the GoDaddy Bowl in January 2015 over Arkansas State by a score of 63 to 44 (above). The women's basketball team also excelled, winning the MAC tournament in 2001, 2010, 2011, and 2013. The team won the Women's National Invitational Tournament in 2011 (right) against the University of Southern California by a score of 76 to 68. This was the first Rocket team to capture a postseason basketball title.

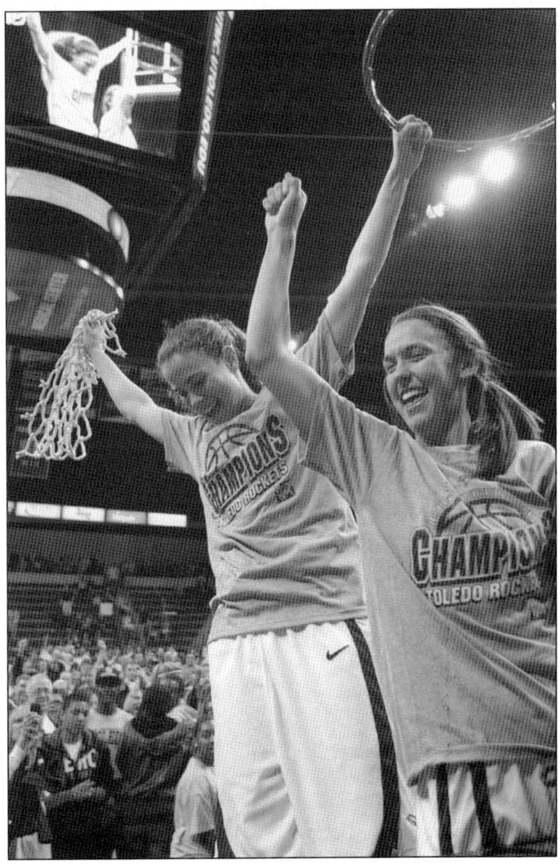

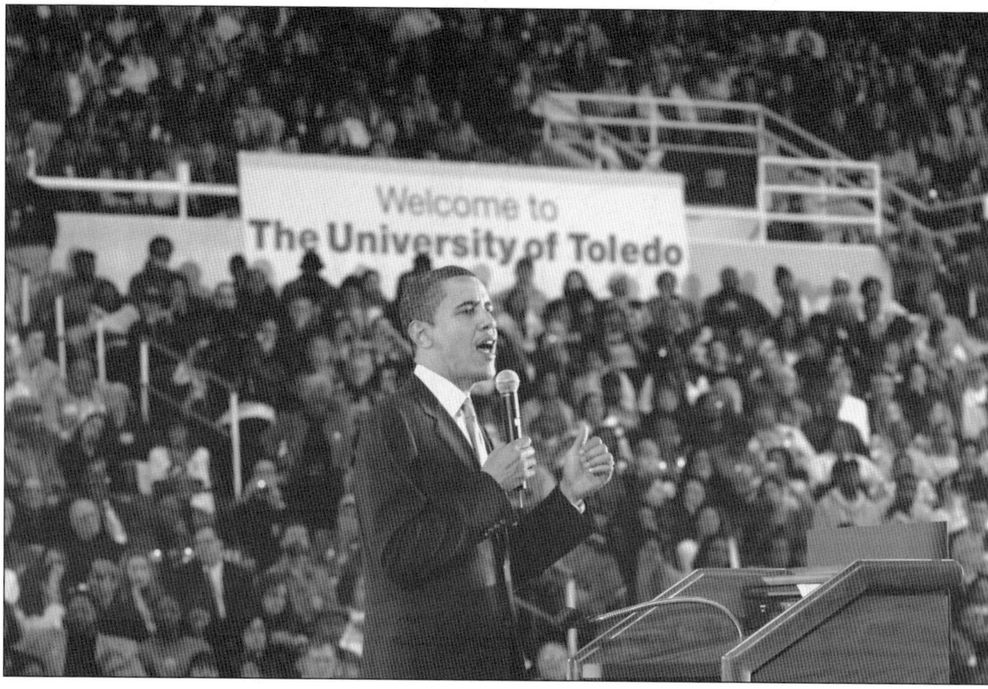

Presidential candidate Barack Obama led a campaign rally in Savage Hall in February 2008. The rally was attended by over 9,000 people.

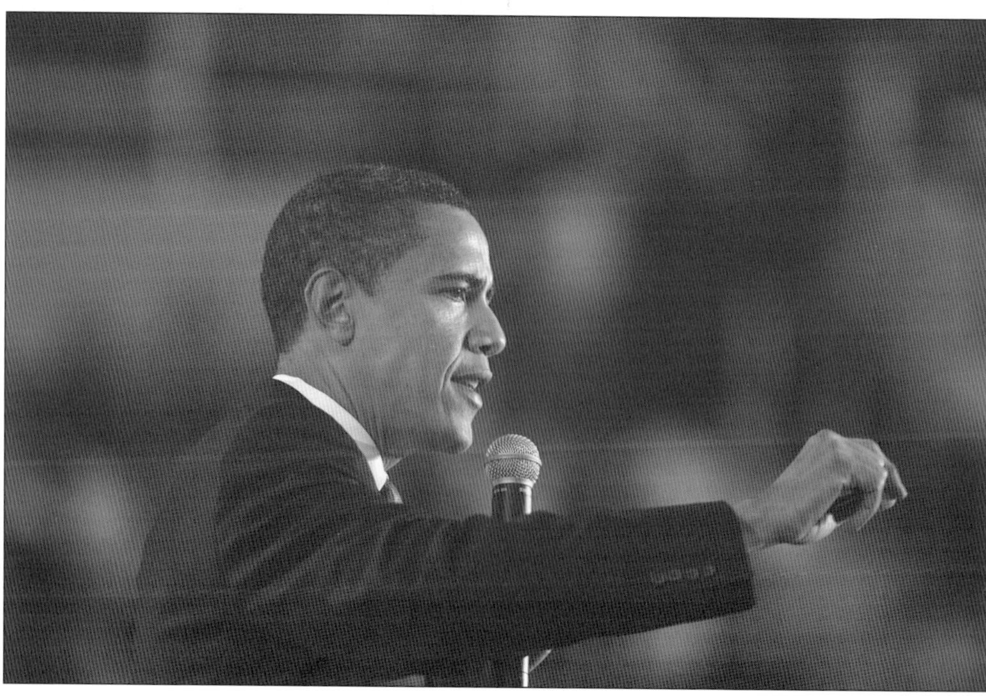

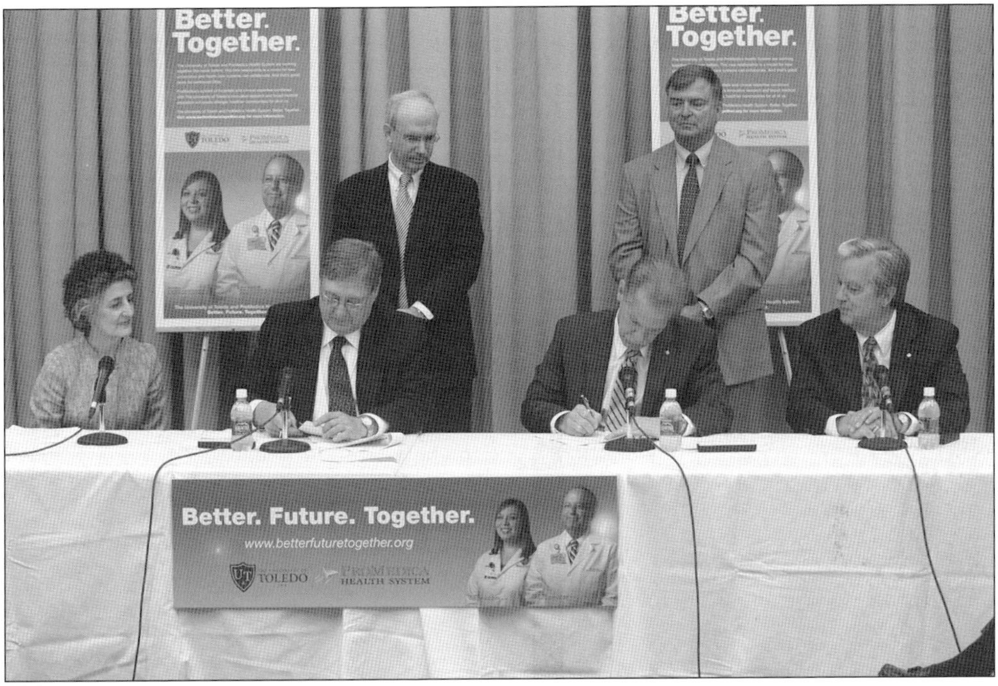

An important collaboration began in 2010 between the medical school and ProMedica Health Systems. UT agreed to serve as the academic medical center for ProMedica, while ProMedica provided clinical experiences for UT health science students.

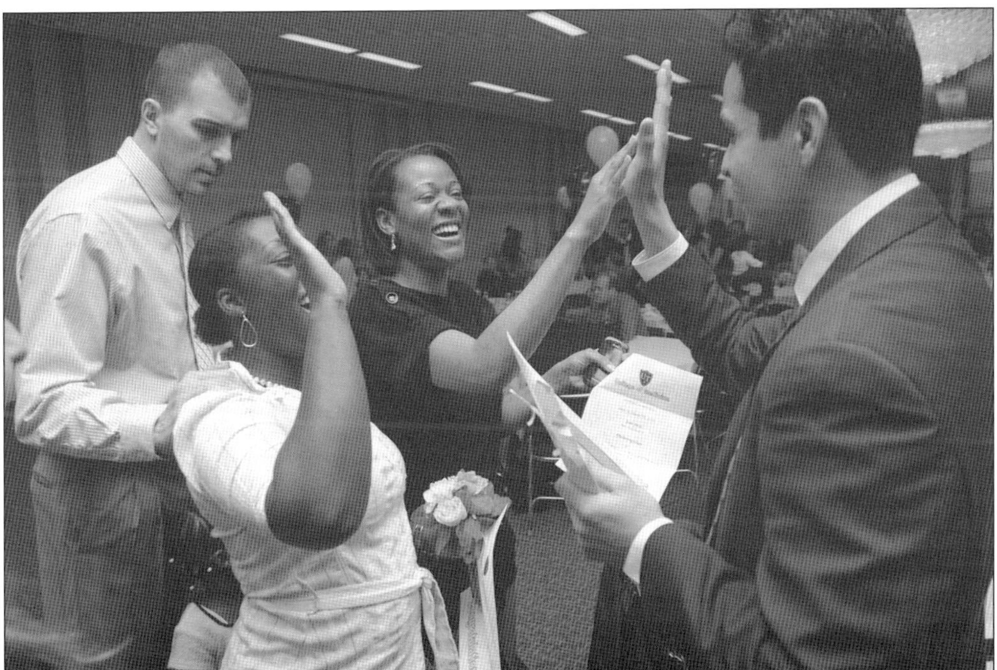

In March of each year, UT medical school students celebrate Match Day. During this event, where the students learn where they will be serving their residencies, emotions run high.

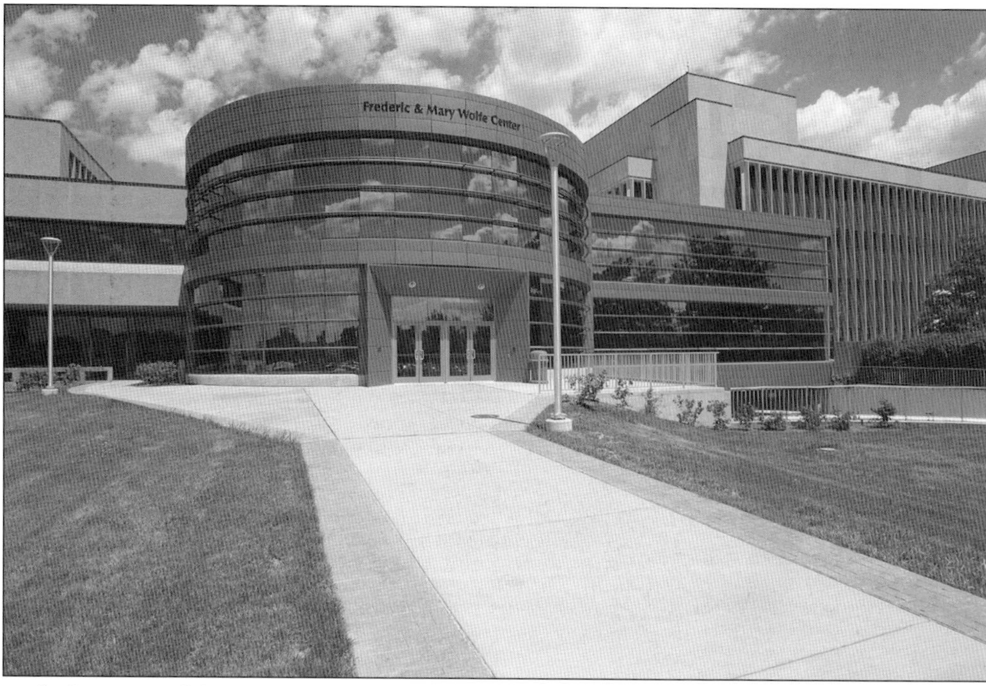

With the move of the professional pharmacy program to the Health Science Campus, a new College of Pharmacy building was constructed in 2010 on that campus. The $25 million building was named the Frederic and Mary Wolfe Center.

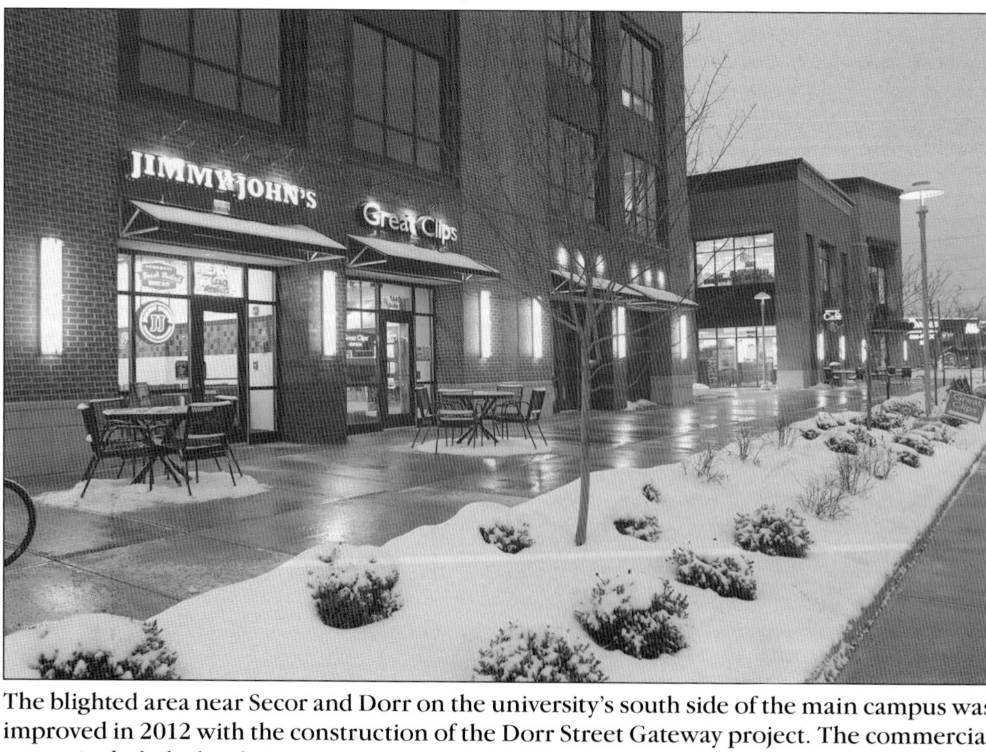

The blighted area near Secor and Dorr on the university's south side of the main campus was improved in 2012 with the construction of the Dorr Street Gateway project. The commercial center included a bookstore, restaurants, and living spaces for students.

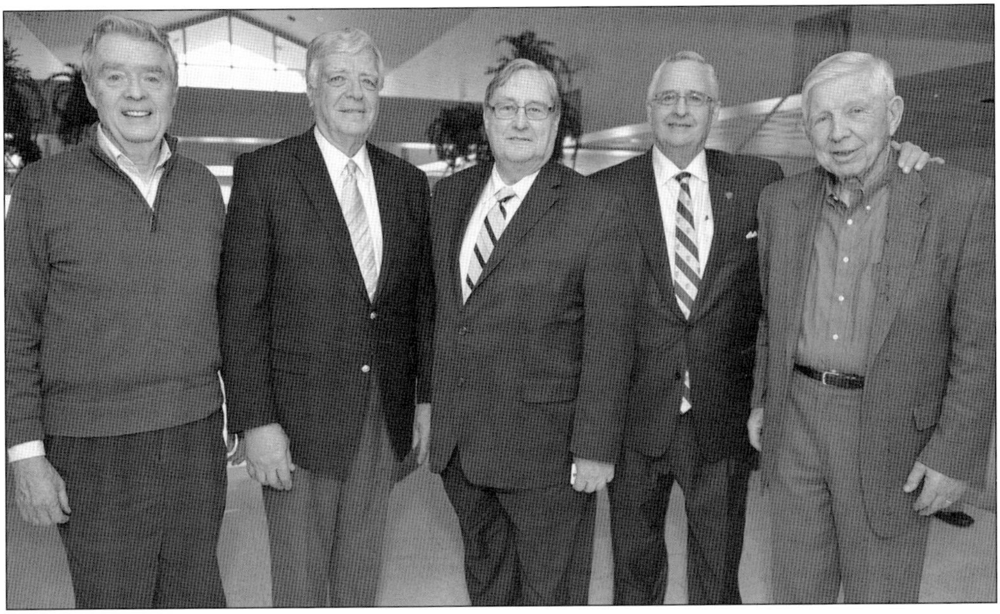

The Crossings, residence halls located on the south side of campus, were renamed in March 2013 as Presidents' Hall. The name was in honor of John Dowd, Philip Nash, Wilbur White, and Daniel Johnson. The dedication ceremony included UT donors Bob Savage (far left) and Richard Anderson (far right), and, from left to right, Dr. Johnson, Dr. Jacobs, and UT board of trustees chairman Joe Zerby. In July of that year, the Dowd-Nash-White dormitory off Campus Drive was demolished.

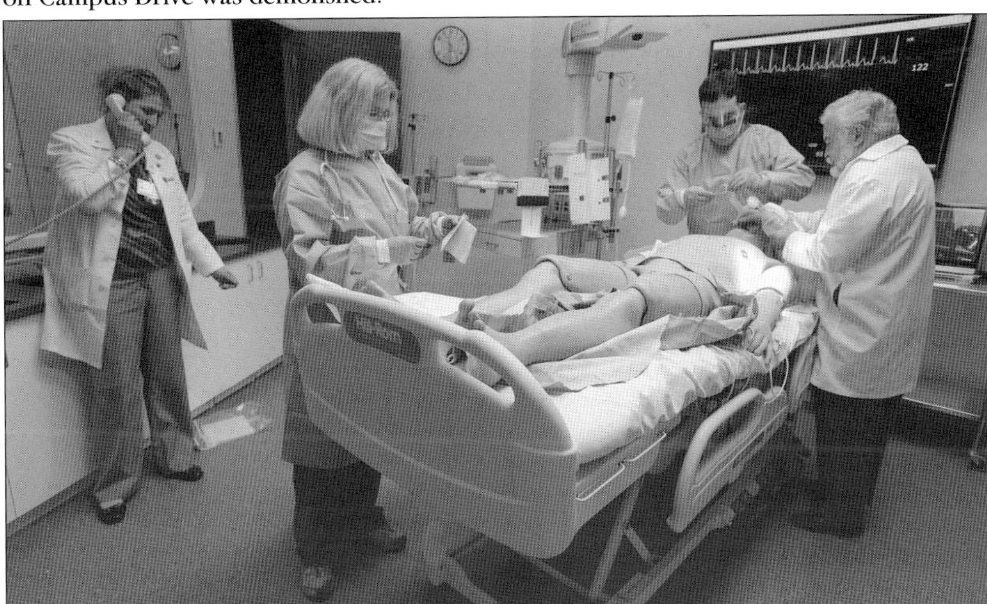

One of the largest construction projects on the Health Science Campus was the $36 million Interprofessional Immersive Simulation Center. Construction began in 2012 on the building that includes state-of-the-art 3D simulation technology allowing physicians and medical students to develop their technical skills. The center was named for Dr. Lloyd Jacobs when it was completed in 2014.

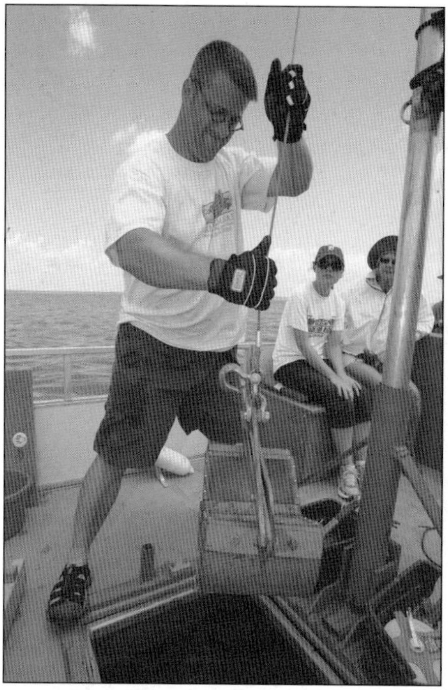

A major crisis in 2014 that caused Toledo to shut down its water supply for several days due to toxic algae blooms in Lake Erie refocused attention on the work of UT researchers on improving the water quality of the Great Lakes. A Water Task Force consisting of experts from the Lake Erie Center, the medical school, and political leaders built on decades of work by UT researchers on water quality.

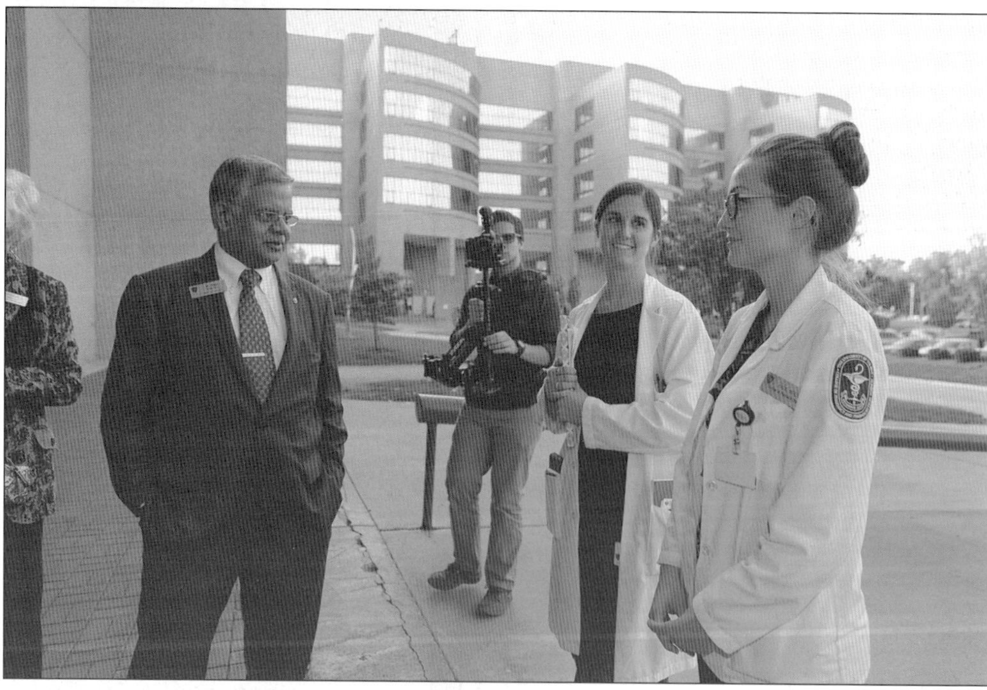

Dr. Jacobs announced he would be stepping down as president of UT as of July 1, 2014. The announcement coincided with a celebration of the 50th anniversary of the former Medical College of Ohio. While a search began for a replacement, Dr. Nagi Naganathan, dean of the College of Engineering, was selected to serve as interim president. "Nagi," as he was affectionately known, had been at UT since 1986, and as dean of engineering was credited with overseeing a successful expansion of the college.

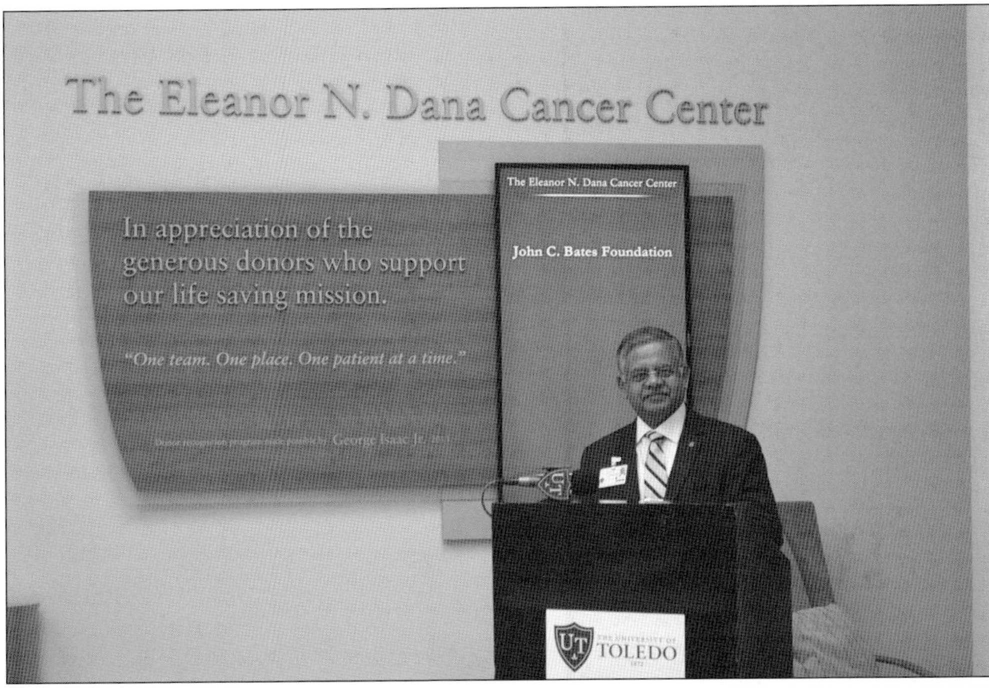

In 2013, the UT Medical Center consolidated its cancer treatment programs into the Eleanor N. Dana Center. The center allowed cancer patients to be guided comprehensively through all aspects of their treatment. The center was dedicated on August 21, 2014, in a ceremony where Dr. Naganathan thanked the donors.

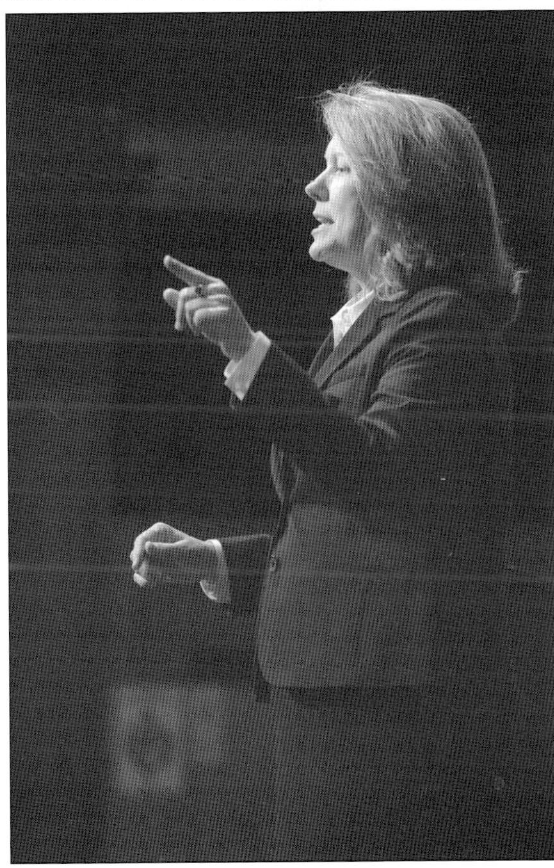

Following a national search for a new president, Dr. Sharon Gaber, provost at the University of Arkansas, was chosen as the University of Toledo's 17th president in March 2015. She was the first female to hold the position. Her academic background was in urban planning.

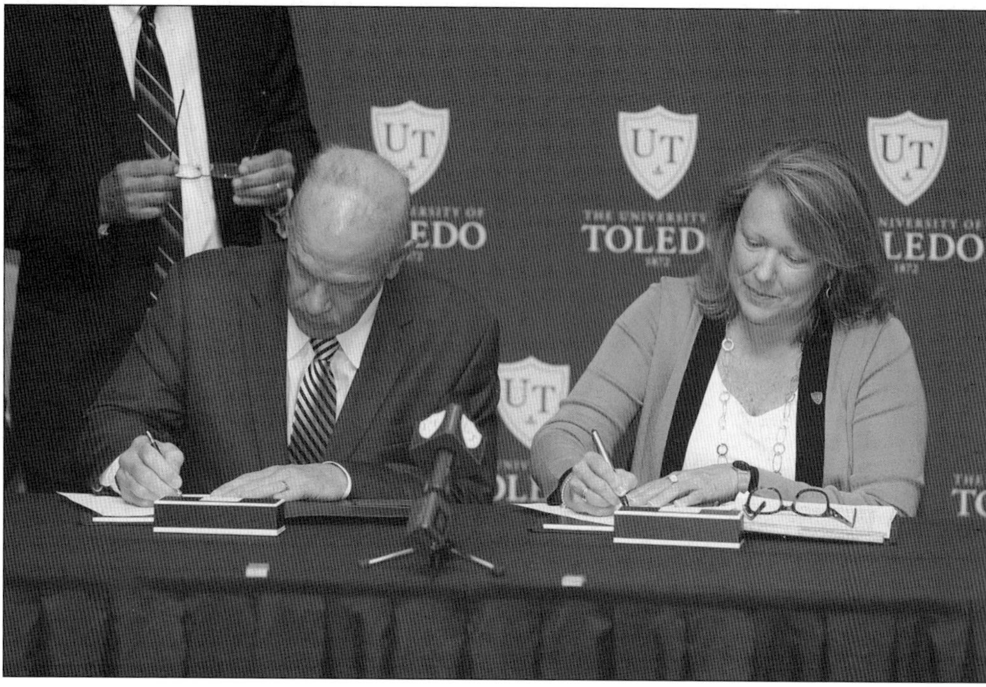

Shortly after assuming her new role, Dr. Gaber signed the agreement creating the academic affiliation between UT and ProMedica. "As we look out at the next half century, this affiliation positions both organizations to be national leaders in health-care education and medical research," Dr. Gaber noted at the signing event with ProMedica CEO Randy Oostra (left).

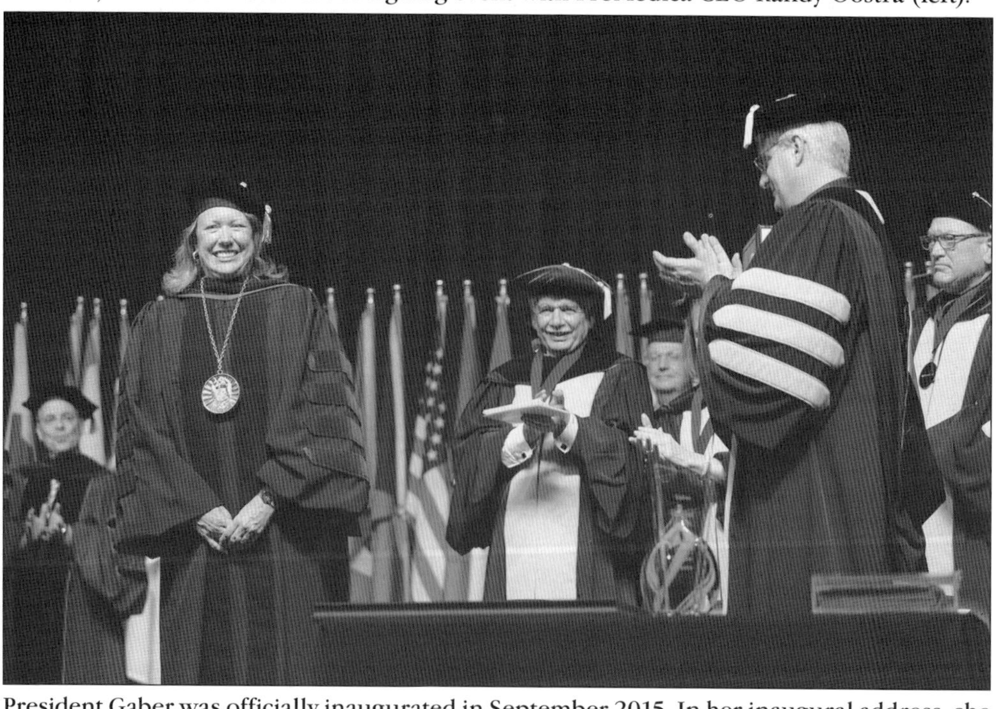

President Gaber was officially inaugurated in September 2015. In her inaugural address, she called UT "a university of us."

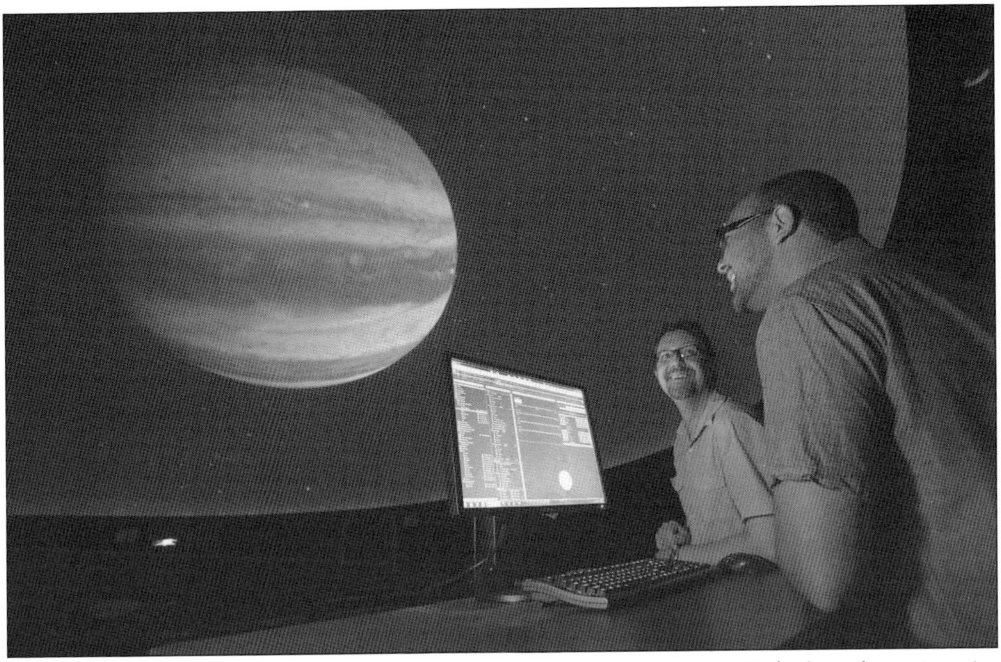

UT's prominence in astronomical research was recognized in June 2016 when the university was selected to join the Association of Universities for Research in Astronomy. The selection was in recognition of UT's research in and facilities for the study of astronomy.

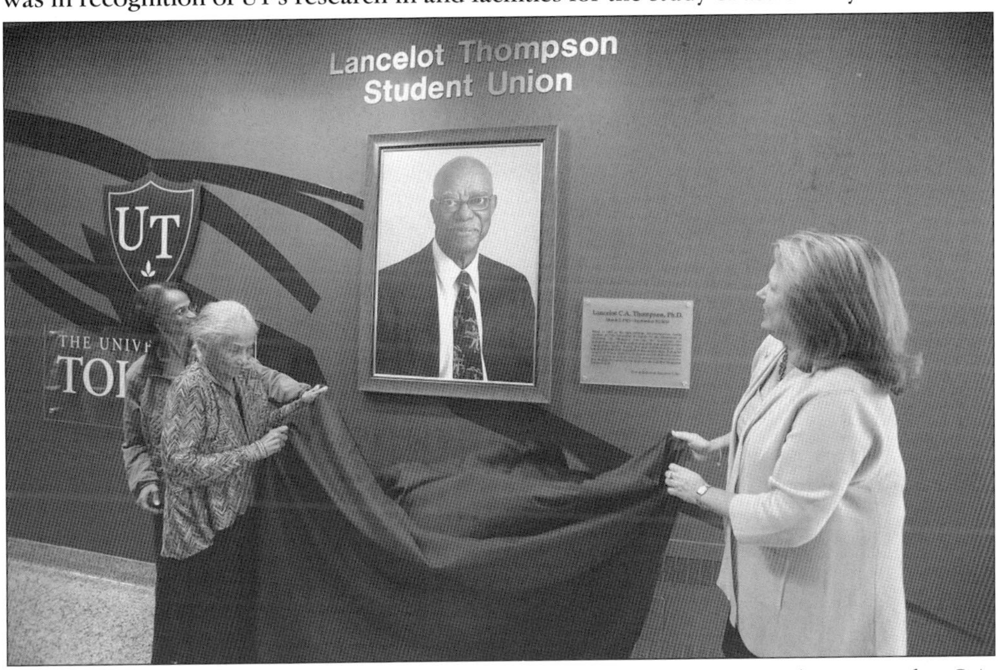

In September 2016, UT lost one of its most beloved administrators when Lancelot C.A. Thompson died. Thompson joined UT as a faculty member in the Department of Chemistry in 1958, and was appointed vice president for student affairs in 1968. He inspired generations of UT students. In honor of his legacy, the student union was renamed the Lancelot C.A. Thompson Union in November 2016.

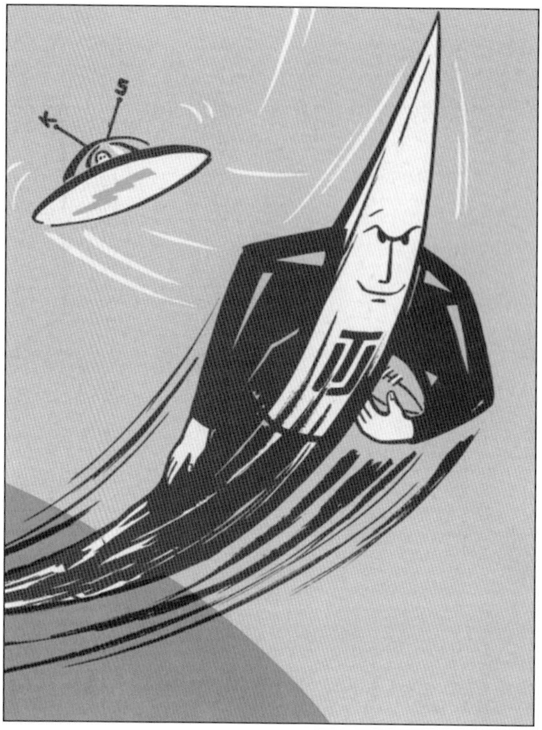

The concept of the UT sports teams' nickname as a personified "Rocket" appears to have developed in 1965 with this depiction on the cover of the football programs that year. In 1966, an actual mascot consisting of a person dressed in costume made his first appearance. While his look changed dramatically over time, Rocky the Rocket, UT's distinctive mascot, celebrated his 50th anniversary at homecoming in 2016. His female counterpart, Rocksy, debuted in 2011.

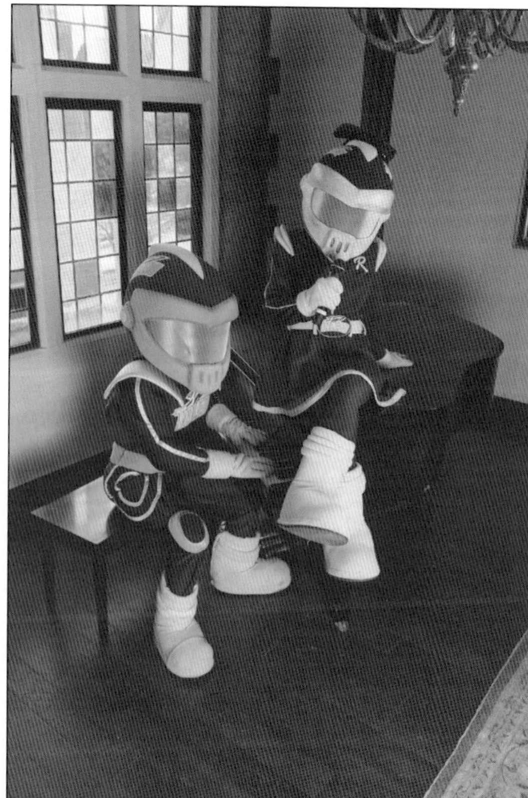

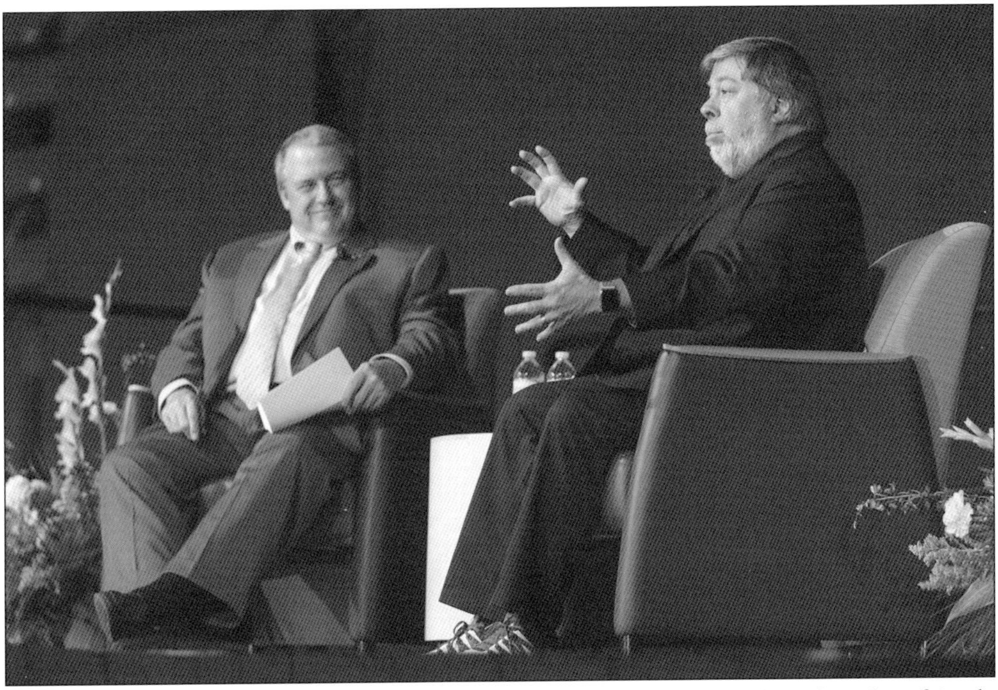

The Jesup Scott Honors College Lecture Series brought Steve Wozniak, cofounder of Apple Inc., to UT on February 1, 2016. Provost John Barrett (left) facilitated the conversation, with over 3,000 people in attendance.

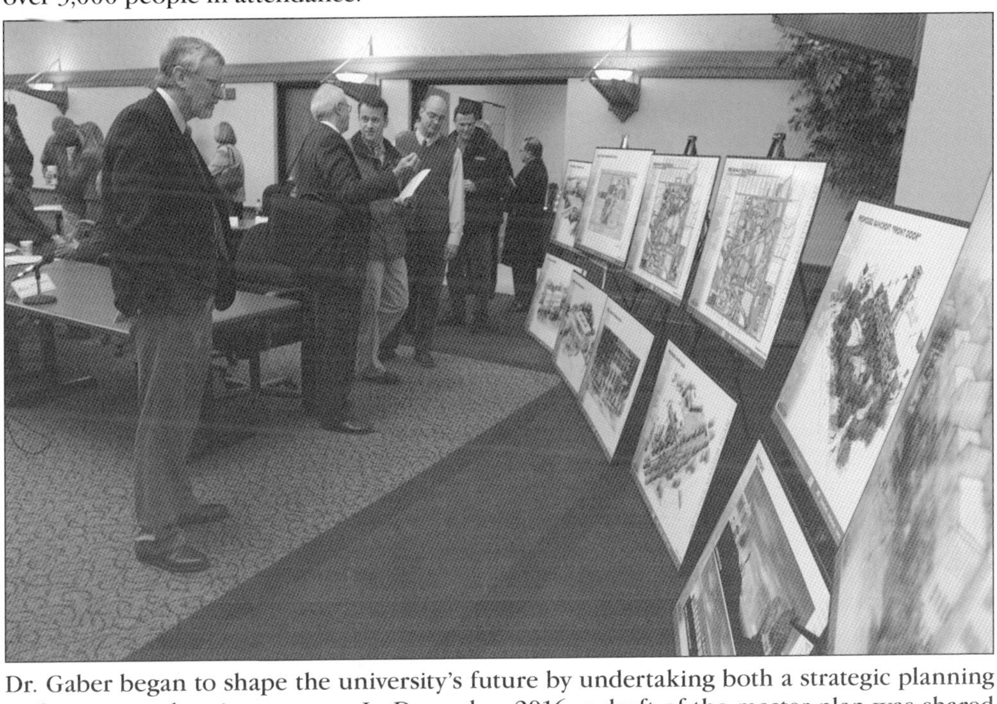

Dr. Gaber began to shape the university's future by undertaking both a strategic planning and a master planning process. In December 2016, a draft of the master plan was shared with the community. The plan seeks to reposition the academic core of the main campus, invest in research, and consolidate athletic facilities.

Consistent with our mission to preserve history on a local level, this book was printed in South Carolina on American-made paper and manufactured entirely in the United States. Products carrying the accredited Forest Stewardship Council (FSC) label are printed on 100 percent FSC-certified paper.

MADE IN THE USA